An Introduction to Political Parties

An Introduction to Political Parties

Gordon G. Henderson

Tougaloo College

Harper & Row, Publishers

New York, Hagerstown, San Francisco, London

Sponsoring Editor: Dale Tharp
Project Editor: Ralph Cato
Designer: Andrea Clark
Production Supervisor: Will C. Jomarrón
Compositor: Port City Press, Inc.
Printer and Binder: Halliday Lithograph Corporation
Art Studio: Vantage Art Inc.

An Introduction to Political Parties

Library of Congress Cataloging in Publication Data
Henderson, Gordon G   Date
    An introduction to political parties.

    Includes index.
    1.Political parties—United States.
2.Political parties.   I.Title.
JK2265.H45   329'.02   75-38601
ISBN 0-06-042778-7

For Eve

The Chapters...

Contents

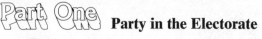

Part Four **Party in Government**   *243*

10 **Party Competition and State Public Policy Outputs**   *245*

Preface

An Introduction to Political Parties tries to mirror the issues which are uppermost among the concerns of students of political parties today: the rise in the number of Independents; the decline in trust; the appearance of policy voting; the relationship of party-organization personality types to the contemporary political environment; the increase in the number of primaries and its meaning for party organization; the identity of the politically nonparticipating and its meaning for parties; the impact of party competition upon policy outputs; the decline in party voting in Congress; and the likelihood of realignment. All these are subjects prominent in the literature on parties. All are subjects which today's student of parties finds exciting and over which debate and disagreement rages.

For the Student Reader . . .

I have also tried to provide the reader with a survey of the best-known high-quality writing that has been done on the subject. The amount of literature is profuse! Much of it is first-rate. If some work is really important, it deserves to be mentioned in the body of the text itself, not merely referred to in the small print of a footnote. That is a rule I have tried to follow here. Since there is no real disagreement among students of parties over which are the more important of the studies that have been done, you will find that most of the books and articles that appear in books of readings on the subject of political parties are indeed discussed in the body of the text.

This book assumes that students will be skeptical of what anybody tells them is the best evidence about parties in the United States and, taking a questioning attitude toward anything they read, that they will on occasion want to do some investigating on their own. For these students the book provides a summary of what is presently accepted as the best available thinking on a given topic, provides references to the existing studies, poses questions that appear not yet to be answered, identifies problems in current research methods, suggests leads for the next stages of research, and generally tries to encourage students to take off from whatever point they like in pursuit of new knowledge about parties. Only from such individual endeavors—which this book assumes college students are quite capable of undertaking—will come a superior understanding of political parties.

The quotations found at the beginning of each chapter are presented with three purposes in mind: to give readers a preview of some of the issues over which writers on the subject of parties disagree; to capture readers' attention—and maybe even fancy— and thus encourage investigation of the work from which the quote was taken; and finally to reveal the diversity of viewpoints that is to be found in writing about parties—to make it clear that not all statements in print on the subject can be regarded as equally valid. The authors of the quotes which appear at the beginning of Chapter 12, for instance, offer strikingly different appraisals of parties. Whose judgment is to be preferred? That must be an individual decision. This book will, I trust, offer some help in reaching such decisions.

A Survey—Not an Encyclopedia . . .

At the same time, the book is intended to be an introduction to the subject, not an encyclopedic survey. I have tried to include here only what I thought could not be left out, to keep the book brief, and to provide leads to additional readings, either within the text or by means of citations in the footnotes.

There are many good questions that can be asked about political parties. For some we have answers. For some we do not. Even the answers we like today may not hold our admiration through tomorrow. I have no doubt that, five years from now, I myself will question some of the things I "know" are true about political parties today. Notions about parties do change. New data, new ways of looking at old data, new techniques of analysis, new questions, new concerns, have led people to reject many ideas about parties that were accepted as truth 20 or 30 years ago.

Students of mine have never been reticent about challenging what I say, matching their observations against mine and against the observations of others whose ideas are reported in this book. My hope is that those who read this book will find that their ideas are better focused if they share them with others, and if any readers are of mind to disagree with me or to know how I react to their ideas, I hope they will get in touch with me personally in care of the Department of Political Science at Tougaloo College, Tougaloo, Mississippi 39174.

GORDON G. HENDERSON

Acknowledgments

A great many people have helped with this book and I have benefited greatly from that help. Don Freeman, Bernie Hennessy, Catherine Rudder, Samuel Eldersveld, and Duane Lockard read the whole of the manuscript at the request of Harper & Row and myself. To the extent that I followed the critical suggestions they offered, the book, I am sure, has become a better one.

The National Center for Education in Politics, an organization that should never have been permitted to die, provided a year's postdoctoral fellowship for study and service in a political office. Sam Goddard, Governor of Arizona, allowed me to serve that year as a full member of his staff. To the NCEP, its director, Bernie Hennessy, and Sam, I shall always be grateful. It was that experience as much as anything that made me decide I had to write this book.

I also want to thank Dean Naomi Townsend of Tougaloo College for giving me time during one January term to work on this manuscript.

As will quickly be obvious to anyone who reads this book, I have drawn heavily upon the data archives of the Center for Political Studies of the University of Michigan. To the Center for Political Studies, whose impact upon the study of political behavior has been enormous and beneficial, I am grateful, as I am to Roland Smith and Ray Wells, who helped in putting together some data from the 1960 and 1972 elections.

Many people at Harper & Row helped, and I am especially pleased with the careful editorial work done by Ralph Cato and with the design done by Andrea Clark.

Through several drafts and years my family has been both supportive and patient and I want them to know that I appreciate that. To Eve, our firstborn, the book is dedicated with love.

An Introduction
to Political Parties

For the free men of this Republic there is only one way to make a new beginning. We must, in Lincoln's words, "meet and overthrow the present ruling dynasty." We the citizens of the Republic must find the means to break up party control of politics and strip the usurpers of their corrupt and corrupting power. . . . The only certain means to overthrow the present ruling dynasty without setting up another is . . . to make it easier for free men to enter public life, to bring issues that interest them into the public arena, to bring forward for elective office independent men who have won their trust [and] make it easier for independent men to win their trust.

We believe that American political parties, whatever their current limitations, offer the best potential means for achieving broad citizen participation in politics and continuing citizen influence in the direction of government.

Over her coffee at her community college snack bar, Sharon speaks intensely about the President. . . . "Would you believe my history professor is trying to give us a big rap on why we should register and vote? He's gotta be kidding!"

What possible difference could it make? Ford and Rockefeller are almost as bad as Nixon! . . . They're all so corrupt, and there just isn't anything you can do about it. Washington politics is just so big, so far out there, I just can't relate. I don't even read about it anymore."

The Study of Political Parties

What is a political party? What influences give parties their distinctive characteristics? What evidence need we look at in our search for an understanding of the political party? What is generally included within the scope of a study of parties? What are the boundaries of the inquiry? What view does this book offer of parties? Those are among the questions examined in this beginning chapter.

Why Study Political Parties?

People are usually attracted to the study of political parties for one or both of two reasons. The first is to gain some useful knowledge about an important political institution. The second is simply to satisfy an intellectual curiosity.

The Search for Useful Information. Parties are important political institutions. There is really no question about that. People who want to bring about social and political change, along with those who prefer to maintain the social and political status quo, have often seen parties as a means to promote or frustrate change.

In 1974 a man interested in government reform in Maine, James Longley, found public and party officials unwilling to give his ideas for fiscal reform what he considered a fair hearing. Undaunted but annoyed he ran for governor, as an Independent. His support came mainly from youth. He defeated both the Democratic and Republican candidates. The media—whose information about politics is generally substantial and reliable—declared the outcome a surprise. It should not be a surprise to anyone who reads this book and digests what is said here about the components of an effective campaign organization, the attitudes (and numbers) of youth, the tendency for college-educated youth today to declare themselves Independents, and the gradual erosion of trust throughout the population that could be observed beginning about 1968. On the other hand, if this event had occurred 20 years earlier, *that would have been a surprise.*

Citizens, party leaders, candidates, and public officials all engage in party activity. Some are clearly more skilled at what they do than others. And some part of a difference in skill is attributable to the quality of the information they possess about politics in general and the political party in particular.

Consider the candidate again for a moment. Any candidate for public office needs help. Part of the help he can use is reliable information. Myths abound, and it is seldom easy to separate myth from fact, and it is often a lot easier and more comforting to believe the myths. Consider these hardy staples, all of which are myths:

> The candidate who has the most television advertising is the one who usually wins.
> Certainly television advertising cannot hurt you.
> Registration rates do not change much from year to year; neither, really, does turnout.
> Issues more than anything else influence the voter's decision.
> Most voters pay close attention to what is said and done in a campaign.
> Republicans are much more likely to turn out to vote than Democrats.
> Mainly old people are attracted to a candidate like George Wallace.

But separating myth from fact is only part of the problem. There is an almost endless number of questions that must be answered during the course of a campaign. Decisions will be made because decisions must be made, whether reliable information is available or not. Senator Abraham Ribicoff of Connecticut, himself a decidedly successful campaigner, offers two "laws" of campaign politics. The first is "Do what has worked before." But what *has* worked before? The second law is "Try everything." [1] What can it mean to try everything? There is surely never enough time nor resources to try *everything*. Campaign resources are always limited. Campaign decision making is a matter of making choices. Choices demand an input of information, answers to questions. What determines whether turnout on election day is high or low? How much do registration rates vary from year to year? Is black voting behavior distinctive? How easy is it to build a coalition, say, of youths, blacks, and poor whites? Do some campaign techniques work better than others? Which ones? Why? Where does the money for a campaign come from? How is it best spent? Does it make sense for a candidate to spend a large portion of his campaign resources on registering voters? The questions are almost endless. But even so, to many of them fairly reliable answers are available. And while reliable information is surely no guarantee ever of election victory, only a fool would argue that the quality of information available has little bearing upon the quality of decision making that is made in the course of a campaign.

This book is not intended to be a sure guide to campaign victory. Such a book does not exist. And besides, many books deal in much greater detail with campaign organization than this one does.[2] What this book does try to offer is an appreciation that some solid, useful information about all aspects of party behavior does exist, and that an acquaintance with it—which this book undertakes to provide—is of value to anyone interested in party politics in America.

Intellectual Curiosity.   A reason which brings people to a study of parties besides the search for useful information is simple intellectual curiosity. Parties are intriguing phenomena. They have so many aspects, and a proper understanding of them requires an investigation of so many possible relationships, that students alternate between despair over ever being able to understand them and great excitement over the discovery of new ways of looking at them, and over new evidence of what they are. The literature on parties includes many writings whose origins lie primarily in a writer's desire to approach the study of parties from a new or simply better perspective than other writers have used. Mastery of a complicated subject matter is a very satisfying accomplishment, and no one would argue that political parties are not complicated phenomena. Parties have long challenged the best efforts of scholars to bring order and sense to an understanding of them. They still do. And scholars continue to be intrigued by that challenge.

The work done by one student stimulates others to pursue the matter further. What is set forth in one study is replicated in a second; the conclusion (or theory) is tested in different circumstances, perhaps employing different definitions of key concepts or different data; a check may be made for the possible influence of time, and the original conclusions challenged, modified, or supported. And the process continues.

EVOLUTION OF A THEORY: AN EXAMPLE. It was such a process as this that gave us a few years ago the view of party organization in America as a "stratarchy." Shortly after the turn of the century, Robert Michels, an Italian sociologist and student of parties, offered what has come to be known as Michels' "iron law of oligarchy"—that there is a tendency within any large organization for decision making to devolve into the hands of a small, cohesive, tight-knit elite.[3] According to Michels, any large organization is inherently oligarchical; that is, any large organization is necessarily led by a small number of individuals who, despite the existence of democratic forms, cannot in any meaningful or effective way be responsible to the rank-and-file membership. Party organizations in America clearly are large organizations, yet for years many students of parties in America insisted that Michels' law simply did not apply to party organizations here. What they saw as the leading characteristic of American parties was an extreme (and perhaps dangerous) decentralization in decision making, which worked against the possibility that American parties could ever be effective in setting and in carrying out national policy goals. Which of these two views was the closer approximation of the truth?

In 1959 Samuel Eldersveld conducted an exhaustive and now well-respected study of party organization in Detroit. As a result of that study, Eldersveld felt obliged to challenge both Michels' view of parties as oligarchical and the more generally held view of American parties as supremely decentralized. He felt particularly obliged to challenge Michels' notion that control of the party structure is inexorably concentrated in the hands of a single leadership corps, the elite managerial nucleus at the top of the structure. Instead, Eldersveld suggested an alternative image of the party as a "stratarchy," a special type of hierarchy in which ruling groups proliferate, and power prerogatives and the exercise of power are diffused. In a stratarchy, rather than centralized unity of command, there exist throughout the structure numerous strata commands, which operate with a varying but considerable degree of independence.[4] Eldersveld's case was buttressed by substantial and convincing evidence. But is what is true in Detroit necessarily true elsewhere? Or is Detroit somehow a special case? Clearly the work done by Eldersveld is just the beginning of a new line of inquiry, not the end.

Other students have ploughed different fields. A great many have searched for the causes of two- or multiparty systems and the effect of each type of party system on political stability. These different searches have arrived at startlingly different conclusions —and thus provided a reason for a fresh search to begin. Any number of students have made serious attempts to develop a theory of the political party. Samuel Barnes is almost certainly correct when he says

> It is evident that *the* theory of the party or indeed of any political institutions or processes does not now and never will exist. There are numerous theories of the party that may be more or less useful, powerful, and reasonable; but there is no theory for all seasons.[5]

Yet at least some students appear not to share Barnes' conviction, for the search for theory shows no sign of letting up.

The subject of political parties *is* amorphous. Its limits *are* poorly defined. One may pick and choose among literally thousands of books and articles, taking special care to read only those which deal with some narrow aspect of party activity, such as election campaign techniques, if that is one's bent. Or, if one is something of a puzzle fancier, one may choose instead to concentrate on those items in the literature that are pathfinders in their use of new tools, new perspectives, new ways to look at parties. Or one may choose, as this book does, to encompass in a few hundred pages a broad-ranging spectrum of the literature dealing with parties.

But even a broad view must have coherent, definable limits. What are the limits of this book?

In this book the evidence on party activity comes from four distinguishable yet related sources.

Party in the Electorate

The first source requires a look at the citizen. This constitutes a study of the "party in the electorate," as many choose to call it.

What Affects Citizen Attitudes Toward Parties?   The political party is a major political institution. It has been with us a long time. It commands widespread public support and has an impact upon the making of public policy. But it is still only one of many political institutions, and it is clear that both its place and its importance in the political system are far from static. How and why is today's party different from yesterday's? Understanding some of the changes that occur requires attention to the impact of citizen attitudes toward party, and knowledge of what affects those attitudes as well as how they may change, especially when they are negative.

THE ACTIONS OF PARTY LEADERS.   Through the decisions they make in the area of public policy, party leaders in Congress can have an impact upon the lives of citizens. The decisions which still other party leaders make at national party conventions every four years always have an impact, because those decisions determine the presidential candidates from among whom the rank-and-file voter gets to choose on election day. If these decisions are not found acceptable by citizens at large—if any considerable part of the public is outraged—there is likely to be a demand for change, and party processes are almost certain to be affected.

UNPOPULAR PUBLIC POLICY.   If public policy is perceived by citizens as wrong-headed, unfair, or just simply inadequate, we know from the record of the past that party fortunes will suffer. The failure of the Herbert Hoover administration between 1929 and 1932 to provide remedies adequate to cope with the Great Depression, transformed a strong majority Republican party into a weak minority party. Gradually increasing public dislike of the conduct of the Vietnam War between 1966 and 1970 moved millions of citizens to decide not to be either Republicans or Democrats but to call themselves Independents instead. It was this same war issue, and especially public reaction to the apparent hostility of too many Democratic party leaders to the antiwar candidacies of Eugene McCarthy and Robert Kennedy, that produced a major reform in the nominating processes of that party.

PARTY RESPONSIVENESS TO CITIZENS.   All citizens may not be equal in their political influence. Indeed they are far from equal (a point that will be closely examined in a later chapter). And the weight of the influence which a single citizen can exercise may indeed be slight. Yet most do have some influence, and the influence of thousands of citizens acting in concert can be considerable.

For decades parties have been perceived by citizens generally as necessary and valuable political institutions. Indeed, there are some students of parties who argue that it is impossible to conceive of a democratically functioning political system without parties. Yet the record of party success and acceptance in the past can be no guarantee of success and acceptance in the future. The citizen is not blind, nor simple, nor a fool. Parties may be important political institutions, but must they be preeminent, say, in the initiation of public policies? (In the United States, have they ever been preeminent?) Must their present and future structure resemble what it has been? Cannot some of their functions be performed better by other institutions? These are open questions. The record of the past two decades alone strongly suggests that the American citizen is capable of great loyalty to a party, but that there is a limit to that loyalty, which may be strained if he sees that parties are becoming unresponsive to his interests or wishes, or if other institutions in the society are better able to perform functions which in times past were assumed to fall within the province of the party.

Citizens have feelings about many things besides parties. Citizens also have feelings about the family, about the broader society, about religion, special interests, justice, constitutional government, the American dream, pollution, abortion, the school system, their duty as citizens, their trust in government, the size of their paycheck, the monotony of work, fishing, football, war, peace, and a million other things. Some of what they believe about parties is easily affected by how they feel about other things. And whether their interest in and support of parties goes up or goes down may well be influenced by how they feel about the other things in their lives that are important to them, as well as their perceptions of party performance.

SOCIAL AND ECONOMIC CHANGE.   More than just attitudes change. So do social and economic factors. More people go to college today than ever before. The median number of school years completed was 12.1 in 1970. At the time of the 1960 census it was 10.6; in 1940 it was 8.6. Median annual family income in 1973 was $12,050. In 1960 it was $5,900. Thirty-five percent of all American families had incomes of $15,000 or more in 1973. Yet 11 percent had incomes below what the government defines as the poverty level. The median age in 1970 was 28.1; in 1960 it was 29.5. It is commonly believed—though some would sharply disagree [6]—that we are much less of a blue-collar people than ever before, that the white-collar segment of the population has been rapidly ascendant since the end of World War II. The number of farmers—there is no dispute about this—has declined dramatically in three decades. Tens upon tens of thousands of field hands and sharecroppers in the hot, steamy acres of the South have been replaced by machines. And increasingly since the 1940s Americans have moved to the cities. We are not, socially or economically, the people we were a mere 10 years ago, and certainly not what we were three or four decades ago. And this has left its mark on what we as citizens believe and how we feel about many things, including politics and parties.

In summary, the study of party in the electorate encompasses a study of citizen attitudes toward parties, the actions of those who are recognized as leaders of the party, citizen response to what is perceived as party action, the possibility of citizen influence upon party action, and how these attitudes themselves are influenced by changes in the social and economic characteristics of the people.

Party as an Organization

The second line of inquiry in our search for an understanding of the political party requires some appreciation of the party as an organization.

Who get to be party leaders? What are they like, how do they differ from the citizen at large? What are their values? What brings them to work for the party, and what sustains their engagement with party work? Corporations and formal party organizations are both creatures of the law, but like corporations, party organizations develop many processes about which the law is silent. What do the laws on party organization say, what is their impact, how restrictive are they, and how permissive? What is the chain of command in the organization? How is the overall organizational structure best described? All these are questions about the party as an organization.

On the subject of party organization, two points in particular need to be made at the outset. First, organizations under whose umbrellas the work of the party gets done are often quite dissimilar from one another. Second, party organization is a hot topic. Students of parties often find themselves engaged in lively debate both over what the party organizations are, and what they might or ought to be.

At the simplest level, the argument is made that one variety of party organization is somehow intrinsically better than some other—"better," say, in the sense that it is more suitable for or compatible with the structure and ends of a modern industrial society. The argument often appears either in a defense of party organizations as we know them in America or as a criticism of those organizations as being ineffective, not responsible, nonmodern, and so forth. Unfortunately there appears to be no easy way to reconcile these conflicting positions, largely because those who hold them usually begin from quite different premises, and their contrasting appraisals of party organization are hardly more than an extension of their different appraisals of the structure and ends of contemporary society. What we can try to do here is to point up the sometimes hidden value premises from which different students approach the analysis of party organization. Hopefully this will make it a little easier to understand what the debate about organization is all about and why it persists, even if this does not move us farther toward a reconciliation of the different viewpoints expressed.

Intellectually, much of our thinking about party organization has been heavily influenced by Maurice Duverger, a French scholar of parties, who offered two contrasting models of party organization. One he called the cadre party; the other he called the mass party. American parties were thought to be more like the first, while the European socialist parties typically were thought to be more like the second.

The Cadre and Mass Parties.   In the cadre party, voters have no formal ties with the organization, nor are they heavily involved in the internal decision-making processes of the party. Control of the machinery of the party, such as it is, rests largely in the hands of an elite or cadre, and it is this cadre that makes the major party decisions and whose performance defines what the party stands for. The preeminent function of the cadre party is electoral, and those of the party who win election to public office are among those who play a large role in the making of party decisions. With only slight exaggeration, one may say that the cadre party represents a them–us relationship, in which the party and its activists stand at some point distant from the rank-and-file voter, and the two encounter one another only infrequently, usually at election times.

The mass party, on the other hand, is designed to involve the rank-and-file members in the decision-making processes of the party. Typically, the organizational structure of the party is both articulated and detailed, with the detail of intraparty relationships often specified in a party constitution and bylaws. Members do feel closely identified with the party of their choice, a feeling that is maintained in part by formal membership in the party and the payment of annual dues. Presumably these organizational characteristics account for the existence of a large pool of talent from which party leaders are recruited.

No one today argues that all existing party organizations are perfect copies of either mass or cadre organizations, but rather that they tend to lean either one way or the other. Why are organizations different? Mainly for these two reasons: First, because they serve the needs of societies with different characteristics and traditions. (This brings us back to the need to look closely at the citizen in order to understand why parties are what they are.) Second, because they are required to perform different functions—a reference both to the citizen and to the place the party occupies in the making of public policy.

The distinction drawn by Duverger between the mass and cadre party remains an important part of the literature on party organization, because it presents with precision and great detail some important features of observed party organization—virtues that, admittedly, may not be evident from the very rough summary of Duverger's model presented above. However, the Duverger analysis is not the only vantage point from which party organization may be viewed. In the literature of the last 20 years, two other major strands of development are evident.

The Structure of Incentives for Party Leadership.   The first strand focuses upon the structure of incentives. Those who work in this field want to know why some people participate much more than others in the work of the party, what brings them there in the first place and what keeps them there, how their work for the party affects them, and whether, as it appears, the party activists of today are in many important respects unlike those of yesteryear. The fruits of this line of inquiry are a collection of studies that provide us with a wealth of detail about party leaders, especially in local organizations, that was next to nonexistent in the literature just 10 years ago.

The Structure of Intra-Party Democracy.   The second new line of inquiry focuses attention upon the structure of *intraparty* democracy. The decade of the sixties was a hard time for parties in America, a time when both their adequacy as representative mechanisms and as effective influences upon the shaping of government policy were called into question. A number of students were encouraged to ask why this was so and what it meant, both for the future of the parties themselves and for the broader society whose interests parties were presumably intended to serve. The resulting studies have told us much that we did not know before about the internal workings of party organizations and have added at least a little to our understanding of how, through parties, citizen influence may be brought to bear upon the making of public policy. Many of these recent studies also contain an element of polemic—blueprints for reform, demands for change, and warnings of terrible things to come if parties do not adapt to changing circumstances and/or recapture a sense of party mission that has for one reason or another been lost in recent years.

This, then, is the stuff of which a study of party organization is made: who belongs, what are the ties that bind, what work gets done, in what respects organizations differ, how best to define the structure of internal and external relationships, how parties influence and are influenced by other political institutions. And always underlying any part of the inquiry is the bothersome problem of discerning change and accounting for it.

Parties in Elections

The conduct of elections is probably the most visible of all party activities. The process of nominating candidates and choosing public officials from among the ranks of those nominated, periodically engages the attention of millions of citizens. The conduct of elections thus serves as a third major source of evidence of what political parties are.

Elections are important. They stand at the confluence of three streams of activity: one that flows from the acts of citizens, one that has its source in the parties as organizations, and one that has its origin in the performance of parties in the government.

The Distinctiveness of American Elections. In some respects the conduct of elections in America is highly distinctive. For one thing, no other polity in the world relies as much as does America upon the direct primary election as a device for nominating party candidates—a fact, as we shall see, that has a definite impact upon the operation and effectiveness of American parties. Further, the fact that millions of Americans are participants in elections for president every four years can easily draw our attention away from another observable fact: that *in most elections* for public office, many fewer Americans participate than turn out in presidential years, in part because some of our electoral arrangements make it quite difficult for people in America to participate in the electoral process. And finally, we must observe that we hold a good many elections in this country. In fact, we elect about 500,000 public officials in America. That alone makes elections here distinctive.

Recent Changes in Elections. No aspect of party activity has changed more during the past two decades than elections. The style of campaigning; the sheer cost of it all and the movement toward public financing of campaigns; the advent and near-primacy of television as the medium of political communication in campaigns; the growing influence of technicians, pollsters, media men, computer craftsmen, and the like; the increase in the use of the primary to nominate party candidates; at the local level, a movement toward nonpartisan elections; the enfranchisement of 18-year-olds; the enfranchisement of blacks, especially in the South; the impact of reapportionment upon party competition for public office—all these are developments that have radically altered the face of elections in America.

Elections are thought to be primarily a device by which public officials may be held accountable to the citizens. Citizens are not exactly what they were 20 years ago. Neither are elections. In the face of these changes, therefore, we must ask whether elections today are more, or less, able to fulfill the function of rendering government accountable than they were yesterday. No question asked in this book is more important. Performance in elections is crucial to the life of parties. Failure to perform as expected could well require major surgery and might even prove fatal. There is solid evidence that citizens have become increasingly unhappy with the condition of their lives and less optimistic for the future than they used to be. If, as seems almost certain, some of the blame for the things that are wrong is laid at the door of government, parties and elections are certain to be affected in turn. Why? Quite simply because it is a staple belief of the American political culture, in which every American child is reared, that elections (and indirectly, parties) are part of the guarantee of responsible government which is every citizen's birthright. And if responsible government is fading away, then elections and parties will surely share some of the blame.

Party in the Government

The fourth line of inquiry taken up here seeks to uncover the influence of party in the making of public policy, an inquiry which is often referred to as a study of "party in the government."

For some students of parties this is at the heart of a study of parties. If parties were not influential in the making of public policy, would there not be much less reason to study them closely? In fact, there is some evidence that parties today have much less impact upon the making of public policy than was once true, or at least thought to have been true. The evidence on this point, however, is far from clear. It may well be that we have not been looking carefully enough at the evidence, or even that we have been looking in the wrong places for evidence, or perhaps have not been asking the right questions. The study of party in government, like the study of organization, is an area around which debate and argument rages.

For all the debate, we are certain of two things. First, party is never the only influence upon policy makers; and second, party is not equally an influence across all areas of public policy.

Party Influence on Congress.   Take the case of Congress for a moment. There are 535 members of Congress, 435 in the House and 100 in the Senate. Since it is the votes of these 535 persons that decide which laws are passed and which are defeated, it can be argued that the behavior of these 535 people is the best evidence of Congressional decision making in public policy. Each of these 535 persons wears a party label. Overwhelmingly, that label is either Democrat or Republican. Because the identity of the policy makers is clear and because their party affiliation is equally easy to determine, finding out how much influence party has upon their behavior should be a relatively uncomplicated business. And for the most part it is. Studies of party influence in Congress tell us that the member of Congress is subject to influence mainly from three sources: (a) his own personal convictions about what public policy ought to be; (b) his constituency; and (c) his political party. These studies also inform us that party is more influential in some areas of public policy and also that the relative influence of party, constituency, and self varies not only by policy area but also through time. Finally, these studies tell us that some aspects of congressional and state legislative organization definitely serve to weaken the influence of party in the making of decisions. Most notable of these organizational aspects is the committee system through which legislation must pass before it comes to the floor of either house for a final vote. The seniority system, thanks to which chairmen of standing committees have gotten to be chairmen not by virtue of the support they have given their party but by their success in winning reelection; the filibuster in the Senate, which enables a committed and hardy third of the membership to prevent a bill from coming to the floor for a vote; the considerable power which the Rules Committee in the House enjoys over the flow of legislation from committees to the floor— all these are elements of organization which for years have reinforced the influence of committees and committee chairmen, and on many notable occasions have served to thwart the power of party leadership in Congress.

Yet Congress is not unchangeable. Elections displace some members, and some new ones come to serve. The election of 1964 saw Democratic gains in Congress greater than at any time since the early 1930s. So much new blood on the Democratic side of the congressional aisles unquestionably facilitated the work of a Democratic President and a Democratically controlled Congress in redefining many areas of public policy. The 1974 elections saw the greatest Democratic gains in Congress since 1964, but the impact of that shift on policy is apt to be minimal, for Congress is easily able to move forcefully only when the occupant of the White House is committed to moving ahead forcefully.

Even the rule of seniority, once thought impregnable, has come under challenge. It all began in January 1973, when Democrats in the House adopted a resolution which gives the Democratic caucus—consisting of all Democrats in the House— power to choose the chairmen of standing committees by majority vote when the Democrats are the majority party in the House. No chairman of any committee lost his job in the secret balloting that followed the adoption of this resolution, but neither did any chairman receive unanimous support. When Congress opened its doors in January 1975, it included a group of 52 Democratic freshmen who had been elected in special and regular elections during 1974. Once again, as had happened two years before, the caucus voted on committee chairmen. This time three chairmen lost their jobs, and others retained theirs only after they promised to make substantial changes in the way they ran their committees. Jamie Whitten of Mississippi, for example, was forced to give up a chairmanship of a subcommittee of the Agriculture Committee dealing with the environment, a post he had effectively used for years to block environmental protection legislation not to his personal liking. Several other chairmen agreed to bring an unaccustomed measure of democracy into their committees by ensuring a more active role for younger members in the substantive work of the committee, including decisions on such matters as the allocation of staff and budget of the committee itself.

Party Influence Elsewhere In Government. *Congress,* of course, is not synonymous with *government,* and a student of party in government must spend at least a little time looking at party influence elsewhere in government. At times this inquiry is quite difficult, as, for instance, when the effort is made to measure party influence upon judges or upon city councilmen who are elected in nonpartisan elections in which party labels are suppressed. The search can also be tricky when one tries to make an assessment of party influence on the totality of public policy or on some very broad policy areas.

Party Impact Upon State Public Policy.   We have in the literature a great many studies which have undertaken to measure the influence of party in the making of public policy in the 50 states. These studies have regularly reported quite opposite findings. None has succeeded in establishing itself as the best study in the field. Indeed, a few older reports appear in retrospect to be so sweeping in design, in measurement, and in conclusions that we must wonder why we did not have the sense to give them a grade of "F" when they first appeared.

FINDING ADEQUATE PUBLIC POLICY INDICATORS.   What is the problem? Actually there are several problems. First is the problem of finding indicators or measures of the public policies being studied. Can a figure of "per pupil expenditure"—the amount of money a state reports spending per pupil each year for public school education—fairly represent the whole of a state's public policy in education? Can the "average monthly payment under the aid-to-dependent-children program" adequately represent a state's public policy in the area of welfare? Probably not. Indeed these figures may obscure a great deal more than they reveal. The conflict within a state over textbooks, busing, capital expenditures for the universities, what to do with unused dormitory space, the tax base used for the support of education, teachers' salaries, the amount of emphasis to be given to vocational education in the high schools and junior colleges, the extent of support to be given to two-year versus four-year colleges, the cost of tuition at state schools, the relative burden for the support of education to be borne by the state and by local government and by different income groups within the population, and a host of other questions subject to differing support from the political parties are poorly expressed, if expressed at all, in "per pupil expenditure" figures. Thus, any study which employs such a gross measure of educational policy runs a grave risk of misleading us by oversimplifying.

THE VARYING IMPACT OF PARTY UPON DIFFERENT POLICIES. Another problem is to discover what public policy areas are most likely to be affected by party differences and competition. Is political party conflict really likely to arise over the *total amount of spending?* Or is it far more likely to be over *who precisely shall benefit* from what is spent? A proposal to allow a tax credit to a family that spends more than $3,000 a year on college tuition for its children is clearly going to be of greater interest and benefit to middle- and upper-income groups than to those whose income is low, while a proposal to extend unemployment benefits or create public service jobs or expand a food stamp program will promise benefits to quite a different income group. This is an important point whose importance is underscored by the long-observed fact that political parties tend to attract different levels of support from people with different levels of income.

THE PROBLEM OF MEASURING COMPETITION. A third problem is finding a measure of political party activity sufficiently discriminating to allow us to assess the impact, if any, of the party on public policy. That has proven to be a tough problem. Suffice it to say for the present that students of parties are far from agreed that an adequate measure has yet been devised. Most of the efforts thus far have concentrated on devising a measure of party strength in a community, using data from elections, and then undertaking to determine whether public policies are significantly different in those places where parties are competitive and in those places where one party seems to be firmly in control. There are difficulties with this, as we shall see when we explore this subject in some detail in a later chapter.

What then is encompassed in the study of party in government? The following items may provide an answer:

A look at party influence in decision making at different levels and institutions of government—Congress, certainly, and state legislatures, courts, the bureaucracy, and so forth.

An appraisal of the circumstances—organizational, social, economic, and other—which appear to encourage or hinder party influence.

A look at the impact party has upon different areas of policy.

A continuous effort to determine how party influence in government can be explained by what we have already observed about the citizen, the party organization, and the conduct of elections.

This book aims to provide an analysis of parties which is a synthesis of the best thinking of the many students who find parties intrinsically interesting and as worthy of study as any other political institution. It aims to reflect the findings and concerns of current research and to suggest new research lines that look fruitful. The goal overall is to provide an introduction to the subject adequate both for those who want no more than an introduction to the subject and for those who will see a reading of this book as just a starting point in understanding political parties.

NOTES

The first quotation at the beginning of the chapter is from Walter Karp, *Indispensable Enemies: The Politics of Misrule in America* (Baltimore, Md.: Penguin, 1974), 294. The second is from John S. Saloma III and Frederick H. Sontag, *Parties: The Real Opportunity for Effective Citizen Politics* (New York: Vintage Books, 1973), 5. The third is from Robert S. Gilmour and Robert B. Lamb, *Political Alienation* (New York: St. Martin, 1975), 2.

1. Abraham Ribicoff and Jon O. Newman, *Politics: The American Way* (Boston: Allyn & Bacon, 1967), 99.
2. There are a great many "how-to-do-it" books on election campaigning. Those that bear looking at are: John Dean, *The Making of a Black Mayor* (Washington, D.C.: Joint Center for Political Studies, 1972); Edward Schwartzmann, *Campaign Craftsmanship: A Professional's Guide to Campaigning for Elective Office* (New York: Universe Books, 1973); Chester G. Atkins, *Getting Elected: A Guide to Winning State and Local Office* (Boston: Houghton Mifflin, 1973); James M. Perry, *The New Politics: The Expanding Technology of Political Manipulation* (New York: Potter, 1968); Frederick Pohl, *Practical Politics* (New York: Ballantine, 1971); Dick Simpson, *Winning Elections: A Handbook in Participatory Politics* (Chicago: Swallow, 1972); Meyer D. Swing, *The Winning Candidate: How to Defeat Your Political Opponent* (New York: Heinman, 1966).
3. Robert Michels, *Political Parties* (New York: Free Press, 1962), especially part 6.
4. Samuel J. Eldersveld, *Political Parties* (Skokie, Ill.: Rand McNally, 1964), especially chapter 5.
5. Samuel H. Barnes, "Party Democracy and the Logic of Collective Action," in William J. Crotty (editor), *Approaches to the Study of Party Organization* (Boston: Allyn & Bacon, 1968), 105.
6. For an unusually clear and persuasive argument on the difficulty of defining membership in the blue- and white-collar classes—a prerequisite for determining growth rates in each class—see Andrew Levison, "The Working-Class Majority," *New Yorker,* September 2, 1974, 36–61.

Part One

Party in the Electorate

Political organization, individual leadership, and the policies of the great parties are important as precipitants and preservatives of political change. However, they rarely, if ever, are capable of producing long-term change independent of some basic change in the political environment.

The patterns of shifting partisan attachment are quite obvious when examined with respect to age, education and region, but the most dramatic change in partisan attachment is found for blacks. Partisan attachment for whites appears almost stable by comparison.

Recent data from France and Italy underscore the conservative impact of religious practice on party choice. In these two classic European cases, where long-established Marxist parties exist in a nominally Catholic culture, participation in religious activities has been strongly linked with moderate and conservative political behavior among workers. Those workers who have little or no Church affiliation register very strong support for Communist and Socialist parties.

The evidence of the foregoing analysis substantiates the assertion that religion remained a potent source of political cleavage in the United States through the 1960s. [However] the analysis of trends in sources of party identification over the eight-year period suggests a relative increase in the importance of respondent's education and a diminution in the impact of religion.

The Social Bases of Partisanship

The suggestion that there is a connection between an individual's social characteristics and his political behavior is hardly news. The question is whether some characteristics have a stronger influence upon behavior than others. This chapter considers the influence of a person's occupation, education, income, religion, ethnic group membership, age, and region upon his partisanship and upon his political participation, with occasional reference made to points of similarity and contrast between the United States and other countries.

Social Cleavages and Politics

Cleavages exist in every society. Some people are richer than others, some are better educated, some belong to a church, and others do not, some work at occupations that carry a lot of prestige, while others do not, some are proud of a black skin while others in their turn are conscious and glad of being white. Cleavages not only exist; they can have political significance. Indeed, in every society where political parties exist, the supporters of each party can be distinguished by their social characteristics.[1] It is this phenomenon which led sociologist Paul Lazarsfeld to say, with only slight exaggeration, that social characteristics determine political preference.[2]

Parties in the United States are no exception. These days, blacks, for example, are far more likely to be Democrats than Republicans.[3] (In 1972 one of every five McGovern voters was black.[4]) So too are members of labor unions, Jews, and people with an eighth-grade education or less, while the Republican Party is likely to be preferred by people 50 years old or more, professional people such as doctors, lawyers, bankers, airplane pilots, and the like, and people who use the long form rather than the short form at income-tax time. Here, then, is evidence of the importance of ethnic group membership, status, religion, education, occupation, and age as influences upon partisanship.

The Relatively Weak Relationship Between Social Factors and Partisanship in America.   Yet it has often been remarked that the history of party politics in America is in some important respects distinctive. For one thing, the country has never seen an effective socialist party. There have been numerous socialist parties, but they have never enjoyed a large membership, nothing even close to the size of the membership of the major political parties, even at times of great economic dislocation, when the appeal of a socialist party might be expected to be at its highest. For another thing, the relationship between social class and partisanship in the United States has never been strong. The major American political parties have drawn support in varying degrees from all social strata, and thus the tendency for groups of partisans to differ in their social characteristics is probably less pronounced in the United States than in any other country.[5] The need here, therefore, is to define as precisely as possible the direction and strength of such relationship as does exist in the United States between the citizens' social characteristics and their partisan preferences.

The Relationship Between Status and Participation.   Studies have shown an interesting relationship between social characteristics and participation. Generally speaking, those low on status— those with few years of schooling, low incomes, who work in low-status occupations—are much less likely to participate in politics than those whose status is higher. The differences are sometimes marked: Figures from the 1972 election showed, for example, that persons with a college education were almost *three times as likely to vote* that year as those who had four years of schooling or less.[6] Students of parties have also observed that public policy is much more likely to be responsive to the demands of some groups of citizens than to others, and this is often explained as being related to the relationship between social characteristics and both partisanship and participation. Further, party organizations themselves are populated by citizens who generally enjoy a significantly higher socioeconomic status than the population as a whole. Is this bias unavoidable? Is it true for America but much less true elsewhere? Does it mean anything—is the bias built into the recruitment patterns of party organizations itself a source of the bias evident in at least some important areas of public policy? These are lines of inquiry which lead some students of parties to be concerned with the relationship between citizens' social characteristics and political behavior.

Finally, the social characteristics of the citizens in this country may not change radically from one decade to the next, but some change does occur. The desire to know what changes are occurring and how these may affect party politics is still another reason why students of parties consider themselves obliged to pay attention to the social characteristics of citizens.

In short, citizens are far from alike in their social characteristics, and there is a connection between various social characteristics and both partisanship and political participation, including participation in party activity; and there is at least an indirect connection between the social characteristics of citizens and the social preferences reflected in public policy. To explore some of these connections is the task of the remainder of this chapter, which considers seven social characteristics which have in the past proved to merit close attention: occupation, education, income, religion, age, ethnic group membership, and regionalism.

Occupation

Some lines of work carry more prestige than others. The job of a banker, a doctor, an actress, a factory owner, a judge, or even a professor, ranks high. The job of a bartender, a charwoman, a garbage collector, or an elevator operator ranks lower. A general in the army ranks high, while an army private has about as much status as a student. In short, our occupations give us varying measures of status. The professions are at the top of the status ladder, white-collar jobs are generally in the middle, and blue-collar jobs are generally located on the bottom rungs.

The number of Americans in different occupations is anything but stationary. Some classes of occupations are growing rapidly. Others are declining just as rapidly. The 1970 census tells us that a greater number of people than ever are to be found in higher-status occupations. In the 20-year period between 1950 and 1970, the proportion of the nation's work force in the professions increased from 18 to 26 percent; in the white-collar occupations, from 20 to 23 percent; but in the manual labor category, the number declined from 50 to 43 percent. At the same time—even more dramatic—the number in farming declined from 12 to 3 percent.

Knowing a man's occupation can usually tell you a lot about his politics. The relationship between occupation and politics can be very close, as it is with lawyers, for example.[7] People in high-status occupations tend to be Republicans. They tend to be more active and involved in politics than people in lower-status occupations. Their ranks constitute a major resource for the recruitment of party workers and candidates,[8] and some of the best-known, best-organized, and most active and effective interest groups are those that represent occupations. In this connection we may call to mind the American Medical Association,[9] the United Auto Workers, the National Education Association, the American Association of University Professors, and the International City Managers Association. No one should have any difficulty thinking of the names of many other such interest groups. The columns of any issue of a major daily newspaper should supply at least a dozen.

Education

More Americans than ever are going to school for longer periods of time. According to the 1950 census, the average number of school years completed was 9; in 1970 the figure was 12. In less than a generation, the "average" American changed from an elementary school graduate to a high school graduate. In this same period, the proportion of adults with only a grade school education declined from 45 to 30 percent, while the number who reported having completed college rose from 8 to 20 percent.

The Low Impact of Education on Party Preference.   Education and occupation tend to be mutually reinforcing, for the plain reason that people with more schooling tend to work at higher-status occupations, while those with less schooling tend to have jobs with lower status. Rarely do we find an instance when this is not so. However, when we do find someone with a college education working in a low-status job, we are likely to note at least one respect in which his attitudes are distinctive: He will differ sharply from his co-workers in his attitudes on foreign policy. In this one instance it is his education, and not his occupational status, that determines his attitudes.[10]

Education alone has little impact upon partisanship. Bankers are generally well educated and Republicans. Those who drive the city sanitation trucks are likely to be poorly educated and Democrats. However, when we find that rare instance where occupation and education are not mutually reinforcing—a banker who never went beyond the sixth grade, or a taxi driver who graduated from Harvard—what we find is this: The banker is most probably a staunch Republican, and the taxi driver a Democrat or Independent.[11]

The High Impact of Education on Participation.   Where education does make a substantial difference is in efficacy and activity. People with more education tend to have a higher sense of political efficacy—a feeling that one can be politically effective —and to be much more active and interested in politics than those who have ended their schooling early.[12] They are also observed to possess more information about politics and government, and to be more likely to talk about politics. They have more group memberships and are exposed to a wider range of social interaction, with a concurrent exposure to a wider and more constant stream of political stimuli. The well educated are also represented in government far out of proportion to their numbers in the total population. It is unlikely that anyone occupying a policy-making position in the bureaucracy will *not* have a college degree, yet even today a degree cannot be claimed by more than 20 percent of the adult population. In this connection, we must not forget one other consequence of exposure to formal schooling: Those who have the most schooling are most likely to have the strongest commitment to democratic values. We will have more to say about that later. Education, in short, does have important political consequences.

Education has been found to be an important correlate of political participation in many countries besides the United States. Its significance has been established in studies of voters in Finland,[13] Italy,[14] Great Britain,[15] and France.[16] In their five-nation study, Almond and Verba found that education was an even better predictor of participation in Mexico, Italy, and Germany than it was in Great Britain and the United States. They found also that education had a greater impact upon political participation in all five countries than did either income or occupation.[17]

Yet even this long-accepted proposition requires a caveat: We may have more confidence in the relationship if we specify the conditions under which the observed relationship is likely to remain strong. A notion that education is related to participation is intuitively appealing. Yet in fact there are those in the upper-income, occupational, and educational brackets who do not participate. To look abroad, for a moment, it has been demonstrated by Rabushka's study of Chinese in two Malaysian cities that an inverse relationship exists between education and turnout in elections—the best educated are least likely to vote. Apparently their education helped them discover that their vote is meaningless.[18] Kim and Koh reported a similar finding from a study of voting behavior in three presidential elections in South Korea.[19] As for the United States, Coveyou and Pfeiffer indicated that turnout among black high school graduates in the presidential election of 1968 was lower than among both those with only a grade school education and those with a college education. This observed difference appears to be a function both of age and region.[20] Therefore, while the long-accepted proposition that education is strongly related to participation may still stand, it is no longer wholly intact. Age and region may modify it. And we should hardly be surprised if a study done today were to reveal that the relationship is further complicated by the level of trust citizens have for political institutions and the political system.

Income

Inequality of income distribution is a feature of American society. Over the past several decades, family income generally has risen, but the growth has hardly been uniform across the nation and for all persons. The South generally remains poorer than the nation as a whole, and within the South some places and persons are much poorer than others. In 1973 the median family income in the United States was $12,050. Quite in contrast is the picture of Tunica County, Mississippi, with a population in 1970 of approximately 3,500 blacks and 2,000 whites. The county economy is predominantly agricultural; cotton is the dominant crop. In 1970 the median family income there was $2,885—less than one-fourth the national figure. Equally pronounced differences are evident in the income figures for the 435 congressional districts. By far the richest is the Eighth Congressional District of Maryland, which in 1970 reported a median family income of over $17,000. The heart of the Maryland Eighth District is Montgomery County, and we shall have more to say later of the characteristics of party leaders in this wealthy suburban community.

People with many years of formal schooling work in higher-status occupations and are likely to earn more money. As is true with education, income is more strongly related to participation than it is to partisanship, although, to be sure, people with higher incomes are likely to be Republicans, while those with less income tend to be Democrats. Why are people with higher incomes more likely than persons with lower incomes to participate in politics? In part, we believe this is because those with an adequate income have time which can be used for political activity. In part, it may also be because people with higher incomes are likely to have a good supply of self-esteem. Some people lacking in self-esteem may hesitate to identify themselves too closely with politics by publicly wearing a campaign button or putting a campaign sticker on their car, but the higher-income individual with high self-esteem will display no such hesitation.[21] It is not true, however, that those with the highest incomes are those most likely to be active in politics, a fact which leads Robert Lane to speak of a "kind of declining marginal productivity of income on voting." [22]

Socioeconomic Status and Partisanship.   Income, education, and occupation together provide a measure of a person's socioeconomic status (SES). Any number of studies have searched for, but none has found, a *close relationship* between SES and partisanship. In neither their ideas nor their memberships are the parties identifiably associated with a particular status group—a point of major significance to which we will return many times in this book. (That is not to say, of course, that all status groups are equally well represented by the major parties. Indeed they are not, and to that point we shall also have occasion to return later.) Yet income inequality, the sharing of the goods of the society, is at the heart of serious political battle in most political systems. It is hard to believe that citizens of Tunica and Montgomery counties have common needs for government policies, or that existing programs offer equal benefits to the people in these two counties. In fact, it is not at all difficult to demonstrate that the structure of government policy offers quite different costs and benefits to high- than to low-income groups.

Socioeconomic Status and Participation. If any significant portion of any status group is, for whatever reason, excluded from participation in party and government activity, dare we assume that their interests will be adequately represented? That seems improbable. Yet the impact of SES is evident precisely in participation. The difference in the rates of political participation among different status groups in America is striking. Status in America, in short, is weak as a correlate of partisanship, strong in its relationship to political participation. Those who rank high on status participate at a rate many times greater than those who are of low status. Figure 2-1 presents the findings from a study of political participation in America, one of a series of studies of political participation in 12 countries. This figure divides those in the American survey sample into five categories, according to a measure of their political participation, and within each category into three categories of SES. The figure shows rather dramatically that those who have low SES are much less likely to participate than those who have high SES. It also shows that the high-SES–highest-participating group is larger than any other SES-participating group—representing in fact 12 percent of the total population. "Participation," say the authors of the study, "is a potent force; leaders respond to it. But they respond more to the participants than to those who do not participate."[23] Those most likely to participate in America are the more affluent, the better educated, those in higher-status occupations. And it is to these upper-strata persons that governmental leaders respond.

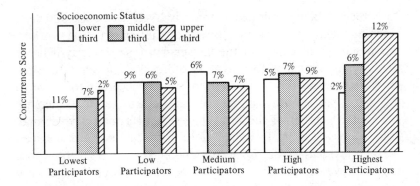

The percentages above each column are the proportion comprised by the particular group within the population as a whole.

The concurrence score measures how frequently leaders agree with a citizen on priorities: the higher the bar, the more the average member of that particular group receives from government.

Figure 2-1   Participation and Concurrence for Three Socioeconomic Groups

Source: Sidney Verba and Norman H. Nie, *Participation in America* (New York: Harper & Row, 1972), Fig. 20-1, p. 337, modified by permission of the authors and publisher.

Socioeconomic Status, Lifestyles, and Attitudes.   What does it mean to have high rather than low socioeconomic status—to be, say, a lawyer instead of a construction worker? They have different lifestyles, certainly, and a different relationship to politics, probably. Let us consider the case of the construction worker first. If there is a common image of the construction worker it is an image of well-being: Earnings of $7 to $10 an hour, 35 hours per week, 52 weeks a year (with three weeks off for vacation) equals a comfortable if modest home, supported on an income of roughly $12,000 to $15,000 per year, not counting overtime. Employment statistics issued annually offer a quite different picture.[24] These employment data show the construction worker as a man often out of work (35 percent of all such workers were unemployed for more than 120 working days in 1973), either because of a slowdown in some area of construction (in 1973 it was in homebuilding) or because of rain (in which case he may not be paid). His wife works at a checkout counter in a supermarket or at another job that pays less than princely wages, and *together,* when times are good, they earn roughly $10,000. If he is black, their combined income is likely to be $2,000 less. Unemployment is a constant threat to the construction worker. It is much less a reality for the lawyer, who, particularly if he or she is young and new to a firm, is quite likely to have to work long hours every day and often on Sunday in order to prove to the senior partners that he or she can be a productive, income-producing member of the firm. The wife of a male lawyer may hold a job, but more likely she does not. The contrasts between the employment patterns of professionals and workers whose status is even lower than that of the construction worker, are even greater. Can there be any doubt that the different lifestyles of professionals and lower-status workers, contrasting as they do in such critical matters as job security and whether the wife in a family must work will be reflected in their political attitudes? Surely not.

It is the degree of contrast in lifestyles of persons of different social status that has political consequence. The problems of their daily lives are at so many points dissimilar. And it strains credibility that a party or government system manned very largely by upper-status persons will easily or strongly reflect the unique concerns of lower-status persons, to whom—to mention just one concern—the problem of uncertain employment has an every-day immediacy.

Religion

Religion can be an important influence upon political behavior. We need only look at the 1960 presidential election to see that. Our general understanding of the 1960 election is that John F. Kennedy lost a little more than he gained because he was a Roman Catholic. It is not always easy to sort out the influence of religion as such. We can say, for example, that among Protestants, Episcopalians are more likely to vote than Baptists, but how much this is the product of religion and how much it is the product of socioeconomic status is hard to say, because we also know that Episcopalians generally enjoy a higher socioeconomic status than Baptists.

Religion and the 1960 Presidential Election.   What we do know is that the impact of religion, like the impact of any group association, will be affected by (1) how strongly the individual himself identifies with the group, and (2) how clearly the perceived object, a candidate, for example, is seen to be identified with the group.[25] In 1960, a roman Catholic Republican who was a devout Catholic and who saw John F. Kennedy first as a Catholic and then as, unfortunately, a Democrat, was likely in the end to vote for him. Similarly, an equally devout Protestant Democrat with a solid prejudice against Roman Catholics was never able to forget or accept the fact that his party had nominated one of "them," and he was likely to end up voting for Richard Nixon.[26]

Our understanding of group influences like religion leads us to expect what we find in the data from the study of the 1960 election. Figure 2-2 presents data to show the relationship between regularity of church attendance among Protestants and the rate at which they defected to support Richard Nixon, while

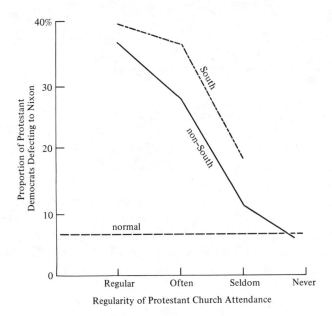

Figure 2-2   Defections to Nixon Among Protestant Democrats as a Function of Church Attendance

Source: Angus Campbell et al., *Elections and the Political Order* (New York: Wiley, 1966), Fig. 5-1, p. 89, by permission of the publisher.

Table 2-1 Offsetting Effects of the Catholic Issue, 1960 Democratic Presidential Vote

Area	Percent of Two-Party Vote in Area
Outside the South: Kennedy's "unexpected" . . .	
Gains from Catholics	5.2
Losses from Protestant Democrats and Independents	−3.6
Net	1.6
Inside the South: Kennedy's "unexpected" . . .	
Gains from Catholics	0.7
Losses from Protestant Democrats and Independents	−17.2
Net	−16.5
For the nation as a whole: Kennedy's "unexpected" . . .	
Gains from Catholics	4.3
Losses from Protestant Democrats and Independents	−6.5
Net	−2.2

Source: Angus Campbell et al., "Stability and Change in 1960: A Reinstating Election," *American Political Science Review* 55 (June 1961), 278.

Table 2-1 summarizes the findings on the net effect of the Catholic issue upon the outcome of the election. The data demonstrate rather handsomely that his Roman Catholicism hurt Kennedy a lot among Protestant Democrats in the South. Those who attended church regularly were much more likely to vote for Nixon than were those who said they never attended. Votes denied him by southern Protestant Democrats were not offset by the sizable gains he made among Catholics in the non-South, with the overall effect that in the nation as a whole his Catholicism cost him an estimated 2.2 percent of the two-party vote.[27]

The Social Bases of Western Parties.   The 1960 election was unusual. Religion seldom plays that large a role in American politics. That makes American party politics distinctive, for in other Western countries religion is by far the most common of all social bases upon which political parties stand.[28] In a study of 76 political parties in 17 Western countries, Rose and Urwin found that parties tended to derive their cohesion mainly from four social bases: religion, class, "communal nationalism" (meaning linguistic or ethnic identity), and regionalism. The cohesion of 35 of the 76 parties studied derived from a common religious or antireligious identification among their members. In 4 of the 17 countries studied, including the United States, there were no religiously cohesive parties. Class (measured by occupation) was next in importance to religion as a basis for party cohesion. Thirty-two of the 76 parties were class based. Three countries, again including the United States, had no class-based parties. Communal nationalism and regionalism were each the basis for only 8 of the 76 parties, while 19 of the 76, including both the Democratic and the Republican parties in the United States, had to be classed as heterogeneous in their base, because no particular social characteristic dominated a majority of their supporters. A summary follows of how these 76 parties were classified:

Table 2-2 Classification of Political Parties in 17 Western Countries

Heterogeneous		19
Single-claim		
Religion		18
Class		20
Mutually reinforcing loyalties including		
Religion	(17)	
Class	(12)	
Region	(8)	
Communal	(8)	19
TOTAL		76

Source: From "Social Cohesion, Political Parties and Strains in Regimes," by Richard Rose and Derek Urwin. Reprinted from *Comparative Political Studies,* Vol. 2, No. 1 (April 1969), pp. 18–19, by permission of the publisher, Sage Publications, Inc.

The weakness of religion as a correlate of partisanship in the United States is further highlighted by the discovery in the Rose and Urwin study that 9 of the 11 countries where a substantial number of Catholics live have a cohesive party based upon Catholicism. The other country, besides the United States, which does not is Ireland, and Ireland is not that great an exception because all parties in Ireland support the special position of the Roman Catholic church in the life of the country. That leaves the United States the only clear exception.

Ethnic Groups

The American "melting pot" has effectively assimilated millions of persons born in other lands. The effects of the huge waves of immigration which brought these people to American shores, made them citizens, and developed in them and in their children an appreciation for the cultural norms of the country, are far from having disappeared completely from sight, however. There are wards and precincts in every American metropolis which are peopled by Poles, Germans, Jews, Italians, Irish, Puerto Ricans, and so on through the list of countries from which immigrants came. It is the voting returns in these wards and precincts which are relied upon to tell how the Polish vote, or the German vote, and so on is likely to go. A tribute to the importance of the ethnic factor in American party politics is the continuing appearance of that campaign ploy known as "balancing the ticket." The belief is that if you care at all about whether your party's candidates do well in an area in which large groups of Poles or Irishmen or Italians are found, then you had best make sure that your party's slate of candidates contains the appropriate proportion of easily recognizable Polish, Irish, or Italian names.

Important Ethnic Groups.   A listing of some of the larger and better-known ethnic groups would have to include the Irish of Boston, the Italians of Rhode Island, the Germans of Wisconsin,[29] the French-Canadians of Maine and Vermont, the Jews, Italians, Irish, Chinese, etc., of New York City, the Japanese of Hawaii, and the Poles of Milwaukee, to say nothing of the blacks found in every southern state and in every northern city. There is no metropolitan area in the United States that does not have its sizable ethnic group, and where these groups exist, there too are politicians ready to court them. Speaking of the importance of ethnic politics, Raymond Wolfinger reminds us that "the political history of New England, the Middle Atlantic states, and the eastern Great Lakes cannot be adequately described without paying considerable attention to this subject [ethnic politics]."[30]

Much like religion, membership in an ethnic group is most likely to influence our political behavior if (1) we feel closely identified with the group and (2) if we have reason (or occasion) to evaluate some element of politics in terms of its relationship to the group.

Ethnic Voting.   There are many places where one may find evidence of ethnic politics, including the making of appointments, the nominating of candidates, and other political decisions, as well as in voting.[31] Members of ethnic groups do not always vote along ethnic lines, but the evidence is substantial that ethnic voting is not an infrequent occurrence.[32] The direction of the voting choices is not always easy to predict. In New Haven, Connecticut, the Nineteenth Ward is overwhelmingly Democratic, while the Eleventh is overwhelmingly Republican. The populations of these two wards are alike in every important social and economic characteristic except that the Nineteenth is black, while the Eleventh is Italian.[33] Italians in New Haven are among the poorest people in that city's population. We might expect them to be Democrats, but they are not. Three decades ago the first Italian candidate for mayor of New Haven was nominated by the Republican party, and in 1945 he was elected mayor. Since that time Italians have been the mainstay of Republican voting strength in the city, even in years when there have been no Italian candidates on the ballot.[34] Italians in New Haven are quite different from Italians elsewhere in New England, the large majority of whom are Democrats.[35]

Newark, New Jersey, a city whose population is roughly one-third first- and second-generation immigrants and roughly two-thirds black and Puerto Rican, provides a good place to study the relative influence of party and ethnic voting. Newark elects its city officials on a nonpartisan ballot. Candidates for seats in the state legislature, however, bear identifying party labels. Denied the opportunity to choose among candidates according to their party labels, voter choices in city elections tend to follow ethnic lines, but no such pattern is evident when voters choose among party candidates running for seats in the state legislature.[36]

What seems true from the New Haven and Newark examples is that, as Gerald Pomper puts it, the political parties do not eliminate ethnic influence, they "manage" it.[37] In the process of designing balanced tickets, they serve to reduce the sharpness of political conflict among competing ethnic groups.

Blacks: America's Largest Ethnic Group.   One of the largest and most conspicuous of all ethnic groups in America is made up of American blacks. They are, even today, far from being fully treated as equal citizens by all other Americans. Because they are often acutely aware of the negative attitudes of many other Americans and because they easily identify with other blacks, the status of American blacks has had and will for some time continue to have major political consequences.

BLACKS AND THE DEMOCRATIC PARTY.   Blacks are presently among the strongest of Democratic party supporters, but the record of recent years indicates that those attachments are far from sturdy. The movement of blacks into the ranks of the Democratic party began in the 1930s, but was much accelerated during the decade of the sixties. It was in part the acts of two Kennedys, one in the White House and the other in the Department of Justice, both of whom were sympathetic to blacks, and in part the decision of the Republican presidential candidate in 1964 to vote against the Civil Rights Act of 1964 that solidified this movement.

Those blacks who support the Democratic party and reject the Republican party do so for much the same reasons that all Democrats do, and their images of the party are much the same whether they live in the North or in the South. In an extensive study of southern political attitudes made in the early sixties, blacks reported having a strongly favorable image of the Democratic party and a correspondingly unfavorable image of the Republican party.[38]

THE INCREASE IN BLACK PARTICIPATION.   For decades, the lack of black participation in politics has been notable. In the South their participation was lowest in precisely those places where blacks were most numerous. The southern white could count and could reckon as well as the next man.[39] In many places, especially where blacks were a majority of the population, whites went to great lengths to prevent blacks from participating in the political process. Times are changing. Millions of black voters have been added to the voting rolls of the South, and blacks have been elected to offices in the South and to the U.S. House of Representatives,[40] thanks largely to the passage of the Civil Rights Act of 1964 and the Voting Rights Act of 1965. In cities of the North, the record from the past decade shows that the rate of participation by blacks in local elections on occasion is even higher than it is for whites.

American blacks have also distinguished themselves from other Americans by their willingness to employ a wide variety of techniques in the pursuit of political ends. Surveys done during the past decade show that more than half of all blacks—and an even higher proportion of black leaders—say they are willing to participate in mass action, including marching in a demonstration, taking part in a sit-in, going to jail, and picketing.[41] Their willingness to participate in direct action does not, however, necessarily mean that all blacks are alienated. Undoubtedly, many of the younger, better-educated blacks do feel alienated from white society, and often from middle-class blacks as well. The emergence of the Black Panthers, the Deacons, and the Muslims, and their strong appeal to youth represent the negative reaction of youth to the National Association for the Advancement of Colored People (NAACP), as well as a rejection of white society and its institutions. On the whole, however, blacks continue to have a broadly favorable image of the Democratic party, and most still choose to maintain an identification with it rather than to move over to the support of a new third party.[42]

SHIFTING PATTERNS IN BLACK PARTISANSHIP.   Yet it would be a serious error to assume that blacks are just as enthusiastic in their support for the Democratic party today as they were earlier. At the beginning of the 1960s a sizable number of blacks were recorded as being either apolitical or Independent. In the South, one in every four blacks fell into this category. But by 1968, no less than 86 percent of blacks in the country called themselves Democrats. After that, the movement reversed, and by 1972 the number identifying with the Democrats in the nation dropped back to 69 percent. The number calling themselves Independents rose from 11 percent in 1968 to 24 percent in 1972. The shift was even greater in the South than elsewhere. Black Democratic identification in the South dropped from 91 percent in 1968 to 66 percent in 1972, while in the non-South the drop was from 79 to 73 percent. In this same period the number of southern black Independents rose from 6 percent to 27 percent, while in the non-South the figure remained stationary at 18 percent. These shifts occurred mainly among blacks with only grade-school educations and lower-income blacks. Those with incomes of over $10,000 and those with some college education showed less change in their party identification.[43]

A number of forces are probably at work here. Two in particular deserve mention: (1) a growing feeling of dissatisfaction with both political parties; and (2) a marked increase in support for black separatism, including a willingness to support black political parties. The Survey Research Center's 1972 election study found that blacks saw the Democratic party as taking less liberal positions on issues than they do. Only 15 percent reported a convergence in their own and the Democratic party's position on major issues. The same study noted an increase (from 24 percent in 1970 to 35 percent in 1972) in the number of blacks who said they would be willing to support a black political party if one were to form. Today, therefore, blacks must be counted both as a major source of potential support for Democrats nationally, but also as a major source of defectors in future elections. Like youth and Independents, blacks are recruited as much by issues, by candidates, and by group appeals as they are by the appeal of party.

Age

Political Differences Between Youth and Older People. Age has impact upon three aspects of political attitudes and behavior: (1) The young are much less likely to vote than older persons.[44] (2) They are much more likely to be Independents than partisans. Voting studies have consistently demonstrated that partisanship increases with aging at least in America.[45] (3) The young are much more liberal on major issues than the population as a whole.[46]

The Youth Vote in 1972. In 1972, 25 million young people were eligible to vote in national elections for the first time. Fourteen million were between the ages of 21 and 24, while the remaining 11 million were those between 18 and 20 who had received their franchise as a result of the passage of the Twenty-sixth Amendment. Their impact upon the outcome of the 1972 presidential election might have been substantial, yet it was not. In 36 states, the number of persons given the vote by the Twenty-sixth Amendment was greater than the number of votes by which Nixon had carried the state in the 1968 election. Among these 36 states were 24 which contributed 258 electoral college votes to the total of 301 which Nixon received in the electoral college. The absence of any sizable impact of the youth vote in 1972 was in part due to low turnout. Only one in two voters between 18 and 20 voted on election day. Since as a group they were noticeably more liberal than older voters, one might have expected they would flock to the support of George McGovern. Yet that did not happen either. They did support the Democratic candidate more than President Nixon, but only by a narrow margin.

Youth: A Potential Source of Change.   In their tendency to be nonpartisan and nonvoters, youth are distinctive from older voters. Yet these are not characteristics of American youth alone. The record from countries in Western Europe indicates that youth represents an important potential for change within the party system *if it can be mobilized.* The rise of the Gaullist party in France during the Fifth French Republic is a good case in point. During the period from 1958 to 1968, the Gaullist party acquired substantial, reliable partisan strength by gradually recruiting support from a large pool of Independents and weak party identifiers that was "available" when Charles deGaulle came to power. Large numbers of these were young people. What began as a demonstration of support for the General himself gradually was transformed into support for the Gaullist party. If there is a lesson here relevant to the American experience, it is that American youth today represent one of the largest identifiable groups of voters available for recruitment by new issues, new candidates, new parties.[47]

Regionalism

There is one other way of grouping citizens which has an association with partisanship, and that is by region. Talk about politics in America frequently contains reference to the distinctive political preferences of a particular area and the influence it can have on party fortunes. We hear mention of the Solid (Democratic) South—which these days is not as solid as it used to be—and of the Republican, once-isolationist, farming Midwest. Sometimes the references are to the politics of areas within a state. Thus we hear mention of the downstate vote in Illinois (Republican) and the upstate vote in New York (also Republican), the preference of the Piedmont in North Carolina (Republican again), and the difference between northern (Democratic) California and southern (Republican) California, and how Vermont, after 107 years of allegiance to the Republican party, finally, in 1958, sent a Democrat to Congress . . . for one term.

The Five Political Regions.   In the scholarly literature dealing with regional politics in America, five regions of the country are identified: the Northeast (and within this region, a major sub-region, New England [48]), the South,[49] and West,[50] the Midwest,[51] and the Border States.[52]

THE NORTHEAST.   The Northeast as a region encompasses the area north of Washington, D.C. and east of the Great Lakes. There is no study of the politics of the whole of the region, although the politics of individual states within it have on occasion been given thorough treatment and there is an excellent study of the politics of New England.[53] All parts of the region, however, are thought to have much in common: early settlement, a common tendency to indulge in ethnic politics, a sizable Catholic segment and a correspondingly widespread use of parochial schools, state constitutions that are old and simple, a tendency to prefer local administration of programs that elsewhere are more likely to be handled by the state, and frequently close competition between the parties.

THE SOUTH.   The South as a region shows considerable variety. The economy of contemporary Texas, for example, has little in common with the economies of either Mississippi or Florida. Yet, however the region is defined, states within it are thought to have at least these elements in common: widespread poverty, a large population of nonwhites, a history of slavery and segregation, low levels of education, low levels of participation in politics, one-party politics, something of a tendency to be conservative politically (though they were admiring supporters of Franklin Roosevelt, even if not that kindly disposed toward his wife, whom they regarded as a "do-gooder"), and relative centralization in the administration of government services.

THE WEST.   The West as a region is no easier to define than any other, but there are still things which states in the region are thought to have in common: a concern with water because it is scarce; an interest in conservation generally; tax troubles and other problems which arise because the federal government still owns so much of the land in the West (in no state east of the Rocky Mountains does the federal government own *more than 13 percent of the land;* in no state west of the Rocky Mountains does the federal government own *less than 29 percent of the land*); a low score on both per capita income and industrialization, but high scores on both competition between parties and voter turnout—both perhaps partly the result of the region's not having a history going back to the Civil War, a time when states in other regions were forced to choose sides between North and South, and between Republican and Democrat; reliance upon generally weak party organizations; and extensive use of some of the mechanisms of popular rule, including the party primary, the referendum, and the recall.

THE MIDWEST.   The Midwest includes those states that are left after the others have been assigned to the Northeast, South, and West. The region extends from about Ohio to the Dakotas, and from the Canadian border to Kansas. The land is flat. In the east the region is industrial and Democratic, while in its western parts it is agricultural and Republican. There are few sharp differences over public policy, both parties are heterogeneous in social composition, and the competition between them tends to center not on the substance of public policy but on personalities, patronage, and contracts.[54]

THE BORDER STATES.   The Border States are distinctive in part because there is a variety of competition between parties here that makes them different both from the South and from the North, which they sit between. Generally thought of as border states are Kentucky, West Virginia, Maryland, and Missouri. These states deserve special notice because they have already been touched by the liberalism of the North and serve, therefore, as a likely image of the transformation which already appears underway in the politics of the South.

Regionalism: A Weak Base for Party Support.   From a survey of regional politics in America, three things are obvious: First, one may legitimately speak of regions within the United States, and not all regions are alike. Second, there are notable variations within regions themselves: The politics of New Jersey is not the twin of politics in New Hampshire, any more than the way things get done in California is precisely the way things are done in

Idaho. Third, unlike the situation in some other countries,[55] regional characteristics and identification provide an insubstantial base for major political cleavages to develop upon. Only the South among the regions has possessed a strongly distinctive brand of regional politics, a brand centered upon race; and even that is on its way to disappearing. In other countries, regionalism may provide a strong base of support for a major political party, but such a thing is much less possible in the United States.

NOTES

The first quote at the beginning of the chapter is from John H. Fenton, *Politics in the Border States* (New Orleans: Hauser Press, 1957), 80–81. The second quote is from Arthur H. Miller and others, "A Majority Party in Disarray: Policy Polarization in the 1972 Election," a paper prepared for delivery at the annual meeting of the American Political Science Association, New Orleans, September 1973. The third is from Brian H. Smith and Jose Luis Rodriguez, "Comparative Working-Class Political Behavior," *American Behavioral Scientist* 18 (October 1974), 59–96. The fourth is from David Knoke, "Religion, Stratification and Politics: American in the 1960s," *American Journal of Political Science* 18 (May 1974), 331–345.

1. Two excellent books which consider cleavage and parties are Erik Allardt and Stein Rokkan (editors), *Mass Politics* (New York: Free Press, 1970), and Seymour Martin Lipset and Stein Rokkan (editors), *Party Systems and Voter Alignments* (New York: Free Press, 1967). A third study of major importance is Richard Rose and Derek Urwin, "Social Cohesion, Political Parties and Strains in Regimes," *Comparative Political Studies* 2 (April 1969), 7–44.
2. Paul Lazarsfeld and others, *The People's Choice* (New York: Columbia University Press, 1948), 27. The need to modify this statement by recognizing the importance of short-term forces such as perception of issues and candidates is argued by Morris Janowitz and Warren E. Miller, "The Index of Political Predisposition in the 1948 Election," *Journal of Politics* 14 (November 1952), 710–727, and by Angus Campbell and others, *The Voter Decides* (New York: Harper & Row, 1954), 84–87.
3. See Philip E. Converse and others, "Continuity and Change in American Politics," *American Political Science Review* 63 (December 1969), 1083–1105, where the authors argue that the 1968 election was probably as polarized along racial lines as any other election in recent American history to that time.
4. Arthur H. Miller and others, "A Majority Party in Disarray: Policy Polarization in the 1972 Election," a paper prepared for delivery at the annual meeting of the American Political Science Association, New Orleans, September 1973.
5. For a careful and detailed investigation into social class as the basis of

party in four nations, Australia, Canada, Great Britain, and the United States, see Robert Alford, *Party and Society* (Skokie, Ill.: Rand McNally, 1963).

6. U.S. Bureau of the Census, *Current Population Reports,* series P-20, no. 253, "Voting and Registration in the Election of November, 1972," (Washington, D.C.: GPO, 1973), table A, 2.

7. The reasons underlying the preponderance of lawyers in politics is the subject explored in Heinz Eulau and John D. Sprague, *Lawyers in Politics* (Indianapolis, Ind.: Bobbs-Merrill, 1964).

8. See Donald R. Matthews, *U.S. Senators and Their World* (Chapel Hill, N.C.: University of North Carolina Press, 1960), and John R. Schmidhauser, "The Justices of the Supreme Court: A Collective Portrait," *Midwest Journal of Political Science* 3 (February 1959), 1–57.

9. For a fascinating account of the lobbying activities of the American Medical Association see Richard Harris, *A Sacred Trust* (New York: Penguin, 1969).

10. Don R. Bowen, *Political Behavior of the American Public* (Columbus, Ohio: Merrill, 1968), 63.

11. Angus Campbell and others, *The American Voter* (New York: Wiley, 1960), 493–498.

12. Ibid., 475–481.

13. Pertti Pesonen, *An Election in Finland* (New Haven, Conn.: Yale University Press, 1968), 76–77, and 94–96. See also Erik Allardt and Pertti Pesonen, "Cleavage in Finnish Politics," in Lipset and Rokkan, *Party Systems and Voter Alignments,* 325–366.

14. Mattei Dogan, "Political Cleavage and Social Stratification in France and Italy," in Lipset and Rokkan, ibid., 129–196.

15. Mark Benny and others, *How People Vote: A Study of Electoral Behavior in Greenwich* (London: Routledge and Kegan Paul, 1956).

16. Philip E. Converse and Georges Dupeux, "Politicization of the Electorate in France and the United States," *Public Opinion Quarterly* 26 (Spring 1962), 1–24. This article also appears in Angus Campbell and others (editors), *Elections and the Political Order* (New York: Wiley, 1966), 269–291.

17. Gabriel Almond and Sidney Verba, *The Civic Culture* (Princeton, N.J.: Princeton University Press, 1963).

18. Alvin Rabushka, "A Note on Overseas Chinese Political Participation in Urban Malaya," *American Political Science Review* 64 (March 1970), 177–178.

19. Jae-On Kim and B. C. Koh, "Electoral Behavior and Social Development in South Korea: An Aggregate Data Analysis of Presidential Elections," *Journal of Politics* 34 (August 1972), 825–859.

20. Michael R. Coveyou and David G. Pfeiffer, "Education and Voting Turnout of Blacks in the 1968 Presidential Election," *Journal of Politics* 35 (November 1973), 995–1001.

21. Lester W. Milbrath, *Political Participation* (Skokie, Ill.: Rand McNally, 1965), 121.

22. Robert E. Lane, *Political Life* (New York: Free Press, 1959), 326.

23. Sidney Verba and Norman H. Nie, *Participation in America: Political Democracy and Social Equality* (New York: Harper & Row, 1972), 336.

24. Employment figures of the kind mentioned here are issued at various times during the year by the Census Bureau and are known as the "annual work-experience data."

25. Campbell and others, *The American Voter,* 306–319.

26. Philip E. Converse, "Religion and Politics: The 1960 Election," in Campbell and others, *Elections and the Political Order,* 96–124.

27. Philip E. Converse and others, "Stability and Change in 1960: A Reinstating Election," *American Political Science Review* 55 (June 1961), 269–280. This article also appears in Campbell and others *Elections and the Political Order,* 78–95.

28. Rose and Urwin, "Social Cohesion," 7–44.

29. Leon D. Epstein, *Politics in Wisconsin* (Madison, Wis.: University of Wisconsin Press, 1959), 40.

30. Raymond E. Wolfinger, "Some Consequences of Ethnic Politics," in M. Kent Jennings and L. Harmon Ziegler (editors) *The Electoral Process* (Englewood Cliffs, N.J.: Prentice-Hall, 1966), 43. There are two excellent collections of readings dealing with ethnic politics. The first is Harry A. Bailey, Jr., and Ellis Katz, *Ethnic Group Politics* (Columbus, Ohio: Merrill, 1969). The other is Brett W. Hawkins and Robert A. Lorinskas (editors), *The Ethnic Factor in American Politics* (Columbus, Ohio: Merrill, 1970). The best single volume on ethnic politics is Mark R. Levy and Michael S. Kramer, *The Ethnic Factor: How America's Minorities Decide Elections* (New York: Simon & Schuster, 1972).

31. For an illustration of ethnic influence in appointments, see Theodore J. Lowi, *At the Pleasure of the Mayor* (New York: Free Press, 1964), 29–54. See also Daniel P. Moynihan and James Q. Wilson, "Patronage in New York State, 1955–1959," *American Political Science Review* 58 (June 1964), 296–301.

32. See for example Robert Dahl, *Who Governs?* (New Haven: Yale University Press, 1961), 55–60; Campbell and others, *The Voter Decides,* 77–79; Edward C. Banfield and James Q. Wilson, *City Politics* (Cambridge, Mass.: Harvard University Press, 1963), 230–231; Gerald M. Pomper, "Ethnic and Group Voting in Nonpartisan Municipal Elections," *Public Opinion Quarterly* 30 (Spring 1966), 79–97; Raymond E. Wolfinger, "The Development and Persistence of Ethnic Voting," *American Political Science Review* 59 (December 1965), 896–908; and Michael Parenti, "Ethnic Politics and the Persistence of Ethnic Identification," *American Political Science Review* 61 (September 1967), 717–726.

33. Dahl, *Who Governs?,* 57.

34. Wolfinger, "The Development and Persistence of Ethnic Voting," 896–897.

35. Ibid. See also Leroy C. Ferguson and others, "Comparative Political Attitudes of Italians and Italo-Americans," *Comparative Political Studies* 5 (April 1972), 85–92. Ferguson provides a brief but exciting comparative study of the attitudes of Italians in three communities: Boston, Massachusetts; and Rome and Palermo, Italy. Those who live in Boston are much higher in efficacy than those in the two Italian cities, while those in Italy are more than twice as likely to report that political events make them feel "indignant" than those in Boston. The marked differences, Ferguson suggests, are attributable generally to differences in cultural norms, and specifically to differences in agencies of civic education in the two countries.

36. Pomper, *Public Opinion Quarterly* 30 (Spring 1966), 94–95.

37. Ibid., 96.

38. Donald R. Matthews and James W. Prothro, *Negroes and the New Southern Politics* (New York: Harcourt Brace Jovanovich, 1966). See also by the same authors, "Southern Images of Political Parties: An Analysis of White and Negro Attitudes," *Journal of Politics* 26 (February 1964), 82–111.

39. Donald R. Matthews and James W. Prothro, "Political Factors and Negro

Voter Registration in the South," *American Political Science Review* 57 (June 1963), 355–367; and by the same authors, "Social and Economic Factors and Negro Voting Registration in the South," *American Political Science Review* 57 (March 1963), 24–44.

40. In 1972, two blacks were elected to the U.S. House of Representatives from southern states, Barbara Jordan of Texas and Andrew Young of Georgia. In 1974, a third was elected from Tennessee, Harold E. Ford.

41. William Brink and Louis Harris, *The Negro Revolution in America* (New York: Simon & Schuster, 1964), 68.

42. David O. Sears, "Black Attitudes Toward the Political System in the Aftermath of the Watts Insurrection," *Midwest Journal of Political Science* 13 (November 1969), 542–544. The literature on black-white relations is massive. Among the better-known works are these: Eldridge Cleaver, *Soul on Ice* (New York: Dell, 1968); Anne Moody, *Coming of Age in Mississippi* (New York: Dell, 1968); Stokely Carmichael and Charles V. Hamilton, *Black Power* (New York: Random House, 1967); Pat Watters, *The South and the Nation* (New York: Pantheon, 1969); Allan P. Sindler (editor), *Change in the Contemporary South* (Durham, N.C.: Duke University Press, 1963); Everett Carll Ladd, Jr., *Negro Political Leadership in the South* (New York: Atheneum, 1966); Charles E. Silberman *Crisis in Black and White* (New York: Random House, 1964); Hugh Davis Graham and Ted Robert Gurr, *Violence in America* (New York: New American Library, 1969); and Hanes Walton, *Black Political Parties* (New York: Free Press, 1970), and *Black Politics* (New York: Lippincott, 1972).

43. See Arthur H. Miller and others, "A Majority Party in Disarray," as delivered to the American Political Science Association, New Orleans, September 1973.

44. Campbell and others, *The American Voter,* 493–494.

45. Gerald Pomper in chapter 6 of his *Voters' Choice* (New York: Dodd, Mead, 1975), offers an excellent discussion of developments in black political attitudes in the postwar period.

46. There are numerous writings by and about youth. Among the better (and livelier) samples are these four: James Simon Kunen, *The Strawberry Statement* (New York: Avon, 1970); Diane Divorky (editor), *How Old Will You Be in 1984: Expressions of Student Outrage from the High School Free Press* (New York: Avon, 1969); John Hersey, *Letter to the Alumni* (New York: Knopf, 1970); and Joseph A. Califano, Jr., *The Student Revolution* (New York: Norton, 1970).

47. Ronald Inglehart and Avram Hochstein, "Alignment and Dealignment of the Electorate in France and the United States," *Comparative Political Studies* 5 (October 1972), 343–372.

48. Duane Lockard, *New England State Politics* (Princeton, N.J.: Princeton University Press, 1959).

49. V. O. Key, Jr., *Southern Politics* (New York: Knopf, 1949), a classic.

50. Frank Jonas, *Western Politics* (Albuquerque, N.M.: University of New Mexico Press, 1960).

51. John H. Fenton, *Midwest Politics* (New York: Holt Rinehart & Winston, 1966).

52. John H. Fenton, *Politics in the Border States* (New Orleans, La.: The Hauser Press, 1957).

53. Lockard, *New England State Politics.*

54. Fenton, *Midwest Politics.*

55. Rose and Urwin, "Social Cohesion," 7–44.

An adult is the lengthened shadow of a child.

Since young people are developing their party identification later in life today than they were in the 1950s, as is suggested by the currently greater percentage of young independents, issues and leadership cues may become more important as determinants of party identification than parental socialization.

The vote has become less determined by sociological characteristics and traditional loyalties and is more affected by the electorate's position on public policy and its corresponding evaluation of the candidates. Such influences bring results as disparate as the Democratic landslide of 1964 and the overwhelming Nixon triumph eight years later.

Unlike the portrayal of the apathetic Independent of the 1950s, we see the Independent and the weak partisan of the 1970s as an aware, informed, concerned voter who is dissatisfied with the alternatives furnished to him by the Democratic and Republican parties.

The Partisan Electorate

An individual's political attitudes and behavior are influenced by social characteristics such as socioeconomic status, religion, and the like. That is easy to understand. It has long been evident that possessing a particular social characteristic predisposes an individual to act and feel like others who possess the same characteristic. Yet it is not true that political behavior, such as a preference for one political party over another, or a vote on election day, can be perfectly or even adequately understood by reference to social characteristics alone.

Consider: The social characteristics of the whole of the population do change through time, some of them more than others. But in the past 20 years, the changes that have occurred have by no means paralleled the changes that have occurred in political party fortunes from one presidential election to the next. The Republican landslide of 1956 was followed in 1960 by a squeaker win for the Democrats, which was followed in 1964 by another landslide, this time for the Democratic candidate, which was then followed in 1968 by a squeaker victory for the Republican candidate, with a landslide victory for the same Republican candidate in 1972. No amount of ingenious unscrambling of the social characteristics of the electorate or of those who turned out to vote can possibly explain these outcomes, each of them a mere four years apart. Some part of the puzzle is missing. Something else must be taken into account if we are to approach an acceptable level of understanding of such events. One of the missing pieces is party identification.

What is party identification? Where does it come from? Why is it important? Does it change? Is party identification unique to Americans, or is it important in other places as well? How crucial is it when it comes to explaining how we respond to other political objects, such as candidates and issues? That is what this chapter is all about.

In America most people acquire membership in a political party at birth, so to speak, by acquiring the party identification of their family, much as they acquire from the family their membership in a particular church. It is of no little importance that they remain at least as loyal to the party with which they were brought up to identify as they do to the institutional church. Even though an American's party identification may not always be as reliable a guide to how he will vote on election day as it is for voters in some other countries,[1] yet it is still true that party identification remains the single best predictor of the way a person will vote in America on election day.[2] That is because *party identification is the single most important influence shaping the individual's political attitudes and behavior*. The attention we give in this chapter to party identification, its development, and its meaning is therefore no more than they deserve.[3]

Party Identification

An individual's party identification may be discovered by asking this series of questions:

Generally speaking, do you usually think of yourself as a Democrat, a Republican, an Independent, or what?

If the respondent replies "Democrat" to the first question, then ask him:

Would you call yourself a strong Democrat, or not a very strong Democrat?

If the respondent replies "Republican" to the first question, then ask:

Would you call yourself a strong Republican or not a very strong Republican?

If the respondent replies "Independent" to the first question, then ask:

Do you think of yourself as closer to the Republican or Democratic Party?

If the respondent answers the first question by giving the name of some political party besides the Republican or Democrat party, or if he insists he has no interest in politics whatever, or if he says he has no preference for any (or either) party, then ask:

Do you think of yourself as closer to the Republican or Democratic Party?

The first question is designed to establish the *direction* of the individual's party identification; the others are asked in order to provide a measure of its *strength*. From this series of questions come the eight categories of party identification shown in Table 3-1. That table provides data on the party identification of the electorate at 13 points in time between October 1952, and November 1974. Into the last category ("Apolitical; don't know") go those individuals who say they have no ties to any party whatever. Because few respondents fall into this category, and because those who do almost invariably have only a tenuous connection with politics, we shall from this point on speak of party identification on the American scene as if it encompassed only the first seven of the eight categories.

The Stability of Party Identification. Stability, rather than change, has been a feature of party identification for most of the period since the end of World War II, and this is reflected in the base support which voters have provided each party in elections during this period. As the authors of the most widely respected study of American voting behavior say:

A general observation about the political behavior of Americans is that their partisan preferences show great stability between elections. [V. O.] Key [Jr.] speaks of the "standing decision" to

Table 3-1 The Distribution of Party Identification General Electorate, 1952–1972
(Range of N = 1,139 to N = 3,021)

	Oct '52	Oct '54	Apr '56	Oct '56	Oct '58	Oct '60	Nov '62	Jan '64	Oct '64	Nov '66	Nov '68	Nov '70	Nov '72	Nov '74
Strong Democrat	22%	22%	19%	21%	23%	21%	23%	23%	26%	18%	22%	20%	15%	17%
Weak Democrat	25	23	24	23	24	25	23	27	25	27	25	24	25	21
Independent-leaning Democrat	10	8	6	7	7	8	8	9	9	9	9	10	11	13
Independents	5	4	3	9	8	8	8	10	8	12	10	13	13	15
Independent-leaning Republican	7	6	6	8	4	7	6	6	6	7	8	8	10	9
Weak Republican	14	15	18	14	16	13	16	14	13	15	14	15	13	14
Strong Republican	13	15	14	15	13	14	12	9	11	10	9	9	10	8
Apolitical, DK	4	7	10	3	5	4	4	2	2	2	2	1	2	3

Source: Center for Political Studies, University of Michigan.

support one party or the other, and this same phenomenon soon
catches the eye of any student of electoral behavior. . . . Few
factors are of greater importance for our national elections than
the lasting attachments of tens of millions of Americans to one
of the parties. These loyalties establish a basic division of electoral strength within which the competition of particular campaigns takes place. And they are an important factor in assuring
the stability of the party system itself.[4]

Indications of Change. Stability may be in evidence in the data
provided in Table 3-1 for the period since 1952, but so are
indications of change, particularly at the end of the period.
Through 1964, Democrats were the majority party by a wide
margin, commanding the loyalty of roughly half the electorate.
Republicans found support from another 25 to 30 percent of the
electorate, while a smaller number were classified as Independents. Since that time, and especially since 1968, support for
Democrats has declined, and Republican strength has remained
fairly constant, while the number of people calling themselves
Independents has increased to the point where they now out-
number Republicans. In October 1952, 22 percent of the electorate were Independents. In October 1964, 23 percent were
Independents. But in November 1974, no fewer than 37 percent
of the electorate called themselves Independents. A posture of
independence of party has clearly developed an appeal since
1964.

Sources of Identification and Change. It is easy to accept the
notion that we pick up our party identification from the family.
So much of what we are seems to reflect our membership in the
family. Perhaps only the school rivals the family in influence,
and then not by shaping our party identification, but rather by
heightening an interest in politics.[5] In America and elsewhere,
children acquire the party identification of the parents most often
in homes where the parents themselves are politically aware and
share a common party identification. No less than two-thirds of
all those who come from such homes report that they identify
with the party with which their parents before them identified.[6]
Where does the family's party identification come from
in the first place? What may prompt someone to change his party
identification? An answer to the first question is probably impossible: The roots of an adequate explanation probably lie

buried in the obscurities of a distant past. Why some people remain steadfast in their loyalty to one party, while others find themselves changing, is somewhat easier to answer.

THE DEFINITION OF PARTY LOYALTY.   Let us understand what we mean by *loyalty* and by *change*. Party identification is an attitude, a *psychological commitment* to party. Its existence and its dimensions can be discovered only by asking an individual the party identification questions listed earlier. As long as the individual continues to give the same response to this set of questions, we say that shows continuing loyalty to a party. That kind of party loyalty requires no legal recognition, nor a formal membership in a party. It does not even require an unswerving support of the candidates of the preferred party on election day. We do not say that individuals have changed party identification merely because they vote in one election for a Democrat and for a Republican in a later one. Only if the individual himself tells us that the party he or she presently identifies with is not the one he or she used to identify with may we properly speak of a change in party identification.

Changing party identification is an uncommon experience for most Americans, and change is reported less often by strong party identifiers than by either weak identifiers or Independents. Better than 9 of 10 strong Democrats say they have never changed their party identification, and a corresponding measure of loyalty is evident among those who call themselves strong Republicans.[7]

SOCIAL FORCES AND CHANGE.   In accounting for change in party identification, it is helpful to distinguish between two sources of change which are readily distinguishable one from the other, largely because of the number of people they affect. The first of these is a social force, of which we have but two examples: the Civil War and the Great Depression. These events produced a massive shift in the party identification of the electorate in a short space of time. The Civil War saw the emergence of the Republican party as the majority party in the country, which it remained until the advent of the Great Depression produced a massive transfer of loyalty to the side of the Democratic party, which thereupon emerged as the new majority party.

PERSONAL FORCES AND CHANGE.   The second source of change is some personal force which tends to derive from circumstances which are highly individual to the person whose party identification is changed. Of personal forces, the two most common are marriage and a change of job. The first is more often reported by women than by men, while the second is more often reported by men than by women.

About 20 percent of the current American electorate report having undergone a change in party identification sometime during their lifetime. It is a mark of the greater importance of social forces as an instrument of change that for every person who attributes such a change to the impact of personal forces, another five attribute such a change to the impact of the Great Depression.[8]

The Evidence of Loyalty in Voting. Americans show a notable measure of loyalty to party in their voting. Figure 3-1 employs data from surveys conducted in five presidential elections, 1956 through 1972, to indicate what percentage of each category of

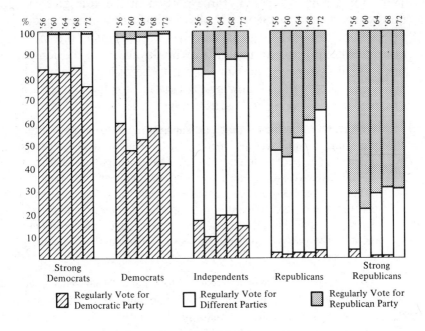

Figure 3-1   Party Regularity in Presidential Voting for Partisans and Independents, 1956–1972

Source: Center for Political Studies, University of Michigan.

party identifiers report having consistently voted for their party's presidential candidate. Strong Democrats and Republicans alike are strong in the loyalty they give their party's candidates for president. Almost none of them report giving their support regularly to the candidate of the opposition party, and very few have even done it occasionally. The story for Independents is quite different. Voting for different parties seems to be the norm for them: In every survey, better than 50 percent of them say they have voted for candidates from both parties. In the election of 1956, for example, 84 percent of the strong party-identifiers said they voted always or most of the time for the same party, while 82 percent of the Independents said they voted for different parties.[9] Sixteen years later, in the election of 1972, a similar report appeared: 76 percent of the strong identifiers said they voted always or mostly for the same party, while 77 percent of the Independents said they voted for different parties.[10]

Loyalty to party appears to be related to the aging process. Those whose loyalty is most likely to be weak are the young. In 1968, for example, a considerable portion of the vote given to third-party candidate George Wallace came from people under the age of 35.[11] The longer a man has been a voter, the more occasions he has had to demonstrate his loyalty, and the longer one is loyal, it appears, the harder it is to be disloyal. Campbell and Valen propose the following explanation for the connection observed between aging and partisanship:

> We incline to the belief that partisanship tends to become more important for the average member of the electorate as he grows older. Concerned with interests of a more personal character during his early years, he may become involved with political affairs as he becomes more fully a member of society as a parent, a worker, a neighbor, a taxpayer. Once drawn into peripheral association with a party, the strength of his attachment to the party is likely to increase as his length of membership increases.[12]

THE IMPACT OF SHORT-TERM FORCES. What will lead someone to vote for the other party? The answer is issues and candidates, short-term forces usually associated with one election. Mississippi has a long record of being hostile to Republican candidates for office, but in 1964 Mississippi gave 87.3 percent of its votes to Republican presidential candidate, Barry Goldwater. That same year it sent a Republican to the House of Representatives, and it might have sent more than one, if more than one had been running. In 1968 great numbers of southern Democrats deserted their party to support George Wallace, bound together by their common concern for the issue of civil rights. In 1972, issues were again crucial to the election outcome. Democrats were deeply divided on issues; indeed it is fair to say they were polarized, not just on a single issue but across a range of issues. That alone was enough to make the 1972 election radically different from elections that had preceded it.[13]

There is consistently closer competition between the parties for the office of president than for almost any other office in America. Republicans and Democrats alike may think their chances of capturing the presidency are good. As elections go, none engage the attention of voters quite as much as do presidential elections. Voters believe the outcome will "count," and, major decisions often do seem to rest upon the outcome.

In these circumstances party loyalty is likely to be put to as severe a test in a presidential election as it is in any other election. Conversely, party loyalty is more likely to remain unimpaired in the voting for more local offices.[14]

Loyalty and Participation. Voting studies have also made us aware of a strong relationship between party identification and political involvement, which may be stated thus: The stronger the individual's attachment to party, the greater his involvement in politics.[15] The existence of a positive relationship between partisanship and involvement is a direct denial of the existence of one of the heroes of civics textbooks writers, the Independent Voter, a noble fellow, active and involved and interested in politics, who weighs the rival appeals of a campaign and reaches a seasoned judgment, unsullied by partisan prejudice. While yon hero may in truth be worthy both of envy and emulation, he does not appear to exist much outside the pages of the textbooks. It is not the Independent, but the strong partisan, who is more likely to be the aware, attentive, informed, and active citizen. The Independent is often among the least involved participants in politics. He is likely to have a poorer knowledge of issues, a fainter image of the candidates, less interest in the campaign, and less concern about the outcome of the election.

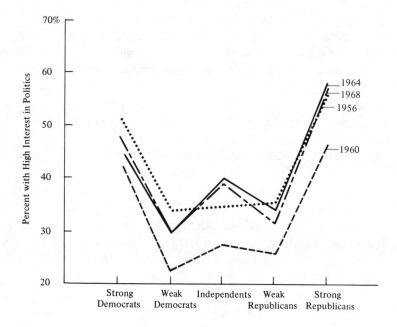

Figure 3-2   Interest Among Partisans and Independents in
1956, 1960, 1964, and 1968

Source: Center for Political Studies, University of Michigan.

Two figures which follow, Figures 3–2 and 3–3, indicate the
strength of the relationship between party identification and
political interest. Employing data from the presidential elections
from 1956 through 1968, Figure 3–2 reports how interested
partisans and Independents said they were in the presidential
campaign during those election years. Figure 3–3 uses the same
data to compare the responses they gave when asked whether
they were concerned about the outcome of the election.

The Independents

While the data of Figures 3–2 and 3–3 support our con-
tention about the relationship between partisanship and involvement, we must take care not to exaggerate the differences between the partisan and the Independent. Actually there are two

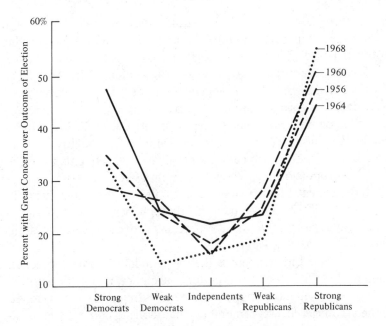

Figure 3-3 Concern with the Outcome of the Election Among
Partisans and Independents in 1956, 1960, 1964,
and 1968

Source: Center for Political Studies, University of Michigan.

distinct categories of Independents. Let us call them type A and
type B.[16]

The Independent of the Past. Type A is the Independent we
have been describing so far. His attitudes are well pictured in
Figures 3–2 and 3–3. He has dominated the Independent ranks
for most of the past generation. To what we have already said, we
need only add that he is also less likely to turn out to vote than
the partisan and is more likely to wait until the last weeks or days
of the campaign to decide what he will do on election day.

The New Independent. Along about 1964 a new type of Independent voter begins to appear in ever-increasing numbers: type
B. This is the voter, definitely on the younger side, who is just
entering the electorate and whose presence accounts for the large
increase in the numbers of Independents that we noted earlier.
The new Independent may easily be as interested and concerned
about politics as any partisan, and certainly he scores as high on

efficacy as the partisan, but it is quite obvious that he does not need the aid of party identification to help him evaluate the political world about him. He often comes from a middle-class home and very often is going to or has graduated from college. This is the new breed of Independent, a new force: young, well educated, comfortable financially and interested.

The definite preference among people under 30 to be Independents is indicated in the data of Table 3–2. Roughly half the people in this age group called themselves Independents in 1968, and the proportion was even higher in 1970 and after. Being an Independent is also attractive to those who have been to college: In 1972, 37 percent of all such persons called themselves Independents, while 32 percent said they were Republicans, and 31 percent Democrats.

This new Independent is the very model of a modern ticket-splitter. This ticket-splitting pattern of choice is not too surprising, considering how many of the new Independents have attended college, if we remember that college-educated persons have always been disinclined to cast a straight-party vote.

Finally we must also note that the new Independent is in-

Table 3-2   Party Identification by Age Groups
1960–1968

Age	1960	1964	1968
UNDER 30			
% Independent	26	32	48
Democrat	49	49	33
Republican	25	19	19
30–49			
% Independent	25	26	27
Democrat	49	52	50
Republican	26	22	23
50 AND OVER			
% Independent	18	16	19
Democrat	48	54	51
Republican	34	30	30

Source: Center for Political Studies, University of Michigan.

clined to be concerned with issues and to take a liberal rather than a conservative view of issues.

The emergence of this new class of voters, the type-B Independent, is a major event of the past decade, equaled in its impact upon parties only by the emergence of television as the principal source of political information and by-the increased importance of issues as determinants of voter choice. Of these developments and the contribution they will surely make to a continued weakening of party influence upon voting behavior, we shall say more later.

Candidates and Issues

Voter Images of Candidates.   Voters usually have clear pictures of the appealing and unappealing qualities of presidential candidates. Only a brief scanning of the data in Tables 3–3 and 3–4 is required to demonstrate this. In any election year there are always points of sharp contrast in the images voters have of rival party candidates. But these differences are scarcely greater than the differences that appear in their images of *candidates of the same party in successive elections.* The Hubert Humphrey visible to the electorate in 1968 was not a carbon copy of the Democratic presidential candidates of previous elections. Indeed, there are more points of contrast than similarity between his image in 1968 and the images of Lyndon Johnson in 1964 and John F. Kennedy in 1960. Both Humphrey and Johnson benefited from their records of service in public life, but in 1960 it was Richard Nixon, not Kennedy who was seen as the experienced candidate. A large number of persons thought Kennedy was not qualified, not experienced. Kennedy also suffered for his religion and for being too young. All three Democratic candidates profited from their close association with the Democratic party. Johnson received favorable mention for being associated with specific policies, including medical care, social security, the antipoverty program, and civil rights; while both Humphrey and Kennedy were ahead of Johnson in their images as men of integrity.

On the Republican side, Richard Nixon's image in 1968 had almost nothing in common with the image projected by the 1964 candidate, Barry Goldwater. Voters had a generally unfavorable

Table 3-3   Favorable References to Candidates
1960, 1964, 1968 [a]

| | FAVORABLE REFERENCES TO | | | | | |
| | Democrats | | | Republicans | | |
	1960 JFK	1964 LBJ	1968 HHH	1960 RMN	1964 BG	1968 RMN
EXPERIENCE AND ABILITIES						
Good man, qualified experienced	290	316	222	528	67	277
Successful record	31	256	98	79	8	52
Government experience	63	115	112	205	4	96
Good administrator	7	57	1	1	8	8
CHARACTER AND BACKGROUND						
Is a leader	26	18	10	24	7	10
Decisive	129	48	16	64	54	76
Will save America	28	21	1	17	11	11
Politician (positive reference)	—	68	10	—	5	9
Independent: No one runs him	9	6	14	8	30	15
A protector: Knows what to do	24	14	40	42	3	43
Man of integrity; principle	125	66	113	83	159	88
Public servant, conscientious	26	27	13	26	7	6
Patriotic	21	25	6	11	24	7
Well-informed, understands problems	58	69	75	77	15	44
Educated, intelligent	253	30	44	99	19	60
Catholic	70	—	—	—	—	—
Protestant	—	—	—	75	—	—
Good family life	9	18	18	—	11	17
Hard-working	21	21	16	26	8	16
Stable, balanced	—	48	—	—	3	4
PERSONAL ATTRACTION						
Like him as a person	114	60	36	64	37	43
Gets along with people	15	40	39	14	3	12
Sincere	98	32	76	61	53	41
Good speaker	72	31	29	16	15	27
Age	153	—	—	41	—	—
Outspoken, forthright	—	—	16	—	—	13
ISSUES, GENERAL, UNSPECIFIED						
I agree with him	92	55	59	60	65	78
Knows where he stands	—	22	11	—	42	12
Will support his party's policies	6	19	29	—	1	4

Table 3-3 (Cont'd)

	FAVORABLE REFERENCES TO					
	Democrats			*Republicans*		
	1960	1964	1968	1960	1964	1968
	JFK	LBJ	HHH	RMN	BG	RMN
STAND ON DOMESTIC POLICIES						
Will support needed welfare activity	—	—	14	—	—	—
Would cut down government activity	1	1	—	8	27	3
Fiscal policy	18	30	—	14	30	45
Will bring better times	49	34	20	10	1	12
For states rights	—	—	—	—	45	10
Liberal	41	30	28	1	3	1
Conservative	—	3	1	19	44	21
Stand on antipoverty programs	—	57	28	—	—	25
Stand on civil rights	14	18	27	5	33	15
For civil rights	7	88	51	—	3	3
Against civil rights	—	1	2	7	48	4
Stand on social security	16	40	28	—	11	7
Stand on medical care	17	56	29	7	5	3
Takes hard line on law and order	—	—	19	—	—	82
FOREIGN POLICY						
Handles foreign policy well	22	21	19	297	9	87
Like his foreign policy	15	20	6	16	26	11
Isolationist	—	3	2	—	24	6
Will stop communism abroad	22	2	1	83	4	9
Will keep the peace	1	55	3	33	22	8
Better chance of peace in Vietnam	—	—	90	—	—	141
Can handle trouble spots better	4	19	1	6	17	3
GROUP ASSOCIATIONS: CANDIDATE IS GOOD FOR						
All the people	24	60	34	15	10	—
Common people	77	104	109	45	7	18
Laboring people; labor unions	28	7	12	—	—	—
Business	3	5	1	—	—	3
Farmers	8	7	1	3	1	3
Negroes	6	34	44	4	—	5
Old people	11	—	16	—	—	2

Table 3-3 (Cont'd)

	FAVORABLE REFERENCES TO					
	Democrats			Republicans		
	1960	1964	1968	1960	1964	1968
	JFK	LBJ	HHH	RMN	BG	RMN
CANDIDATE AS PARTY REPRESENTATIVE						
He's a Democrat/ Republican	193	131	169	84	53	70
I like his speeches	74	27	24	—	22	46
I like the people he's close to	20	35	24	50	3	29
Eisenhower's boy	—	—	—	99	—	—
OTHER						
I just like him	67	110	28	73	34	29
Don't change horses in midstream	—	203	21	—	—	—
Time for a change	26	—	—	—	18	158
Lesser of two evils	—	—	54	—	—	58

[a] The sample size in each year was: 1960, *1807;* 1964, *1571;* and 1968, *1673.*

Source: Center for Political Studies, University of Michigan.

image of Goldwater. The 1964 election study done by the Survey Research Center of the University of Michigan contains almost twice as many unfavorable as favorable references to the Republican candidate, an unusual feature during any election. Some people questioned did say he was a man of integrity (153 responses), well qualified (67 mentions), sincere (53 mentions), decisive (54 mentions), a Republican (53 mentions) and a man with whose ideas they could agree (65 mentions). But they were by far more responsive when asked to say what they did *not* like about him. They said he was impulsive (167 mentions), conservative (106 mentions), too warlike and militaristic (186 mentions), and a man who took wrong stands on issues in general (185 mentions), and in particular on social security (156 mentions) and on civil rights (70 mentions). And 260 responses came from persons who said simply that they just did not like him!

How Images Change. Nixon's image in 1968 not only had little in common with Goldwater's in 1964 but had little in common with his own image in 1960. In both election years he received favorable mention for being a good man, generally qualified and experienced, and for his ability to handle world problems, but fewer persons said these things of him in 1968 than had in 1960. The list of unfavorable comments indicates a similar loss of support. In 1960 many people said they did not like him because he was a Republican, and because he lacked integrity, but the number in 1968 was even greater. Further, in 1968, a number of persons said they did not like him because he was a loser—a charge that was not made against him in 1960. Despite this visible fall from grace, Richard Nixon won the presidency in 1968, after having lost it in 1960 to a Democratic candidate who on the whole had a less favorable image than did Nixon's 1968 competitor, Humphrey; obviously, voters' images of candidates is not the only factor influencing the choices voters make on election day. In summary, voters can find many reasons to like or dislike a candidate. They have different images of candidates, and the image they have of a candidate one year may be quite different from the image they have of the same candidate another year.

How Partisans Differ in Their Images. Voters differ not only in their appraisals of candidates but in their appraisals of political parties and current issues as well. And these differences—no real surprise here—are often found to be closely related to differences in voters' party identifications. Partisans in one party are inclined to view the candidates offered by their party more favorably than partisans in the other party, and to associate their party with policies that are more to their liking than the policies they associate with the opposition party. Data given in Figure 3–4, taken from the election study of 1956, provide a rather nice demonstration of the relationship. They show that Democrats are inclined to give a more positive evaluation of the Democratic party's candidates and their party's handling of issues than are Republicans, while Republicans lean in an opposite direction regarding Republican party candidates and issues. In their evaluations, Independents fall midway in between.

Voters can have many different reasons for liking or disliking parties, candidates, and issues, and the data in Figure 3–4 in-

Table 3-4 Unfavorable References to Candidates
1960, 1964, 1968

	UNFAVORABLE REFERENCES TO					
	Democrats			Republicans		
	1960	1964	1968	1960	1964	1968
	JFK	LBJ	HHH	RMN	BG	RMN
EXPERIENCE AND ABILITIES						
Not a good man, not qualified	173	22	80	45	71	70
Unsuccessful record	14	14	42	20	20	43
Not enough experience	38	—	—	5	—	—
CHARACTER AND BACKGROUND						
Not a leader	—	—	32	11	3	11
Weak, indecisive	20	17	95	50	25	47
Politician (negative reference)	2	92	25	4	10	20
Not independent, not own boss	9	28	70	31	9	17
Lacks integrity	48	116	104	74	34	152
Impulsive	51	11	18	7	167	40
Poorly informed	—	7	6	—	32	14
Too rich	88	26	1	—	8	2
Not humble enough	48	—	—	15	—	—
Corruption, immorality in government	—	87	—	—	—	—
Craves power	—	35	4	—	7	11
Fanatic, unstable, dangerous	—	—	3	—	94	—
He's a loser	—	—	—	—	—	90
He's a Catholic	380	—	—	—	—	—
Catholic church would control him	107	—	—	—	—	—
PERSONAL ATTRACTION						
Don't like him as a person	20	27	19	49	29	14
Hard to get along with	—	4	21	4	14	29
Insincere	5	32	24	13	19	18
Age	128	—	—	10	—	—
Not outspoken	—	25	14	—	21	83
ISSUES, GENERAL, UNSPECIFIED						
Don't like his policies	—	14	42	27	78	29
Don't know where he stands	—	40	61	—	185	69
He supports the party's platform	—	—	74	—	—	3

Table 3-4 (Cont'd)

	UNFAVORABLE REFERENCES TO					
	Democrats			Republicans		
	1960	1964	1968	1960	1964	1968
	JFK	LBJ	HHH	RMN	BG	RMN
STAND ON DOMESTIC POLICIES						
Favors welfare state	—	10	—	—	—	—
Dislike his fiscal policy	22	18	—	10	6	—
Favors big government	—	13	6	—	—	—
Too liberal	31	—	24	—	2	1
Too conservative	1	1	—	—	106	16
Stand on antipoverty programs	—	18	—	—	7	—
Don't like his stand on civil rights	7	30	2	4	48	16
For civil rights	8	63	2	4	5	1
Against civil rights	4	16	1	—	70	16
Farm policy	3	1	3	15	8	—
Labor policy	11	6	1	13	19	4
Soft line on law and order	—	—	24	—	—	7
Stand on social security	—	—	8	3	156	12
Stand on medical care	—	12	2	4	42	14
STAND ON FOREIGN AFFAIRS						
Wouldn't handle foreign affairs well	42	12	7	62	18	15
Don't like his policies	5	19	1	11	29	3
Too isolationist	—	—	—	—	16	1
Wouldn't stop communism abroad	23	11	1	30	2	1
Can't handle trouble spots	10	19	2	11	12	1
Warlike, too militaristic	—	2	—	—	186	4
Won't get us out of Vietnam	—	—	49	—	—	42
GROUP ASSOCIATION: WILL KEEP IN CHECK						
The people	—	5	1	3	11	7
Common people, poor people	15	2	5	37	41	39
Labor, labor unions	6	—	—	11	20	7
Negroes	—	—	2	4	25	27
CANDIDATE AS PARTY REPRESENTATIVE						
He's a Democrat/ Republican	58	27	28	170	44	112
Don't like his associates	22	21	6	5	5	5

Table 3-4 (Cont'd)

| | UNFAVORABLE REFERENCES TO | | | | | |
| | Democrats | | | Republicans | | |
	1960 JFK	1964 LBJ	1968 HHH	1960 RMN	1964 BG	1968 RMN
Don't like his speeches	86	50	29	58	206	33
Too critical of opponents	—	—	50	—	—	20
His connection with LBJohnson	—	—	188	—	—	—
OTHER						
I just don't like him	82	93	271	100	225	260
Disapprove of his stand on extremism	—	3	8	—	29	2
It's time for a change	—	—	85	—	—	—
Lesser of two evils	—	—	58	—	—	—

Source: Center for Political Studies, University of Michigan.

dicate rather nicely that partisans in different parties do not necessarily attach the same importance to the reasons they have for liking or disliking a party and its candidates. In 1956 strong Republicans were inclined to be pro-Republican primarily because of the identities of the two candidates, being enthusiastic about their party's choice of Eisenhower, and almost equally unenthusiastic about the opposition candidate, Stevenson. Strong Democrats, on the other hand, were generally inclined to be pro-Democratic not because of the way they evaluated the candidates that year but primarily because of the social groups with which they saw their party identified, and after that for their party's handling of domestic issues. To the extent that they were pro-Republican at all it was for the Republican handling of foreign affairs first, and then for the Republican party's choice of Eisenhower as its candidate.

The Impact of Party Identification on Voter Images. Data such as those given in Figure 3–4 have been used to argue that party identification is an important supplier of cues by which the voter may evaluate the many elements of politics which he himself cannot be acquainted with firsthand.[17] (How many presi-

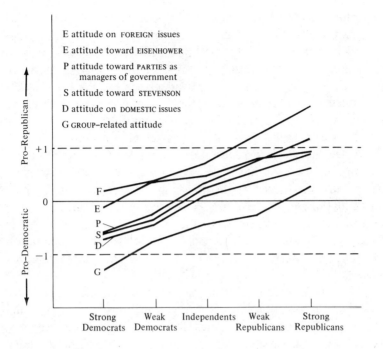

E attitude on FOREIGN issues

E attitude toward EISENHOWER

P attitude toward PARTIES as managers of government

S attitude toward STEVENSON

D attitude on DOMESTIC issues

G GROUP–related attitude

Figure 3-4 Relation of Party Identification to Partisan Evaluations of Elements of National Politics, 1956

Note: The values indicated by plus and minus signs are the average of respondents' scores across attitudes.

Source: Angus Campbell et al., *The American Voter* (New York: Wiley, 1960), Fig. 6-2, p. 130, by permission of the publisher.

dential candidates have you had as neighbors?) The authors of the most respected of the early voting studies express it this way:

> [A] party undoubtedly furnishes a powerful set of cues about a political leader just by nominating him for President. Merely associating the party symbol with his name encourages those identifying with the party to develop a more favorable image of his record and experience, his abilities and his other personal attributes. Likewise, this association encourages supporters of the opposite party to take a less favorable view of these same personal qualities.[18]

That argument has undoubted merit—the data given in Figure 3–4 are quite impressive—yet one should not accept it without caution. One can be convinced that here is evidence of a strong relationship between party identification and a voter's perception of candidates and issues and yet not be wholly convinced that it is the party identification itself that is directly accountable for those evaluations. If we believe that most Americans adopt the family's party identification, we must also recognize that the individual may also be exposed within the home to attitudes toward issues and candidates as well.[19] Attitudes are learned. There is no reason not to believe that, for some Americans at least, attitudes toward issues and some general preference for what is desired in the way of candidates can as easily be influenced by the family as is the acquiring of a party identification. Further, if preferences in partisanship, in issues, and in candidates are things one learns, they can also be influenced by the learning that goes on elsewhere than in the family, including the learning that is acquired through the media and in school.

Issues and candidates do change from election to election, and that fact of politics offers the possibility that voters may radically change in the ratings they give candidates, even the candidates of their own party. How much change can occur is well demonstrated by Table 3-5, which summarizes voter perceptions of candidates for the period 1952 through 1972. Clearly, some candidates are a great deal more popular than others. John-

Table 3-5 Summary of References to Candidates
1960, 1964, 1968

1960				
$N = 1807$	Pro-Kennedy	2678	Pro-Nixon	2790
	Anti-Kennedy	1836	Anti-Nixon	1214
1964				
$N = 1571$	Pro-Johnson	3271	Pro-Goldwater	1306
	Anti-Johnson	1275	Anti-Goldwater	2468
1968				
$N = 1673$	Pro-Humphrey	2259	Pro-Nixon	2378
	Anti-Humphrey	2081	Anti-Nixon	1893

Source: Center for Political Studies, University of Michigan.

son in 1964 was by far the most popular of all Democratic candidates, being helped no doubt by running opposite the most generally disliked Republican candidate in this 20-year period. McGovern in 1972 was far and away the most unpopular Democratic presidential candidate. The election of 1964 constituted a Democratic landslide, that of 1972 a Democratic disaster. Voter evaluation of candidates doubtless played a part in the making of these election outcomes. So, probably, did issues, which are a common feature of any election.

How Voter Images of Parties, Candidates, and Issues Are Related. Voters do not get to vote three times, voting once to indicate their party identification, once to indicate their perceptions of candidates, and once to indicate their perceptions of issues. Somehow the voter must express all three attitudes in a single vote. In shaping electoral decisions, what is the relative importance of party, candidate, and issues? That question was the focus of a major study of voter attitudes employing data from the 1968 election study. The data relied upon consisted of responses which people gave when they were asked to rate a number of political figures using a "feeling thermometer." This is a simple chart which enables someone to express his feelings about candidate by giving him a rating that may range from 0° to 100°, near 100° if he likes the candidate a lot, near 50° if he is rather neutral, and near 0° if he dislikes him a lot.[20]

Rating the Candidates in 1968. Respondents in 1968 were asked to rate several political figures prominent that year, including the three presidential nominees, Humphrey, Nixon and Wallace; the three vice-presidential nominees, Muskie, Agnew and Lemay; the incumbent president, Johnson; and other figures, including on the Democratic side Eugene McCarthy and Robert Kennedy, and on the Republican side, George Romney, Nelson Rockefeller, and Ronald Reagan.

What did the ratings look like? Most people were able to give these 12 people a rating. Few said they did not know anything at all about a candidate or that they had no feelings about him. Eleven of the 12 received a generally favorable rating. The exception was George Wallace. Sixty percent of the people gave him the lowest score they gave to any of the 12, and his average score of 31° was well below the neutral rating of 50°. The highest average rating, a score of 70°, went to Robert

Kennedy. Not all candidates were equally well known. Johnson, Humphrey, Nixon, and Kennedy were much better known than the others and evoked a much wider range of responses than did the others.

Two kinds of variation were evident in the responses. The ratings received by the candidate themselves varied. Some were much more favorably received than others. Then too, the ratings given the 12 candidates varied from voter to voter.

The average range of scores given by a respondent to the candidates was 73°; that is, the score which respondents gave to the person they liked most was, on average, 73° higher than the score they gave to the person they liked least.

DIMENSIONS OF CANDIDATE EVALUATION IN 1968. What do the ratings mean? Use of a procedure known as multidimensional scaling revealed that in 1968 the ratings of candidates involved two dimensions. The first dimension—no surprise here—was one of partisanship. A respondent's party preference surfaced first in the response people gave to a party identification question and then in the responses they gave to two questions which have been found to be closely associated with party identification. The first question deals with whether the government in Washington is getting too powerful. Democrats during the past 20 years have been inclined to think it is not. The second deals with the responsibility for guaranteeing full employment. Democrats in the same period have thought this should properly be the responsibility of the federal government. Republicans' reactions to these same two items tend to be the exact opposite of the Democrats'.[21]

The second dimension involved four items dealing with issues distinctive to the politics of 1968: the Vietnam War, urban unrest, desegregation, and the treatment of protestors.[22] On each of these four items a "liberal" and a "conservative" position could be readily identified. A close correspondence appeared between the position taken on these four items and the respondent's evaluation of the candidates. Here follows a listing of the 12 candidates positioned along this second dimension, from most liberal to most conservative.

McCarthy
Kennedy
Humphrey
Rockefeller

Muskie
Romney
Johnson
Nixon
Agnew
Reagan
Lemay
Wallace

Respondents who took a liberal position on the four issue items tended to give the most favorable rating to candidates at the top of this list and the least favorable rating to those at the bottom. Both dimensions of candidate evaluation in 1968 are displayed in Figure 3-5. The vertical dimension is the dimension labeled "partisanship." The horizontal dimension represents the position taken on the four issue items.[23]

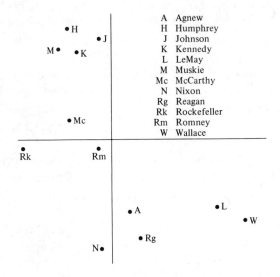

A	Agnew
H	Humphrey
J	Johnson
K	Kennedy
L	LeMay
M	Muskie
Mc	McCarthy
N	Nixon
Rg	Reagan
Rk	Rockefeller
Rm	Romney
W	Wallace

Figure 3-5 Candidate Space in Two Dimensions: The Election of 1968

Note: In this figure the horizontal axis represents more or less an ordering from left to right of least to most pro-Wallace. The vertical axis represents an ordering of the parties from Democratic (at the top) through Wallace's American Party to Republican (at the bottom).

Source: Herbert F. Weisberg and Jerrold G. Rusk, "Dimensions of Candidate Evaluation," *American Political Science Review,* 64 (December, 1970), 1176. Used by permission.

What conclusions dare we draw? Once again, as we saw earlier in the case of the 1956 election, party identification emerges as a crucial factor in candidate evaluation. Those who identified with one party tended to have favorable images of the leaders of that party and to have less favorable images of leaders in the opposition party, and strong party identifiers were more likely than weak party identifiers to feel that way. The continuing importance of party identification, then, is the first thing to note.

NEW ISSUES OF CONCERN TO VOTERS.   Also notable is the emergence of new issues of concern to voters. Since at least the days of the Great Depression and the New Deal—in other words, since the beginning of the latest Democratic era—the two major parties have been aligned on more or less opposite sides of the great issues of the day. Included among the issues have been such questions as federal regulation of the economy; a government commitment to full employment; the protection of labor; support for the farmer; provision of social services, including social security, welfare assistance, medical care, and the like; and in the area of taxation, a commitment to a broadly progressive rather than a regressive taxing system. These issues—sometimes spoken of as the bread-and-butter issues—have dominated the rhetoric of political campaigns for a generation.[24]

But in 1968 we see the emergence of a cluster of issues that have no strong partisan associations. It is not possible to guess how a man will feel about these four issues—Vietnam, urban unrest, desegregation, and protestors—just by knowing what his party identification is. Will this new cluster of issues which were so evident in 1968 remain on the scene? Reports we have about voting in 1972—which we will look at in detail in a later chapter—definitely suggest that possibility. At the same time, the daily attention given since 1973 to wages, prices, unemployment, development of a national health insurance plan, and the energy crisis prompts us to guess that the older, more partisan-related issues will demonstrate an even greater capacity for influence than was evident in the 1960s, with perhaps this one difference: that a perceived party failure to provide policies adequate to deal with even the older issues may lead to a further disrespect for and disregard of parties.

THE SOURCES OF NEW ISSUES.   National and international events—particularly in the period between the 1964 and 1968 elections—helped to make the new issues salient to large number of voters. During this period, urban unrest; the continuing problem of desegregation of the schools, public accommodations, and housing; the Vietnam War and protests against it and against other things, held a prominent place in every day's news. Moreover, between 1968 and 1972 the electorate increased by the addition of 24 million new voters, including 11 million persons between the ages of 18 and 21 who were added to the electorate by passage of the Twenty-sixth Amendment.[25] For most of these new voters the older ties of party and the older social and economic issues were hardly as appealing as the newer issues of war, urban unrest, and the like.

It was not only events that helped to give these newer issues relevance in 1968. The response of the parties helped too. So did the response of party candidates. And so too did the failure of parties and candidates to respond. Wallace found an electorate, and in the American Independent party that electorate found a home, when each discovered the other's thinking on urban unrest, desegregation, and protestors. Nixon too benefited (see Table 3-3) from being perceived as the candidate who promised a chance of peace in Vietnam and who took a hard line on law and order.

If both parties continue to shy away from taking a position on such issues while events keep them in the news, this most certainly will encourage the development of still another third-party movement on the style of the American Independent party, and perhaps even a fourth party, to accommodate those on the left, particularly the young, college-educated Independents and left-of-center Democrats, who find the essentially centrist position of the two major parties unappetizing.

Issues in the Seventies

The politics of the seventies are not the same in many respects as the politics of earlier decades. The rather unexpected and, for some people, disturbing discovery of a heightened voter interest in issues has itself raised an issue among those who study political parties: Have we entered a period in which issues will be dominant in the determination of the outcome of electoral contests? Is this to be the era of the "policy voter"?

The Earlier Nonimportance of Issues.   The early voting studies from the 1940s and 1950s stated that issues played little if any role in the voter's decision. Some voters were found to have a high level of conceptualization, to be interested in issues, to be able to discern accurately issue differences between the parties, and their voting choices accurately reflected both their own issue preferences and their choice of party. But there were few such people, no more probably than 12 percent of the electorate. For most voters, there was no more than a modest association between personal issue preferences, the perception of issue differences between the parties, and their choice of party. For such voters, who constituted the overwhelming majority of the electorate, the single most important influence upon the vote was party identification.[26]

The Recent Importance of Issues.   The early view of the unimportance of issues in voting is no longer accepted as definitive. A deluge of later studies indicates that issues may influence voting. The election of 1964 and, even more, the election of 1972 stand as convincing evidence of this. In both elections candidates were at pains to point out their differences on issues, and voters proved capable of perceiving and responding to the issue choices offered them. Does this mean that the earlier studies were in error? Not at all. It now seems clear that issues are important in some elections (like 1972) and not in others (such as 1952 and 1956). The question, as we see it now, is not whether issues are an important influence on voting, but rather under what circumstances they may be.[27]

Circumstances Affecting the Role of Issues.   There are at least three possibilities.

1. There will always be some people, perhaps a small number in the electorate, who are interested in issues in any election. But if issue differences between the parties are muted or are not raised to voter consciousness, either by candidates during the campaign or by those who are received as spokesmen for a party, such as an incumbent president, then issues are unlikely to play a significant role in the decision of most voters.

2. When voters perceive issue differences between parties, and these perceived differences reinforce party preferences, both issues and party will be influential upon the vote. Issues and party will be mutually reinforcing, we suspect, when the issues

of a particular election are staples—reoccurring issues on which, for several elections past, the parties have taken stands with which they have become identified. In this era the staple issues are jobs, federal regulation of the economy, prices, medical care, favoring of the common man versus favoring big business, and the like.

3. Issue voting may be said to occur only when voters manifest an interest in issues, when they accurately perceive issue differences between the parties and relate those differences to their own personal issue preferences, and when a concurrence of perceived personal and perceived party issue preferences is measurably the best predictor of the vote. Issue voting is most likely to occur when events themselves and/or an election campaign bring new issues to the fore. The election of 1972 was clearly such an election, and it is no surprise, therefore, that issue voting was in evidence in 1972, but not in the elections of 1952 and 1956, in which no major issues were successfully developed, either by events or by candidates. Part of the evidence of the presence of issue voting in 1972 comes from the observation that voters generally responded to issues that year regardless of age, level of education, and so forth. The appearance of issue voting, in other words, was not merely a result of an increase in the number of better educated, young people participating in that election.

The possibility that issue voting will become more common hinges partly upon events (actions by Congress, the length of the line at the unemployment office, the decisions of the president), as well as upon the decisions of candidates running for office. Some newer issues, including compensatory treatment of blacks and women, protection of the environment, and busing, are visible, and over these no small number of voters are agitated. But then, the long familiar bread-and-butter staples are as relevant to a period of inflation and recession as they ever were, and if these issues rather than the newer ones dominate the next presidential election, and if candidates from the political center win the nominations of both parties, the influence of issues may well be less than in 1972.

We may ask, finally, what the appearance of issue voting means for parties. Issue voting can occur only when issues force some significant number of voters to vote contrary to their party identification. Since this in itself would tend to weaken party identification, issue voting is most likely to occur at a time such as the present, when the number of Independents in the electorate is also increasing. These simultaneous occurrences provide still another indication that the citizen's regard for parties is declining. We may reasonably estimate that the trend can be reversed only if substantial numbers of citizens change their party identification, or if parties develop commitments on issues more to the liking of their identifiers.

NOTES

The first quote at the beginning of the chapter is from James C. Davies, *Human Nature in Politics* (New York: Wiley, 1963), 175. The second quote is from Arthur H. Miller and others, "A Majority Party in Disarray: Policy Polarization in the 1972 Election," as delivered to the American Political Science Association, New Orleans, September 1973. The third is from Mark A. Schulman and Gerald M. Pomper, "Variability in Electoral Behavior: Longitudinal Perspectives from Causal Modeling," *American Journal of Political Science* 19 (February 1975), 1–18. The fourth is from Gerald Kent Hikel, *Beyond the Polls* (New York: Heath, 1973), 90.

1. Great Britain is one country where party identification is an even better predictor of a man's vote than it is in the United States. See David Butler and Donald E. Stokes, *Political Change in Britain* (New York: St. Martin, 1969), 40.
2. Chapter 6, "The Impact of Party Identification," in Angus Campbell and others, *The American Voter* (New York: Wiley, 1960), contains an excellent discussion of the relationship between party identification and voting behavior. On pages 142–143, the authors say: "Evidently no single datum can tell us more about the attitude and behavior of the individual as presidential elector than his location on a dimension of psychological identification extending between the two great parties."
3. Three works in particular contain an extensive discussion of party identification: Campbell and others, *The American Voter;* Angus Campbell and others, *The Voter Decides* (New York: Harper & Row, 1954); and Angus Campbell and others, *Elections and the Political Order* (New York: Wiley, 1966).
4. Campbell and others, *The American Voter,* 120–121.
5. Robert Hess and Judith V. Torney, *The Development of Political Attitudes in Children* (Chicago: Aldine, 1967), and M. Kent Jennings and Richard G. Niemi, "The Transmission of Political Values from Parent to Child," *American Political Science Review* 57 (March 1968), 169–184, are among those who admit the importance of the family as a socializing agent but offer compelling evidence that it has formidable competitors, especially where the development of interest and awareness are concerned. In short, they argue that in the matter of political attitudes, the 18-year-old is not simply a carbon copy of his parents. Allan Kornberg and Norman C. Thomas, "The Political Socialization of National Legislative Elites in the

United States and Canada," *Journal of Politics* 27 (November 1965), 761–775, and Allan Kornberg and others, "Some Differences in the Political Socialization Patterns of Canadian and American Party Officials: A Preliminary Report," *Canadian Journal of Political Science* 2 (March 1969), 64–88, and Allan Kornberg and Hal H. Winsborough, "The Recruitment of Candidates for the Canadian House of Commons," *American Political Science Review* 62 (December 1968), 1242–1257, all make the same point as Jennings and Niemi, and offer intriguing data that reveal that Canadian legislators mention the family, while American legislators mention the school, as the most important agent in developing their interest in politics.

6. Campbell and others, *The American Voter,* 146–148.

7. Ibid., 148.

8. Ibid., 150.

9. Ibid., table 6–2, 125.

10. Center for Political Studies, Survey Research Center, University of Michigan, 1972 Election Study. Data supplied through the Inter-University Consortium for Political Research at the University of Michigan. See also Walter DeVries and V. L. Tarrance, *The Ticket-Splitter: A New Force in American Politics* (Grand Rapids, Mich.: Berdmans Publishing, 1972).

11. Philip E. Converse and others, "Continuity and Change in American Politics: Parties and Issues in the 1968 Election," *American Political Science Review* 63 (December 1969), 1083–1105.

12. Angus Campbell and Henry Valen, "Party Identification in Norway and the United States," in Campbell and others, *Elections and the Political Order,* 251, by permission of the publisher.

13. Arthur H. Miller and others, "A Majority Party in Disarray," as delivered to the American Political Science Association, New Orleans, September 1973.

14. This is certainly true in Great Britain. See Butler and Stokes, *Political Change in Britain,* 38–39.

15. Campbell and others, *The American Voter,* 143.

16. V. O. Key, Jr., cautions us not to exaggerate the differences in his *The Responsible Electorate* (Cambridge, Mass.: Harvard University Press, 1966), as does William Flanigan, *Political Behavior of the American Electorate,* 2nd ed. (Boston: Allyn & Bacon, 1968), 40–44. The "new" Independent is also on view in Everett Carll Ladd and Seymour Martin Lipset, *Academics, Politics and the 1972 Election* (Washington, D.C.: American Enterprise Institute for Public Policy Research, 1973), in Everett C. Ladd and others, "A New Political Realignment?" *Public Interest* 23 (Spring 1971), 46–63, in Gerald Pomper, *Voters' Choice* (New York: Dodd Mead, 1975), and in Gerald Kent Hikel, *Beyond the Polls* (New York: Heath, 1975), especially chapter 5.

17. Campbell and others, *The American Voter,* 128.

18. Ibid.

19. R. Wayne Parsons and Allen H. Barton, "Social Background and Policy Attitudes of American Leaders," a paper prepared for delivery to the 1974 annual meeting of the American Political Science Association, New Orleans, La., September 1974, 21.

20. Items in a survey employing the feeling thermometer are introduced this way:

As you know, there were many people mentioned this past year as possible candidates for President by the political parties. We would like to get your feelings toward some of these people.

I have here a card [a replica of the card appears below] on which there is something that looks like a thermometer. We call it a "feeling ther-mometer" because it measures your feelings toward these people. You probably remember that we used something like this in our earlier inter-view with you.

Here's how it works. If you don't feel particularly warm or cold toward a person, then you should place him in the middle of the thermometer, at the 50 degree mark.

If you have a warm feeling toward a person, or feel favorably toward him, you would give him a score somewhere between 50° and 100°, de-pending on how warm your feeling is toward that person.

On the other hand, if you don't feel very favorably toward that person—that is, if you don't care too much for him—then you would place him somewhere between 0° and 50°.

Of course, if you don't know too much about a person just tell me and we'll go on to the next name.

Our first person is George Wallace. Where would you put him on the thermometer?

"FEELING" THERMOMETER

Warm 100° = very warm or favorable
              feeling for candidate

       85° = good warm or favorable
              feeling for candidate

       70° = fairly warm or favorable
              feeling for candidate

       60° = a bit more warm or
              favorable than cold
              feeling

       50° = no feeling at all for
              candidate

       40° = a bit more cold or
              unfavorable feeling

       30° = fairly cold or unfavorable
              feeling

       15° = quite cold or unfavorable
              feeling

Cold   0° = very cold or unfavorable
              feeling

21. The wording of the first item was:

Some people are afraid the government in Washington is getting too power-ful for the good of the country and the individual person. Others feel that the government in Washington is not getting too strong for the good of the country. Have you been interested enough in this to favor one side over the other? [IF "YES":] What is your feeling, do you think. . . .

The wording of the second item was:

In general, some people feel that the government in Washington should see to it that every person has a job and a good standard of living. Others think the government should just let each person get ahead on his own. Have you been interested enough in this to favor one side over the other? [IF YES":] Do you think the government should see to it. . . .

22. The wording of these other four items was as follows:

[Question 33.] Which of the following do you think we should do now in Vietnam, pull out of Vietnam entirely, keep our soldiers in Vietnam but try to end the fighting, take a stronger stand even if it means invading North Vietnam?

[Question 17, 17a.] Did you happen to hear anything about what went on between the police and demonstrators in Chicago at the Democratic Convention? [IF "YES":] Do you think the police used too much force, the right amount of force, or not enough force with the demonstrators?

[Question 66.] There is much discussion about the best way to deal with the problem of urban unrest and rioting. Some say it is more important to use all available force to maintain law and order—no matter what results. Others say it is more important to correct the problems of poverty and unemployment that give rise to the disturbances. And, of course, other people have opinions in between. Suppose the people who stress the use of force are at one end of this scale—at point number 7 [SHOW CARD 3 TO R.]. And suppose the people who stress doing more about the problems of poverty and unemployment are at the other end—at point number 1. Where would you place yourself on this scale?

23. Herbert F. Weisberg and Jerrold G. Rusk, "Dimensions of Candidate Evaluation," *American Political Science Review* 64 (December 1970), 1167–1185. Another work which stresses the importance of issues in the 1968 election is Samuel A. Kirkpatrick and Melvin E. Jones, "Vote Direction and Issue Cleavage in 1968," *Social Science Quarterly* 51 (December 1970), 689–705.

24. A good discussion of voter attitudes on these bread-and-butter issues may be found in Ben J. Wattenberg and Richard M. Scammon, *The Real Majority* (New York: Coward-McCann & Geoghegan, 1970).

25. The Twenty-sixth Amendment was ratified on June 30, 1971. It gives 18-year-olds the right to vote in all elections. *The Congressional Quarterly Weekly Report* for July 2, 1971, 1436–1439, quoting the U.S. Bureau of the Census, estimates the number of newly enfranchised voters eligible to vote in 1972 at 25 million, of which 11.5 million resulted from the passage of the Twenty-sixth Amendment.

26. Paul Lazarsfeld and others, *The People's Choice* (New York: Columbia University Press, 1948); Bernard Berelson and others, *Voting* (Chicago: Chicago University Press, 1954); Campbell and others, *The Voter Decides;* Eugene Burdick and Arthur Brodbeck (editors), *American Voting Behavior* (New York: Free Press, 1959); Campbell and others, *The American Voter;* Philip Converse, "The Nature of Belief Systems in Mass Publics," in David Apter (editor), *Ideology and Discontent* (New York: Free Press, 1964).

27. See in particular Key, *The Responsibile Electorate;* Robert Lane, *Political Ideology* (New York: Free Press, 1960); Steven R. Brown, "Consistency and the Persistence of Ideology," *Public Opinion Quarterly* 34 (Spring 1970), 60–68; J. O. Field and R. E. Anderson, "Ideology in the Public's Conceptualization of the 1964 Election," *Public Opinion Quarterly* 33 (Fall 1969), 380–398; John G. Pierce, "Party Identification and the Changing Role of Ideology in American Politics," *Midwest Journal of Political Science* 14 (February 1970), 25–42; David E. RePass, "Issue Salience and Party Choice," *American Political Science Review* 65 (June 1971), 389–400; Gerald M. Pomper, "From Confusion to Clarity: Issues and American Voters, 1956–1968," *American Political Science Review* 66 (June 1972), 415–428; Richard W. Boyd, "Popular Control of Public Policy: A Normal Vote Analysis of the 1968 Election," *American Political Science Review* 66 (June 1972), 429–449; Norman Nie and Kristi Andersen, "Mass Belief Systems Revisited: Political Change and Attitude Structure," *Journal of Politics,* 36 (August 1974), 540–591.

They aren't doing enough for the people. The country is going down the drain. There's no confidence in the President. The government is spending more than it takes in. We still haven't any leaders in sight. They will all sell us out.

I'm afraid my children and grandchildren won't be able to walk or play in peace. I want the best things for them. Now they don't have good housing or schools, and, most of all, they don't have equality.

I will not take a Molotov cocktail, but I am as mad as the rioters are.

The American response to the severest loss of incomes, careers, and hopes in the 1930s was a model of orderliness. Aside from an almost pathetic Bonus Army march on Washington, and the usual quotient of industrial strikes, the comparative resignation with which Americans accepted "everybody's tragedy as nobody's tragedy" stood in humble contrast to the street riots and violence, the ideological warfare, and the mass political upheavals elsewhere. President Roosevelt is credited by historians as a "savior of capitalism." In the current mood of political alienation and matter-of-fact acceptance of violence, in a similarly depressed economy, it seems unlikely that even a Roosevelt could save the political and economic systems as we have known them.

4

Citizen Perception of Parties, Trust, Efficacy, and Information

Partisanship is a vital force at work in many political systems, including the United States. In most places, the family is the principal transmitter of partisan preferences, and the party identification which the child receives from the family remains remarkably stable over time, although not all the time or in every place (American youth today, France in the 1950s). Stable party loyalties can develop quickly (India since gaining independence) and sometimes, apparently, in response to political leadership cues (France under de Gaulle). But party loyalties can also be eroded, as is evidenced by the remarkable discovery that young people in America today are developing party loyalties later than young people used to, and by the equally remarkable discovery that Independents now constitute the second largest "party" in this country. And while knowing something about a people's party identification may offer a surer clue to their political behavior than information about their social characteristics, even this knowledge does not always provide us with a satisfactory understanding of many of the important things in politics we need to understand. Pieces of the puzzle are still missing. The importance of candidates and issues was explored in the last chapter and the circumstances identified under which issue voting would occur. But still other influences are at work. One other major source of influence, which is the subject of this chapter, is citizens' feelings about the political system itself, its institutions, and their place in it. Here we shall consider three such attitudes: (1) citizen perceptions of the political party as an institution, (2) feelings of trust, and (3) feelings of efficacy —feelings that one can be effective in politics and can have influence. In a final section of the chapter, we shall consider how much information citizens have about the elements of their political world and what contribution varying levels of information make both to partisanship and to support for the political system.

The two major American political parties have often been accused of being Tweedledum and Tweedledee. Their 1968 party platforms were said by an editorial writer for the *New York Times* to be so similar that only a minor codicil or two would be necessary to render them identical.[1] That same year, presidential candidate George Wallace said that there wasn't a dime's worth of difference between the two major parties, and many people were ready to agree with him.[2] The American historian Clinton Rossiter said in his book about political parties that whenever he lectured abroad, no matter what his subject, one of the first questions from the audience was always a request to explain the difference between Democrats and Republicans.[3]

Citizen Images of the Political Parties

How do citizens see the parties? One source that tells us a lot about the image citizens have of the parties is the responses given in election studies to a series of questions known as the party image questions.[4] Tables 4-1 and 4-2 array the responses given to the party image questions by Americans interviewed in the 1960, 1964, and 1968 elections. Table 4-3 provides a convenient summary of these same responses.

Even a brief look at the data of these three tables makes it clear that in all three years the number of responses favorable to the Democratic party was greater than the number favorable to the Republican party. The difference is not unexpected, considering that many more people call themselves Democrats than call themselves Republicans.

Table 4-1 Favorable Images of Parties
1960, 1964, 1968 [a]

	FAVORABLE REFERENCES TO					
	Democrats			Republicans		
	1960	1964	1968	1960	1964	1968
LIKE PEOPLE ASSOCIATED WITH PARTY						
Johnson	7	25	15	—	—	—
Kennedy, John	—	54	29	—	—	—
Kennedy, Robert	—	—	26	—	—	—
Roosevelt	34	40	19	—	—	—
Truman	4	—	2	—	—	—
Humphrey	—	5	13	—	—	—
Muskie	—	—	33	—	—	—
Party has good leaders	27	18	21	57	12	34
Eisenhower	—	—	—	80	27	32
Nixon	—	—	—	—	—	32
Goldwater	—	—	—	—	32	3
Rockefeller	—	—	—	6	—	15
Agnew	—	—	—	—	—	9
GOVERNMENT MANAGEMENT						
Good administration	6	19	9	13	15	31
Honest government	3	7	2	14	23	6
Spend less money	4	5	1	98	63	115
Spend more money	19	5	7	—	2	2
Have done (would do) good job	26	32	43	44	4	19
GOVERNMENT PHILOSOPHY						
Like their ideas	49	60	30	57	35	33
Are against welfare state	—	—	—	7	15	16
Are for less government activity	—	—	—	22	75	56
Favor social reform	57	29	41	7	3	2
Like their liberal philosophy	58	31	44	7	8	5
Like their conservative philosophy	6	4	2	110	115	103
DOMESTIC POLICIES						
Like their stand on welfare	71	34	15	—	1	7
Are doing something about welfare	—	—	31	—	—	1
Like stand on social security	—	94	73	15	—	5
Like stand on aid to education	13	7	28	7	3	4

Table 4-1 (Cont'd)

| | Favorable References to | | | | | |
| | Democrats | | | Republicans | | |
	1960	1964	1968	1960	1964	1968
Like stand on medical care	34	49	45	10	7	2
Times are better under them	143	79	63	74	10	15
They favor lower taxes	—	—	—	—	—	22
Would do something about inflation	12	4	2	23	3	14
They are good for employment	109	58	—	34	2	—
Like stand on civil rights	13	20	16	8	12	5
They are more for civil rights	11	58	46	9	1	5
They are less for civil rights	5	1	2	1	18	2
Would do something about law and order	—	—	1	—	—	14
Foreign policy						
Good foreign policy, unspecified	17	34	5	54	31	5
Better chance of peace with them	13	29	5	164	35	69
Better chance of peace in Vietnam	—	5	18	—	2	43
Group association: Party is good for						
All the people	58	87	52	17	21	14
People like me	—	—	16	—	—	1
Common people, working people	437	322	360	16	10	10
Labor unions	40	28	32	—	1	9
Farmers	41	18	10	4	2	—
Negroes	1	38	56	7	1	4
Old people	—	5	23	—	—	2
Party responses						
"I've just always been a . . ."	206	197	237	111	84	67
General positive reference to party	7	7	14	25	15	15
They keep their promises	18	13	17	35	12	36
Party is well organized	1	11	8	16	4	17
Like their platform	55	21	—	48	22	10

Table 4-1 (Cont'd)

	FAVORABLE REFERENCES TO					
	Democrats			*Republicans*		
	1960	1964	1968	1960	1964	1968
OTHER						
"I just like them"	95	96	56	75	35	27
It's time for a change	59	—	—	—	18	85
Need for two-party system	—	—	—	—	—	12
Don't know anything about them	—	—	94	—	—	84

[a] The sample size each year was: 1960, *1807;* 1964, *1571;* and 1968, *1673.*

Source: Center for Political Studies, University of Michigan.

Also readily apparent in the data is the consistency of the responses. They are not exactly the same from year to year for either party. New candidates, new issues, new events, and new concerns do arrive on the scene from time to time, and the image the electorate has of the parties reflects the attitude with which they greet these new arrivals. Even so, these party images are at least as remarkable for the amount of continuity they show as for the amount of change they reveal.

Some change, however, is evident. The electorate's image of the Republican party was much more favorable in 1960, when Richard Nixon ran and lost, than it was in 1968, when he ran again and won. Clearly, party and candidate images do not always run on parallel tracks. Yet it cannot be without significance that the least favorable image of the Republican party appeared in 1964, a year when the party's presidential ticket of Goldwater and Miller—though supported by 27 million votes—was buried by a Democratic landslide. On the Democratic side, the change between 1960 and 1968 is even more dramatic. Americans could find many more favorable than unfavorable things to say about the Democratic party in 1960 and in 1964. In 1968, however, the number of unfavorable responses increased sharply—indeed to the point where they outnumbered the favorable responses.

Table 4-2 Unfavorable References to Parties

| | UNFAVORABLE REFERENCES TO | | | | | |
| | Democrats | | | Republicans | | |
	1960	1964	1968	1960	1964	1968
DISLIKES PEOPLE WITHIN PARTY						
Johnson	5	22	62	—	—	—
Roosevelt	—	13	3	—	—	—
Humphrey	—	10	66	—	—	—
Eisenhower	—	—	—	33	14	12
Goldwater	—	—	—	—	119	5
Miller	—	—	—	—	14	—
Agnew	—	—	—	—	—	41
GOVERNMENT MANAGEMENT						
Would give bad administration	6	22	47	13	8	5
Would give dishonest government	31	74	24	3	19	5
Would spend too much money	154	87	129	—	2	4
They do (have done) poor job	3	13	54	19	19	19
GOVERNMENT PHILOSOPHY						
Don't like their ideas	18	15	25	16	24	21
Too much like the other party	—	11	84	4	15	93
Want too much social welfare	16	18	37	—	—	—
Are a give-away party	—	—	46	—	—	—
Are destroying moral fibre of people	—	—	21	—	—	—
Opposed to social change	—	—	—	15	25	25
Don't like socialistic philosophy	62	69	33	—	2	1
Don't like liberal philosophy	41	24	20	11	3	2
Don't like conservative philosophy	10	22	9	44	45	50
DOMESTIC POLICIES						
Don't like welfare programs	11	18	4	20	33	6
Don't like stand on medical care	31	17	7	13	12	13
Don't like stand on fiscal policy	49	19	51	56	9	25
Times are bad under them	11	—	6	47	45	76
They are bad for unemployment	21	1	30	26	14	36

Table 4-2 (Cont'd)

	UNFAVORABLE REFERENCES TO					
	Democrats			*Republicans*		
	1960	1964	1968	1960	1964	1968
Don't like their stand on poverty	2	10	50	40	3	24
Don't like stand on civil rights	17	27	18	35	10	5
Are too much for civil rights	23	64	17	27	4	3
Not enough for civil rights	6	3	4	18	16	24
Don't like their farm policy	33	14	9	48	4	—
Soft on law and order	—	—	74	—	—	9
FOREIGN POLICY						
Bad foreign policy, unspecified	10	9	7	57	8	4
Weak, ineffective, foreign policy	—	30	7	—	4	3
Spend too much on foreign aid	3	32	35	22	3	1
Would handle trouble spots badly	1	28	1	18	5	1
They are the war party	106	23	75	4	22	4
Won't get us out of Vietnam	—	—	131	—	—	16
GROUP ASSOCIATION: PARTY IS TOO GOOD FOR						
Labor unions	43	20	13	2	—	—
Big business	7	—	—	291	160	189
GROUP ASSOCIATION: PARTY IS BAD FOR						
The people	—	4	—	7	15	—
Common people, working people	6	6	18	145	117	144
Labor unions, laboring men	1	—	2	17	15	12
Negroes	5	—	2	20	14	26
PARTY RESPONSES						
"I could never be a . . ."	7	3	5	13	13	14
Negative reference to party	—	17	14	16	17	10
They can't be trusted	53	19	61	37	32	54
Dislike party organizations	2	5	30	4	52	8
Don't like their campaigns	44	43	88	10	85	26
Dislike local party	15	14	13	3	7	10
Dislike party bosses, politicians	2	21	27	4	4	10

Table 4-2 (Cont'd)

	UNFAVORABLE REFERENCES TO					
	Democrats			*Republicans*		
	1960	1964	1968	1960	1964	1968
OTHER						
I just don't like them	46	29	36	55	68	71
It's time for a change	3	11	55	5	—	—
Only interested in power	4	17	11	5	4	9
Don't like extremists in party	—	5	1	—	11	2

Source: Center for Political Studies, University of Michigan.

Factors Affecting Party Image.

GROUP-RELATED FACTORS. A major source of strength for the Democratic party is its identification in the minds of a great many citizens with certain groups. Literally hundreds of people in the sample—representing millions of citizens in the population—speak of it in favorable terms because they see it as being for the common man, for the working man, for all the people, for the little guy, for the poor, and so on. Dozens more see it as

Table 4-3 Summary of References to Parties
          1960, 1964, 1968

1960				
$N = 1807$	Pro-Democratic	2032	Pro-Republican	1621
	Anti-Democratic	1199	Anti-Republican	1486
1964				
$N = 1571$	Pro-Democratic	1819	Pro-Republican	982
	Anti-Democratic	1132	Anti-Republican	1281
1968				
$N = 1673$	Pro-Democratic	1872	Pro-Republican	1327
	Anti-Democratic	1985	Anti-Republican	1533

Source: Center for Political Studies, University of Michigan.

being good for labor unions, for farmers, and for black people. This image is buttressed by the tendency of many people to dislike the Republican party because they picture it as being against or not as good for these same groups, as well as being too much the servant of big business.

TRADITIONAL ASSOCIATION.   Another key element in the Democratic party's favorable image comes from a traditional association which many people say they have with the party. "I've just always been a Democrat," they say, and often they add, "Everybody in our family has been for a long time."

POLICY-RELATED FACTORS.   The two preceding elements —an association with the "common man" and a feeling of traditional loyalty—account for roughly one-third to one-half of the favorable images the electorate has of the Democratic party. The party also gains more favorable than unfavorable notice for its association with certain programs and policies, which are more often than not described in broad terms, with people saying they like it for its stand on social security, or on civil rights, for example. Others couch their responses in even broader terms, saying they like the party simply because times are better when the Democrats are in office.

LEADER-RELATED FACTORS.   Leaders may give a party either a favorable or unfavorable image. We cannot fail to be impressed with how many people in the sample still remember Franklin D. Roosevelt with favor, though his death occurred almost a generation ago. We must also be impressed with the number who mentioned Johnson and Humphrey in 1968 when they explained what they disliked about the party. The point is given added emphasis—see Table 3-6 in the previous chapter— by many who mention Humphrey's connection with Johnson as one thing about Humphrey that might make them want to vote against him.

OTHER FACTORS.   Similarly, both parties receive favorable and unfavorable mention in the sample as managers of government. On the whole, in this pre-Watergate period, the image of the Republicans is more favorable, in part because a number of people have particular things they associate with the Republicans in this connection and in part because many people—129 in the 1968 sample—think the Democratic party is the party of the big spenders. Likewise, both parties have admirers and critics of their ideas and philosophies. Some say they just generally like the Democrats for their ideas, and others say they like the party because it is liberal, while a substantial number—more than 100 in both 1964 and 1968—say they like the Republican party because it is conservative. On two specific issues, the images of the two parties in 1968 are different, and in both cases it is the Democrats who are the losers. They stand accused of being soft on the issue of law and order, faulted for not getting us out of Vietnam, and generally disapproved for being the war party. Republicans on the other hand are praised for their hard line on law and order, for offering a better chance of peace in Vietnam and generally for being the party of peace.

Group Identification and Party Loyalty. So much for the specifics. What are the broader implications of the surveys? A notable feature of responses to the party image questions since 1952 has been the large number of persons who incline to see parties in terms of how they benefit or slight social groups. The importance of this perception cannot be overstated. A person who believes that one of the parties is in general sympathy with groups with which he himself identifies is likely to remain firm in his allegiance through thick and thin, particularly if the only option available is to support a political party that is *out of sympathy* with those same social groups. Such has been the case for millions of Democrats who see their party as benefiting the common man, the working man, the people in general; and see Republicans as having opposing group affiliations.

For such a Democrat, if his party is out of power, there is always a next time. And when the Democratic party is in power, the individual Democrat can tolerate policies about which he is less enthusiastic provided he and his group are not unfavorably affected. If the oil depletion allowance is a tax gimmick out of Texas, it can be shrugged off, as long as Texan Lyndon Johnson provides leadership for the passage of Medicare and increased social security benefits. If the rich get away with murder at tax time, that's not right; but it can be tolerated if wages and prices are right. If billions of dollars go for defense, that too is bearable, as long as the country's actions abroad do not require the protracted involvement of millions of American young men.

If blacks are making demands which are resulting in busing in the South, that is understandable; busing in the South is only making up for past injustices. But if busing goes North, if Vietnam divides the nation as well as the majority party, if food cans accumulate price stickers on top of price stickers, and if unemployment hits communities and industries where it has never really hit before, the working-man Democrat may wonder if his party is really as steadfast in its loyalty to him as he has been to it. Hard times and government policies that hurt can quickly erode party loyalties if party members make the connection that their political party is responsible or is helpless to provide acceptable remedies for the problems.

The Effect of Policy Voting on Party Image.   The potential for erosion is heightened by the existence of policy voting. The bulk of the party image responses in a survey fall into four broad categories: (1) group-related, (2) traditional loyalty, (3) idea- and policy-related, and (4) leader-related. Some concern with policy is already evident in the responses from the sixties, a good deal more than was evident in responses from the fifties. If policy voting is on the increase, as it seems to be, what should we expect to see happen to the responses to the party image questions in future years? First, the number of responses in the third category should increase. Surely that much is obvious. What will happen to the number in the fourth category is not clear. The number in *any* of the four categories is certain to be affected by the stands the parties take on public policy, and how the policy-attuned voter appraises those stands. It is conceivable that a political figure could emerge in either party to whom the policy voter might react particularly strongly, either favorably or unfavorably. Failing that, the number of responses in the fourth category will most likely remain stationary: Leaders are always highly visible, presidents particularly, and do attract favorable and unfavorable comments at all times.

The first and second categories are the most interesting by far because the number of responses in either may increase or decrease, and what happens to them may say much about the course of party politics. One can guess, that the number in both categories will most likely decrease, with (a) an overall decrease most likely to occur in the second, the "traditional loyalty" category, while (b) in the first category, the number of favorable responses will most likely decrease and the number of those unfavorable will most likely increase.

Why? For one thing, with young people tending to strike a posture of independence of party, an increase in the number of persons saying things like "I've just always been a Democrat" could hardly increase. About the only circumstance one can think of that might keep the number of responses in the second category stable is the possibility that older people will discover fewer things they can find to say in favor of their party and fall back on such a response. If such a development occurs, it will surely parallel a further weakening among the party identification of older people such as has been observed underway since 1968.[5]

Our estimate of a decrease in the number of responses falling into the first category rests upon our understanding of the distinguishing characteristic of the policy voter: that *his orientation is toward policy* much more than it is to group or party, and that he is disinclined to respond to a question about parties in any other except policy terms. It is not necessarily that he is unaware of parties or how group interests relate to party and policies. He can respond to a question which asks, for instance, how close he thinks such-and-such a candidate or party is to the way he feels about an issue. He can discriminate between parties and candidates by reference to his own preferences and their preferences in policies (as he sees them). An understanding of his perceptions of this relationship is the single best predictor of his vote, more reliable by far than any other of his characteristics, including party identification. That is the hallmark of the policy voter. He may also make a connection between policies and groups, particularly if he recognizes the impact of a failure of policy upon some identifiable group within the population, especially a group with which he himself identifies closely. For the policy-oriented voter, policy concerns are first. Parties, candidates, and groups as such are secondary and are evaluated by reference to policy. And for some policy voters at least, it is important *not* to think of policies merely by reference to which groups within the population they may or may not benefit. They need some broader standard of fairness and rationality.

Citizen Support for the Political Party

How do Americans feel about parties as institutions? This is a subject on which we have only a little direct evidence. Some of what we know comes from two fine studies, the first reporting the results of a sample survey of the adult population of Wisconsin done in 1964,[6] and the other reporting on follow-up studies done in Wisconsin at two-year intervals, beginning in 1966 and continuing through 1974.[7] For these studies a number of statements were written dealing with how political parties are organized and function (there were 16 statements in the original 1964 survey). Each respondent was asked to say whether he agreed or disagreed, strongly or weakly, with each statement. The following six items give some idea of the ground covered by the questions used in these surveys:

1. It would be better if, in all elections, we put no party labels on the ballot.
2. The best rule in voting is to pick the man regardless of the party label.
3. Democracy works best where competition between parties is strong.
4. The party leaders make no real efforts to keep their promises once they get into office.
5. A senator or representative should follow his party leaders even if he doesn't want to.
6. The conflicts and controversies between the parties hurt our country more than they help it.

Seven of the original 16 items, including the first 3 on the above list, were included to tap feelings toward the general norm of partisanship. Six of the items, including the fourth and fifth on the above list, were included to test judgments about the adequacy of the parties. Three items, including the last on the list, were included to test judgments about how "responsible" the parties are.

Public Support for Parties is Limited.   The most important finding from the 1964 study was that people were willing to support political parties as institutions, but that support was both limited and qualified. How limited that support was can be appreciated by looking over Table 4-4 below, which summarizes the re-

Table 4-4   Responses on Items Pertaining to Support for the Party System

	PERCENT WHO:					
Item	Strongly Agree	Agree	Agree Dis-agree	Dis-agree	Strongly Dis-agree	Don't Know
1. No party labels on ballot	3%	19%	7%	54%	13%	3%
2. Pick the man, not the party	23	59	6	9	1	2
3. Democracy needs party competition	7	61	12	11	1	7
4. Party leaders don't keep promises	6	30	28	31	2	3
5. Congressman should follow party leaders	1	22	9	56	7	4
6. Party conflicts hurt country	3	44	14	33	2	3

Source: Jack Dennis, "Support for the Party System by the Mass Public," *American Political Science Review* 60 (September 1966), 600–615. Used by permission.

sponses people gave to 6 of the 16 items. The highest measure of support for the party system appears in the responses to the first item. Thirteen percent say they *strongly disagree* with the statement that in all elections it would be better if we put no party labels on the ballot. Another 54 percent say they disagree with the statement, making a total of 67 percent who reject the idea of removing party labels from the ballot. On the other hand, nearly half the respondents say conflicts between the parties hurt the country (item 6), while only 35 percent line up behind the opposing view. On the second item, which incorporates another nonpartisan norm, only 10 percent disagree, while an impressive 82 percent endorse it. Roughly one-third disagree with the statement that party leaders do not keep their promises when they get into office, slightly more than one-third agree with it, and something less than one third take an ambivalent position.

We do not find much support for any kind of reform which would attempt to make the parties more responsible by encouraging each party to display more cohesion among its members. Only 23 percent of those surveyed agree that a senator or representative should follow his party's leaders even if he doesn't want to. To a slightly softer version of the same idea—that senators and representatives ought to follow party leaders more than they do—41 percent agree, while 30 percent say they think we would be better off if all the Democrats in government stood together and all the Republicans did the same.

There is support here from some measure of party competition, although it is mixed and qualified. Sixty-eight percent agree that democracy works best where competition between parties is strong, but only 31 percent agree that things would be better if the parties took opposite stands on issues more than they do now, while 53 percent endorse the idea that government efficiency would be improved by ridding the system of the conflicts between the parties. Party competition may be desired, but as is true of many political arrangements in America, it is desired only at an abstract level.

Public Evaluation of the Parties. By way of summarizing the findings from the 1964 study, we may say again that popular support for political parties in America is something less than firm. Some features of the parties are approved; others are not. The parties stand accused particularly of having leaders who cannot be trusted to keep promises, of stirring up trouble needlessly and creating conflict, and of interfering with the efficiency of government. Toward party competition, feeling is equally mixed. As a notion, it receives support. As applied—incorporated in a suggestion, for example, that legislators should go along with party leaders, or a suggestion that members of one party should stick together more than they do in opposition to members of the other party—the notion loses a lot of its appeal. If these observations have meaning beyond the population of Wisconsin—and there is no reason to believe they do not—then it is clear that Americans accept parties as institutions and are willing to support them, but with a spirit that falls far short of enthusiasm. As the author of the report on the 1964 study says:

> The general public apparently does not greatly approve party competition and controversy; nor does it regard the party leaders as particularly reliable keepers of campaign promises. In these senses, opinion is unfavorable. It is hard to conclude from these data therefore that the general population is thoroughly supportive of the party system. Rather, the general image which

emerges is that public feeling is somewhat lukewarm and somewhat mixed.[8]

Of course, that was in 1964. What has happened since?

The Decrease in Public Support for Parties.   Subsequent surveys indicate that *in succeeding years mass support for parties as institutions has become even weaker.* Recall that in 1964 the strongest public support for parties was to be found in the responses to the statement which asserted that it would be better if party labels did not appear on the ballot. Sixty-seven percent declared themselves opposed to the idea that year. By 1974 the number opposed had dropped to 38 percent—by any standard a massive shift in attitude. In the 1964 survey the responses to the other items indicated no more than minimal support for parties. The subsequent follow-up studies revealed that these initially minimal support levels remained about the same.[9]

The findings from the Wisconsin studies are in line with data from other studies. Election surveys conducted by the Survey Research Center at the University of Michigan have included questions which touch upon several aspects of party performance. Responses to these questions show that parties rate well below elections as devices for making government responsive to citizens, though *both* elections and parties have fallen in public esteem in the last decade. Parties are believed to "do what they want" once elections are over, rather than feel obliged to keep their promises; to be interested only in people's votes, not in their opinions; and to be largely beyond the reach of ordinary citizen influence. Parties, further, receive a markedly lower performance rating than other political institutions, including the U.S. Supreme Court, Congress, and interest groups; in the fall of 1973, right in the midst of the Watergate scandal, they receive a rating even lower than that given the presidency. Clearly, parties are not among the most highly prized of American political institutions. Mass support for parties has declined steadily since 1964 and in the decade of the 1970s is weakest among younger citizens. From time to time, reformers in and out of government get behind measures—campaign financing legislation, internal party organizational changes, and such—designed to do something about the condition of our national parties. In light of the observed long-term decline in citizen acceptance of parties, one may properly wonder if such measures do anything to arrest that decline.

Trust

Is it only, or mainly parties that have fallen from favor, or is the decline in citizen feeling for parties only one aspect of a general citizen disenchantment with the broader political system within which these institutions function? The evidence we have indicates that parties have lost more in public esteem than other institutions, but that their decline is only part of a falling-off in citizen regard for the American political system generally.

The Record of the Past.   For most of the past generation, surveys of public opinion have told us in unmistakable terms that Americans love America. Even those critical of politics and government have still been able to say they are proud to be Americans, and few have said they could think of any reason that might make them want to leave their country and go elsewhere to live. Americans have also been distinctive in the reasons they give for liking their country: Asked in one cross-national survey what they liked about America, almost 9 in 10 Americans mentioned something about government and politics—a figure far higher than that reported for other countries.[10]

A study conducted in 1964 produced high ratings for all three branches of the national government, with the presidency coming out slightly ahead of the other two.[11] Measured on a scale which ranged from 0 to 10, with 0 representing an expression of no confidence at all in government, and 10 representing the greatest possible confidence, the average rating given each branch was

President	7.43
Congress	7.23
Supreme Court	6.89

Four years after that, a study of southern attitudes toward a number of institutions suggested that the agreement evident in the attitudes of whites and blacks was even more remarkable than the few points of conflict observed.[12] Both whites and blacks were generally disposed to accept the acts of government as legitimate and more willing to accept the actions of government as legitimate than the acts of private groups such as labor unions and business associations. There was one notable difference: Southern blacks were much more willing than whites to accord legitimacy to decisions handed down by the U.S. Supreme Court.

The Decline in Trust.   But from the periodic surveys done by the Survey Research Center come findings that indicate that while trust in government was clearly high through at least 1964, it showed a decline in 1968, and an even more marked decline by 1972. On each of their surveys, people were asked how much they thought the government in Washington could be trusted to do what is right. Table 4-5 displays the responses given in four of these national surveys.[13] The decline in trust evident here also stood out in a 1971 survey, the broad purpose of which was to define and articulate the hopes and fears of the American people. This study indicated that Americans were reasonably well satisfied with their own private lives, but that they believed the nation was in trouble, that it had slipped backward during the course of the previous five years. Some saw the tensions and divisions within the nation as serious enough to lead to a "real breakdown in the country." How did respondents explain this state of things? Some blame was placed at the feet of protestors and troublemakers. But quite as often, the fault was found to lie in institutions that did not work and leaders who did not provide adequate leadership.[14]

With all the attention given Watergate in 1973 and 1974, combined with the resignation of a president and a vice-president and problems of recession and inflation, there is no reason what-

Table 4-5   Trust of the Federal Government
             1964–1972

Q. How much of the time do you think you can trust the government in Washington to do what is right?	1964	1968	1970	1972
Always	14%	7%	6%	7%
Most of the time	64	56	46	46
Some of the time	21	37	48	46
None of the time	*	*	6	*

* Less than 1%.
Source: Center for Political Studies, University of Michigan.

ever to believe that the decline in trust which has been apparent since 1968 has been reversed.

The Importance of Trust.   Why is trust important? It is important because without it authorities lose a measure of their freedom to act in pursuit of collective goals.[15] Political trust is a diffuse support which "forms a reservoir of favorable attitudes or good will that helps members to accept or tolerate outputs to which they are opposed or the effect of which they see as damaging to their wants." [16] When trust is high, public officials find it relatively easier to fulfill the obligations of their offices; when it declines they may well find it difficult to govern effectively.[17]

The Dimensions of Trust.   Thus trust—that reservoir of good will—is undoubtedly important for the functioning of a political system. What meaning are we to give to the downward movement in trust apparent in the last decade? Let us first highlight some of the dimensions of that decline. The decline is not distributed equally throughout the whole of the population. It is closely related to race, age, and status mobility. In the early 1960s, blacks and whites were about equally trusting of government. In 1964, trust among blacks was at an all-time high. In the next four years, trust among both groups declined. In the four years after that, trust among whites continued to decline, but among blacks it plummeted! Two age groups in particular, those under 30 and those between 50 and 60, are conspicuous for showing a decline in trust between 1968 and 1972. Aging appears to foster discontent, while the young today enter the electorate with a noticeable lack of favorable attitudes toward existing institutions. Among whites, upwardly mobile individuals are generally more trusting than the downwardly mobile or those whose status is stationary. However, upward mobility does not preclude the development of attitudes of mistrust. Since 1964 upwardly mobile blacks have become far more distrusting than other blacks. The implication seems undeniable: The people most likely to be critical of the system are *those who feel they get less than they deserve, no matter what their status.* What counts is not any absolute measure of affluence or status change or expectations, but rather how the individual assesses his own standing in relation to the wealth, status, or opportunities enjoyed by others. Equity counts. (Widespread publicity given to the fact that an incumbent president paid only nominal taxes on an annual salary of $200,000 is not likely to be perceived as a model of equity, though it may well be perceived as an example of what the existing tax structure defines as equitable). An individual can easily develop hostile attitudes toward political institutions if he comes to believe that the institutions are providing better rewards and opportunities for people who are no more, and perhaps less, deserving than himself.[18]

When political discontent rises rapidly over a short period of time, there is reason to be concerned. Evidence exists which links discontent with the potential for radical change or revolution.[19] Nonvoters are much more likely to be mistrustful of government than voters, and turnout in elections has been declining. Independents are much more likely to be mistrustful than partisans, and the number of partisans has been declining. The rapid rise in discontent suggests that the needs of some significant part of the population are not being met by existing institutions, and that the blame is directed not just at leaders but at institutions. Hence, there has been a drop both in turnout and in party identification. At the least, what all this suggests is that the means that exist to moderate social conflicts have failed or are beginning to fail, and that when the stress which produces the discontent attains a high enough intensity the demand will come to change the institutions or discard them in favor of others.

Efficacy

If things are wrong and the system and its institutions are not working well, can the citizen do anything about the situation? This is a question about the citizen's efficacy, his ability to be effective, to have influence. Affection for institutions is down. Trust is down. What is the current status of citizen political efficacy?

A sense of political efficacy has usually been defined as "a feeling that individual political action does have, or can have, an impact upon the political process, i.e., that it is worthwhile to perform one's civic duties." [20] It is not necessary for the citizen to feel that the government responds to his wishes every day, nor to feel that the average citizen plays a large role in the actual making of public policy to have a sense of political efficacy. It is only necessary that the citizen feel that he could be influential *if he needed to be*. The Massachusetts supermarket clerk made manifest his sense of efficacy when he said,

> Aw come on, you really think we have much to say about the way the laws are made in this state? Hah. It's them. It's the big guys that do that. I was talking to a friend of mine the other day about just this thing [voting], and I told him those politicians can try to do whatever they want to do, but we little guys have one very powerful little thing in our favor—a vote. If we have to we can get together and vote any rotten politician out on his heels.[21]

Measuring Efficacy. Efficacy, though admittedly an important concept, is one of the trickiest, because it is both difficult to measure, and its social origins are only imperfectly understood. A crucial measurement problem is whether it is better to focus on inputs or outputs when measuring efficacy. It is easily conceivable that an individual could feel strongly alienated from government—could have strong negative reactions to the substance of public policy and conclude that the government must certainly not care much about what people like him think—and would thus score low on feelings of efficacy if our measurement of it concentrated on government outputs—that is, upon the impact government policies have on the individual. A similarly situated individual might, however, feel assured that he could have influence with government officials if he really wanted to, and such a person would score high on efficacy if our assessment of it concentrated upon inputs—that is upon the individual's ability to have influence upon the political system.[22]

Developing Feelings of Efficacy. Nor is the process by which a feeling of political efficacy is developed well understood. We do know that children develop an awareness of political authorities at an early age, at least in America. An early study of schoolchildren in New Haven found that children developed a benevolent image of the president of the United States and could say something about what he did in that job as early as the second grade.[23] A much larger study of the attitudes of elementary school children reported an increase in feelings of political efficacy from the third through the eighth grades, with the sharpest increase occurring in the fourth and fifth grades. In the eighth grade of

school most children express feelings of efficacy equal to that
reported by their teachers.[24] Other studies have reported similar
findings.[25]

We must also count as important the strong relationship that
studies have found between efficacy and personal competence.
Adults and children alike who feel they are personally effective,
that their life is likely to work out the way they would like it to,
are most likely to score high on feelings of political efficacy.

All of this accumulating evidence suggests that the development of feelings of efficacy is an unusually complex process,
closely related to the individual's environment and likely to be a
creature of a wide range of experiences, not all of which have a
political context. We do not expect every bad experience an individual has at the hands of a policeman to lead him to reject the
entire system. But we are not surprised when a southern black
says he does not believe he can have much influence over what his
local government does. Neither are we surprised to discover that
black children of low socioeconomic status are far more likely
than white children generally to score low on feelings of political
efficacy, or to discover that they also score low on feelings of
personal competence. Nor are we surprised, however, if black
children and adults in the South today say they believe they have
a capacity to influence the government and that their vote can
count for something: Hundreds of local black officeholders have
been elected in the South in the past decade. Nor, finally, can
we be surprised to find young radicals on college campuses who
call the vote a sham, an establishment trick, but who believe
they can have considerable influence upon government, and thus
score high on efficacy; they have learned that, for their immediate
purposes, a timely demonstration can sometimes be more effective than the ballot box. Perhaps for the time being, all we dare
say about feelings of political efficacy, besides saying that they
deserve our continuing attention, is that in combination with trust
and information, they are capable of having a considerable impact upon the functioning of a political system.

Information

Finally we come to the question of information. Thus far we have
concentrated upon feelings, usually expressed in terms of liking
or disliking a political object. Now it is time to consider not what

Americans like or dislike about their political system and institutions, but simply what they know about them.

Lack of Knowledge Among the Electorate.   Most Americans get by with a minimum amount of information about their government. Surveys of public opinion have regularly shown that less than half the adults in the country know the number of senators that represent their state in Washington. Far fewer know the names of their two senators. As recently as 1965 less than half the adults interviewed in a Gallup poll could supply the name of their congressman when asked, fewer than one-third knew when he next came up for reelection, fewer than one in five knew how he had voted on any major bill that year, and an even smaller number could think of anything he had done for his congressional district.[26]

A study of adult citizens of voting age in the South in 1961 included a short political information test. The results are indicated in the data presented in Table 4-6.

The level of information among whites was somewhat higher than among blacks. Both groups did best when asked to supply the name of the governor of their state. Their poorest

Table 4-6   Political Information of Southerners
                1961

	Percentage Answering Correctly	
	Negro	White
Do you happen to remember whether Franklin Roosevelt was a Republican or Democrat? [Which?]	57%	87%
Who is governor of [this state] now?	68	90
About how long a term does the governor serve?	65	67
About how many years does a United States senator serve?	8	20
Do you happen to know about how many members there are on the United States Supreme Court?	8	21

showing came on the question about the size of the U.S. Supreme Court. Only one person in five in the white sample, and fewer than one person in ten among blacks, knew that the Court consists of nine justices.[27] Ten years later, the same set of questions was used in a study of attitudes in a metropolitan area in the Southwest, with similar results.[28] There is no suggestion here that the information level of the citizenry increased significantly in the intervening decade.

Nor is it only facts about the structure and process of government that the citizen seems to lack. The citizen frequently has little information even about issues which *he* says he believes are important and about which *he* says he has an opinion. A 1956 election study reported the number of the electorate who said they had an opinion on a number of current issues of public policy and did know what the government was doing; the number who said they had an opinion but knew nothing about what the government was doing in that area; and the number who said they had no opinion on the matter and knew nothing about what the government was doing. In every instance, the number falling into the third category was higher by far than the number falling into the first two. On some issues, such as tax cuts and racial equality in jobs and housing, the number who had an opinion about the issue but *did not know* what the government was doing, was almost four times the number who had an opinion and *did know* something about what the government was doing. For many voters that year, having information about some aspect of policy was not deemed to be an essential prerequisite either for manifesting an interest in a matter or even rendering an appraisal of it.[29] The American voter is probably not alone in this regard. The Gallup Poll in England tells us that at a time when public attention there was focused strongly upon Britain's possible entry into the European Common Market—a commitment that would have a considerable impact on the daily lives of people in the British Isles—68 percent of those interviewed had an opinion on the issue, but only 31 percent knew that Great Britain was not then a member of the European Common Market, but was actually a member of its competitor, the European Free Trade Area! [30]

In order not to mislead—for indeed there is no intention here to suggest either that the American citizenry is woefully ill-informed at all times about all aspects of politics, or that there is something terribly wrong about that—we must point out that at least a majority of Americans say they are interested in politics, especially elections, and say they do pay attention to what is going on in politics. Exactly how well informed the electorate will be at any given moment about a given issue is not at all easy to predict. Take the case of New Hampshire, just before the occasion of the much-noticed and important presidential-preference primary held there in 1968. A survey of adult citizens of voting age in January 1968, taken two months before the scheduled date of the primary, indicated a high level of information, even about some of the details of the mechanics of the primary. For instance, 86 percent knew when it was to be held, while 95 percent knew that paper ballots rather than voting machines would be employed on election day.[31] (And to give the British electorate its due, let us also note that in the general election of 1966, 85 percent of the voters indicated that they had watched some of the campaign broadcasts on television . . . although they said that they liked them in part because they were brief! [32])

Information, Trust, and Efficacy. On the score of information, one thing we need to note and remember is the relationship one can probably expect to find between trust and information. When trust is high, information levels among the electorate may be low: There is no overpowering need to know about the government precisely because it is trusted. That it what trust is all about. When information levels are found to be increasing, it may be a warning of danger, for it may signal that trust is being withdrawn. In a study of rioters in Newark, New Jersey, Jeffrey Paige found that the rioter, who had little trust for the government of Newark, scored higher than his nonrioting counterpart on the score of information, leading Paige to remark that in this instance it appeared that the more that was known about the government, the more it was distrusted!

There may also be a connection between levels of information and feelings of efficacy. Paige also discovered that the better-informed rioter also scored markedly lower on feelings of efficacy than did the nonrioter. The rioter found little reason to feel that he could have influence upon government or that government was concerned about him.[33] Yet another study found that one in three black students who rated high on feelings of political efficacy also had strongly negative feelings toward the police.[34] A third study—of attitudes in Watts, California, follow-ing the riots there in 1965—revealed considerable political dis-affection and lack of trust for elected officials, and indicated that the most disaffected of all were the young and the better edu-cated. But this study also indicated, interestingly enough, that the overall response of people in Watts in the aftermath of the riots was racial partisanship and mobilization, *not estrangement from the political system.*[35]

Schools are information-providing vehicles, and an increase in the number of people going further along in school in America means a generally increasing level of information throughout the citizenry.[36] Can increased levels of education threaten the sys-tem? Does it encourage some people to lose trust in the system? The record of the sixties, a record of involvement of large num-bers of college students in the confrontation politics of that decade, suggests that for some, at least, that is precisely what does happen.

NOTES

The first two quotations at the beginning of this chapter are taken from inter-views reported in William Watts and Lloyd A. Free, *State of the Nation* (Wash-ington, D.C.: Potomac Associates, 1973), 223, 232, 249. The third is from Robert M. Fogelson and Robert B. Hill, "Who Riots?" in Charles M. Bonjean and others (editors), *Community Politics* (New York: Free Press, 1971), 136–149. The fourth is from Robert S. Gilmour and Robert B. Lamb, *Political Alienation in Contemporary America* (New York: St. Martin, 1975), 157.

1. The *New York Times.*
2. Table 4-2, which follows later in this chapter, indicates that 93 responses to one of the party image questions criticized the Republican Party in 1968 for being too much like the Democratic Party.
3. Clinton Rossiter, *Parties and Politics in America* (Ithaca, N.Y.: Cornell University Press, 1960), 107.
4. The standard party image questions are asked this way:
   Is there anything in particular that you like about the Democratic Party? (What is that?)
   Is there anything in particular that you dislike about the Democratic Party? (What is that?)
   Is there anything in particular that you like about the Republican Party? (What is that?)

Is there anything in particular that you dislike about the Republican Party? (What is that?)

5. See Norval D. Glenn, "Class and Party Support in the United States: Recent and Emerging Trends," *Public Opinion Quarterly* 37 (Spring 1973), 1–20; and by the same author "Sources of the Shift to Political Independence: Some Evidence from a Cohort Analysis," *Social Science Quarterly* 53 (December 1972), 494–519, and "Class and Party Support in 1972," *Public Opinion Quarterly* 39 (Spring 1975), 117–122. See also Paul R. Abramson, "Generational Change in American Electoral Behavior," American Political Science Review 68 (March 1974), 93–105.

6. Jack Dennis, "Support for the Party System by the Mass Public," *American Political Science Review* 60 (September 1966), 600–615.

7. Jack Dennis, "Trends in Public Support for the American Political Party System," a paper prepared for delivery at the 1974 annual meeting of the American Political Science Association, Chicago, September 1974.

8. Dennis, "Support for the Party System," 606. Used by permission.

9. Dennis, 1974 American Political Science Association paper.

10. Gabriel Almond and Sidney Verba, *The Civic Culture* (Princeton, N.J.: Princeton University Press, 1963), 101–105.

11. Lloyd A. Free and Hadley Cantril, *The Political Beliefs of Americans* (New Brunswick, N.J.: Rutgers University Press, 1967), 192–193. The wording of the question was:

Our federal government, as you know, is made up of three branches: the Executive Branch, headed by the President; the Judicial Branch, headed by the U.S. Supreme Court; and the Legislative Branch, made up of the U.S. Senate and the House of Representatives. [Hand card showing ladder to respondent.] I'd like you to show me on this ladder how much trust and confidence you have in each of these three branches under present circumstances. The top of the ladder in this case means *the greatest possible confidence;* the bottom, *no confidence at all.*

First, how much trust and confidence do you have in the Executive Branch, headed by the President?

Secondly, in the Judicial Branch, headed by the U.S. Supreme Court?

And finally, in the Legislative Branch, made up of the Senate and House of Representatives?

12. Robert G. Lehnen, "Mass Opinions About the Legitimacy of Some American Institutions," a paper prepared for delivery at the annual meeting of the Southern Political Science Association, November 5–7, 1970, Atlanta, Georgia. Also worth reading is David Easton and Jack Dennis, *Children in the Political System: Origins of Political Legitimacy* (New York: McGraw-Hill, 1969), especially chapter 11, which discusses the role of the policeman in the development of a child's attitudes toward authority. See also Harrell R. Rodgers and George Taylor, "The Policeman as an Agent of Regime Legitimation," *Midwest Journal of Political Science* 15 (February 1971), 72–86, and by the same authors, employing data from the same study, "Pre-Adult Attitudes Toward Legal Compliance: Notes Toward a Theory," *Social Science Quarterly* 51 (December 1970), 539–551.

13. Center for Political Studies, Survey Research Center, University of Michigan. Data for these election studies were obtained through the Inter-University Consortium for Political Research. The wording of the question was: "How much of the time do you think you can trust the government in Washington to do what is right—just about always, most of the time, or

only some of the time?" The most comprehensive study of trust as revealed in these election studies is to be found in Arthur H. Miller, "Political Issues and Trust in Government, 1964–1970," *American Political Science Review* 68 (September 1974), 951–972.

14. Albert H. Cantril and Charles W. Roll, Jr., *Hopes and Fears of the American People* (Washington, D.C.: Potomac Associates, 1971), 11–12. And see the latest in a line of such studies, William Watts and Lloyd A. Free, *State of the Nation, 1974* (Washington, D.C.: Potomac Associates, 1974).

15. William A. Gamson, *Power and Discontent* (Homewood, Ill.: The Dorsey Press, 1968), 39–48; and by the same author, "Political Trust and Its Ramifications," in Gilbert Abcarian and John W. Soule (editors), *Social Psychology and Political Behavior* (Columbus, Ohio: Merrill, 1971), 41–48.

16. David Easton, *A Systems Analysis of Political Life* (New York: Wiley, 1965), 263.

17. Perhaps relevant here is Lipset's reminder that in Germany and Austria, the normally high turnout reached its greatest heights in 1932–1933, in the last election before the destruction of the democratic system itself. See Seymour Martin Lipset, *Political Man* (New York: Doubleday, 1963), 195.

18. On the decline of trust and its possible meaning, see especially Arthur H. Miller and others, "Social Conflict and Political Estrangement, 1958–1972," a paper prepared for delivery at the 1973 Midwest Political Science Association meeting, Chicago, May 1973; and Miller, "Political Issues and Trust in Government, 1964–1970." See also Richard Schacht, *Alienation* (New York: Doubleday, 1970), 246–252; Joel D. Aberbach and Jack L. Walker, "Political Trust and Racial Ideology," *American Political Science Review* 64 (December 1970), 1199–1219; and Ada W. Finifter, "Dimensions of Political Alienation," *American Political Science Review* 64 (June 1970), 389–410. Robert S. Gilmour and Robert B. Lamb, *Political Alienation in Contemporary America* (New York: St. Martin, 1975), present a careful and thorough analysis of alienation (distrust, powerlessness, meaninglessness). They note a dramatic increase in alienation in the past two decades and offer a believable estimate of the meaning of that increase for the future of the American political system.

19. See in particular Ted R. Gurr, *Why Men Rebel* (Princeton, N.J.: Princeton University Press, 1970), and Edward N. Muller, "A Test of a Partial Theory of Potential for Political Violence," *American Political Science Review* 66 (September 1972), 928–959. See also Andre Modigliani, "Hawks and Doves, Isolationism and Political Distrust: An Analysis of Public Opinion on Military Matters," *American Political Science Review* 66 (September 1972), 960–978.

20. Angus Campbell and others, *The Voter Decides* (New York: Harper & Row, 1954), 187. Appendix A of *The Voter Decides,* 187–194, provides a good, brief discussion of the Survey Research Center's political efficacy questions. And see Philip E. Converse, "Change in the American Electorate," in Augus Campbell and Philip E. Converse (editors), *The Human Meaning of Social Change* (New York: Russell Sage Foundation, 1972), 327.

21. Edgar Litt, *The Political Cultures of Massachusetts* (Cambridge, Mass.: The M.I.T. Press, 1965), 73–74.

22. Almond and Verba, *The Civic Culture,* 183–189.

23. Fred I. Greenstein, *Children and Politics* (New Haven, Conn.: Yale University Press, 1965), 33–35. See also Dean Jaros, "Children's Orientations

Toward the President: Some Additional Theoretical Considerations and Data," *Journal of Politics* 29 (May 1967), 368–387.

24. David Easton and Jack Dennis, "The Child's Acquisition of Regime Norms: Political Efficacy," *American Political Science Review* 61 (March 1967), 25–38.

25. The more recent studies include Kenneth Langton, "Peer Group and School and the Political Socialization Process," *American Political Science Review* 61 (September 1967), 751–758; Kenneth Langton and M. Kent Jennings, "Political Socialization and the High School Civics Curriculum in the United States," *American Political Science Review* 62 (September 1968), 852–867; Schley R. Lyons, "The Political Socialization of Ghetto Children: Efficacy and Cynicism," *Journal of Politics* 32 (May 1970), 288–304; Kenneth Prewitt, "Political Efficacy," in the *International Encyclopedia of the Social Sciences* (New York: Macmillan, 1968), 225–228.

26. Gallup Opinion Index, 1965.

27. Donald R. Matthews and James W. Prothro, *Negroes and the New Southern Politics* (New York: Harcourt Brace Jovanovich, 1966), 271–275.

28. My study of voters in Lubbock, Texas, in 1970 indicated that 75 percent knew that Franklin D. Roosevelt was a Democrat, 58 percent that the governor of the state served a four-year term, 35 percent that a U.S. senator served a six-year term, and that 25 percent knew there were nine justices on the U.S. Supreme Court; on the latter item the range in guesses was from 3 to 141.

29. V. O. Key, Jr., *Public Opinion and American Democracy* (New York: Knopf, 1961), 192–195.

30. Richard Rose, *People in Politics* (New York: Basic Books, 1970), 126.

31. Audits and Surveys, Inc. Data for the 1968 New Hampshire primary study was obtained through the Inter-University Consortium for Political Research.

32. D. E. Butler and Anthony King, *The British General Election of 1966* (New York: St. Martin, 1966), 144.

33. Nathan Caplan and Jeffrey Paige, "A Study of Ghetto Rioters," *Scientific American* 219 (August 1968), 15–21.

34. Rodgers and Taylor, "The Policeman as an Agent of Regime Legitimation," 80.

35. David O. Sears, "Black Attitudes Toward the Political System in the Aftermath of the Watts Insurrection," *Midwest Journal of Political Science* 13 (November 1969), 542–544.

36. In 1939 there were 1,350,000 students enrolled in America's colleges and universities; in 1968 the figure had risen to 6,900,000.

Part Two

Party as an Organization

There are those who see the party as a major social structure mediating directly between the individual citizen and national, state, or local government. They see public policy as influenced by the party and its platform, interest groups aggregated through the party, social conflict resolved, public support mobilized, and public opinion represented. . . . On the other hand, others see parties today as obsolete, ineffective, atrophied, and incompetent. They point out that the looseness of the party structure, the tenuousness of membership, the fluidity of affiliation mean that parties seem to be organizations in name only. . . . Since no great body of evidence can be marshaled on either side of this controversy, we clearly need more exact study of the relationships between our parties and American society, and of the effectiveness of our parties in influencing political behavior.

On balance, it appears that direct access to the decision-makers—both elected and appointed—in the American political system is limited, for both individuals and noninstitutionalized groups, by virtue of traditional institutional patterns and power relations. Recognizing this as a fact of American political life, new groups that lack economic and other resources have attempted recently to reach the loci of power through protest tactics, including violence, and the development of new forms of political organization.

5
Party
Organization

State statutes prescribe multilevel units of party organization, which typically include organizations from the precinct level up to and including the state central committee, and what these statutes say can be important. Knowledge of the role prescribed by the law for these organizations in the selection of delegates to national party conventions is of the greatest value, for example, to the candidate in search of delegate support. What the law says about matters of party organization, and what kind of party results both from the law's prescription and its silence, are the major concerns of this chapter.

In their attitudes toward parties, as we have seen, citizens are ambivalent. At one level, many of them identify with parties, though not as many do as used to. Yet they trust them less than other institutions. Parties are not without their critics. Yet on questions of whether they are appropriate, effective, and responsible, parties also have their defenders. How, where, and why critics and defenders disagree is the subject of the concluding section of the chapter.

The structure of the formal party organization in America is prescribed by state law, by rules of the national party convention, and by state and local rules and customs. In form, it resembles a pyramid. At the top are the national committee and convention. At the bottom are thousands of precinct and district organizations. In between are county, congressional district, municipal, and ward organizations. These thousands of party organization units are tied together in a loose union that leaves an important measure of autonomy to each of the units. Such an organization is scarcely a hierarchy; much better call it a stratarchy.[1] The glue that holds it together is, on the one hand, the status given the organization by law and custom, and on the other, the sharing by those who hold party positions of a commitment to and identification with their political party.

As a general rule, the nearer a position is to the top of the pyramid, the more prestige it carries and the fewer such positions there are. But prestige and scarcity must not be taken for political power. Many a national committee member has found that his or her influence within the state party organization is much less than the influence enjoyed by others lower down in the structure, or even completely outside the party organization. One of the most frequently made points about today's party organization is the weakness of state and local organizations compared with the personal organizations of mayors and governors. The latter operate largely apart from the formal party organizations,[2] as indeed do most campaign organizations. In short, the formal party organization is not unfairly described as a paper pyramid. It should not be confused with informal organizations which operate sometimes within, sometimes cooperatively with, and sometimes completely in disregard of the formal organization. The sinews of political power are as likely to be found in these working organizations as in the hands of the formal organization. This is not to say that the formal party organization is either ineffective or moribund. It is only to suggest that we dare not take the formal party organization at face value or assume that the formal organization represents the chief mechanism through which the work of the party is done.

The National Committee and Chairman

At the top of the organizational pyramid stands the national committee. The Democratic party has had a national committee since 1848, and the Republican party since 1856.[3]

Until very recently the national committees of both parties consisted of one man and one woman from each of the 50 states plus members from the territories. But demands within the parties for more democracy in the choosing of national committee members has radically changed both the size and composition of the membership of these committees. As a result of changes made on several occasions during the period from 1968 to 1974, the Democratic National Committee of 1975, for example, became a body of 360 persons. 104 of them represent opposite sex pairs from the 50 states, the District of Columbia, and Puerto Rico. 200 members are apportioned among the states on the same basis as are delegates to the national convention, a basis which attempts to reward states which have elected democrats to major public offices. 31 members represent important groups within the party including the Democratic Governors' Conference, the Young Democrats, the Democratic Mayors' Conference, and so forth. And a final group of 25 are at-large members chosen by the remaining 335 members of the National Committee.

How Committee Members are Chosen.   Membership on the national committee is for a four-year term, from the adjournment of one national convention to the adjournment of the next—a recognition that, in form at least, members of the committee are chosen by the national conventions of their respective parties. In practice, the choice is actually made by the states. In some states the choice is made by the state's delegation to the national convention; in others it is made by a direct primary election, by a state convention, or by the state committee of the party.

A great many considerations may enter into the choice of national committee members. The choice may reflect a serious political contest between rival candidates or factions within the party. The committee member chosen may be a major political figure in his or her own right within the state or may be chosen as a compromise candidate acceptable to major factions within the party. The committee member may also be an elder politician in the party whose selection as national committeeman is a reward for many years of faithful service to the party, or, more likely, a reward for a recent substantial contribution to the party war chest.

These various selection criteria leave their impact on the membership of the committees. Some members clearly belong to the roster of the politically influential. More often, however, the committeemen and committeewomen selected have little, if any, voice in the state party, and are sometimes unknown even to the lower-echelon leadership of their own state party.[4]

Committee Functions.   The functions of the national committee are largely what the members decide they will be. They normally include playing some role in the party's presidential campaign, filling vacancies on the party ticket caused by death or other disability,[5] giving policy guidance to the national headquarters, conducting public relations programs on behalf of the party, fund-raising, and making arrangements for the quadrennial national party convention. These last arrangements include selecting the city in which the convention will be held, issuing a call for the convention, preparing a temporary roll of delegates, and recommending a slate of temporary officers.[6] If the party does not control the presidency, that is if it is the "out" party, the committee's decisions on convention arrangements can be crucial. Representatives of a major contender for the presidential nomination are not likely to succeed in persuading the committee to issue an outright endorsement of the candidate, but they may succeed in persuading the committee to make decisions on certain arrangements for the convention—such as the designation of temporary officers and chairmen of crucial committees— favorable to the strategic interests of their candidate within the convention.

Apart from these decisions on convention arrangements, the national committee as such is unlikely to make any important decisions, political or otherwise. Indeed, the committee may seldom meet. The committees of both major parties have been known to go for months without meeting.

The National Chairman.   With the national committee meeting irregularly and infrequently, such daily work as must be done for the committee falls upon the shoulders of the national chairman and the headquarters staff. Considering that this post is, in a formal sense at least, the highest post in the party structure, the rate of turnover is surprisingly high. In the period from 1940 to 1966, the Republican party had 14 chairmen, and the Democrats 11. In form, the national committee selects the chairman; in practice, he is chosen by the party's nominee for president. If, as has happened frequently, the party chairman is given a post in government by the victorious presidential candidate, the president selects his replacement. In the case of the party of the defeated presidential candidate, the national committee actually does select a national chairman if that post becomes vacant. In this case the national chairman is likely to be someone who is acceptable to all major factions in the party.

As the process of his selection indicates, the national chairman is expected to have close ties to the incumbent president. In this instance, the chairman's power can scarcely be more than an extension of the president's power, to the extent that the president has confidence in his national chairman and has a job for him to do. When his party does not win the presidency, the party chairman is likely to find that his power is strictly limited to performing one major function: serving as caretaker of the skeletal national party structure (and incidentally as a spearhead in fund raising) in the interim between national party conventions.

The practice of making the party chairman the hand-picked designee of the party's presidential candidate has a definite impact upon the work of both the national committee and the headquarters staff. Commonly, the party chairman is chosen immediately after the party convention and is thrust at once into the major effort of giving overall direction to the presidential campaign—unless, of course, the presidential nominee has other plans in mind.[7] Once appointed, he is likely to bring his own personal choice of lieutenants into the headquarters staff, which, for the period of the campaign, may mushroom to several times its normal size. The effects on both the national committee and the headquarters staff are obvious. Continuity in organization and staff under these circumstances is next to impossible. And considering that the chairman's primary assignment is usually direction of the presidential campaign (and perhaps later, fund raising), other functions which the committee and staff might usefully perform—research, candidate recruitment, general party organization, public information, program development—necessarily take second place.

Congressional Campaign Committees

Both the Republicans and the Democrats maintain a campaign committee within each house of Congress, a total of four campaign committees in all. These committees exist independently of the national committees of the two parties. As if to emphasize this independence, the *Democratic Manual* specifically states that these congressional committes have "no organic connection with either the Democratic National Convention, or the Democratic National Committee." Exactly when these committees first came into being is uncertain, but they have been in existence since at least 1866.

Selection of Members. As their titles suggest, each of these committees exists primarily to assist in the election or reelection of members of that party to Congress. The selection of members of the committee is roughly the same for both parties. In the House of Representatives, each state party delegation is entitled to choose one of its members to serve on the party campaign committee in that house. This selection process generally produces a committee of between 35 and 40 people. The two Senate campaign committees are smaller bodies, appointed by their respective party leaders in the Senate. The Democratic committee has seven to nine members, the Republican committee from four to ten. Ordinarily, committee members are chosen only from among those senators who are not themselves running for reelection and who do not have colleagues of their own party in their states running for reelection.

Functions. The campaign committee and its staff directs its energies into four main tasks: research on elections—particularly elections in marginal districts, those in which the vote secured by winning candidates normally falls between 45 and 55 percent; maintenance of a speaker's bureau; distribution of campaign funds; and assistance in the public relations aspects of campaigns. In this last undertaking the Republican Congressional (House) Campaign Committee has been particularly innovative and active. It has designed and produced a wide variety of campaign materials, including campaign letters, general newsletters, throw-aways, cards, television and radio spots, and other materials for use in the mass media. It has also designed layouts for newspapers and magazines, and produced films of varying length, both ready-made (on Republican accomplishments, suitable for use by any congressman in any district), and tailor-made (designed especially for a particular candidate's use or for use in certain kinds of districts, e.g., farm districts).

On rare occasions, the decisions of a campaign committee in

one of the houses may prove to be a sore point with party members in that house, but the complaints seldom pass the point of public grumbling. Such was the case in 1970, when the Senate Republican Campaign Committee, headed by John Tower of Texas, allocated more than twice as much in funds to George Bush, a candidate for the Senate from Texas, as to any other candidate running for the Senate. (Bush received $73,000, while the next largest amount, $37,000, went to Senator Ralph Smith of Illinois. Both candidates lost. Senator George Murphy of California and Leonore Romney of Michigan, both of whom lost, received $31,907 and $8,195 respectively, while two who won, incumbent Senator Hiram Fong of Hawaii and challenger William E. Brock in Tennessee, received $13,188 and $4,640, respectively. Another challenger who won, Glenn Beall in Maryland, received no funds from the committee.) Several Republicans in the Senate complained of what looked like a marked display of favoritism on Senator Tower's part for his fellow Texan, while others—noting that the largest sums went to candidates who lost, while very small sums went to candidates who won—wished aloud that Senator Tower had shown better political acumen. There, however, the matter ended.[8]

State Committees: Variable Creatures of the Law

Unlike the national party committees, which exist extra-legally, the party state committee is ordinarily the creature of state law. Its existence, its membership, and its powers are, therefore, largely determined by the prescriptions of state law. As a result of differences in the laws of the 50 states, the party committees in the 50 states differ greatly in their composition and powers. The committee may be large, numbering several hundred, or it may be small, having only a few dozen members. It may be a powerful policy maker, enjoying considerable discretion in its direction of the party apparatus and exercising effective control over various aspects of the party machinery and programs. Or it may be limited to performing purely ministerial functions of no great consequence politically.

Variations in Size. Size by itself is probably a determinant of the effectiveness of the state committee. When a committee consists of several hundred persons, who meet infrequently, in a place large enough to hold a body of that size, the air of the proceedings is apt to be that of a fiesta or reunion of graduates of the old political school. When the committee consists of a handful of people who know one another, when its very size is apt to make a position on it prestigious and important, and when everyone has a chance to contribute to the discussion and decisions, the chances are better that the state committee will deal with meaningful issues.

Selecting Members.   Membership on the state committee is apportioned according to electoral subdivisions. In some states, members are chosen within state legislative districts, and in others, within counties, or within congressional districts. Members may be selected in primaries or in conventions, or they may hold their office *ex officio,* e.g., by virtue of being chairman or vice-chairman of a party county committee.

Functions assigned to the state committee also vary considerably from state to state. A list of these functions—not all of which are assigned to any one state committee—includes management of election campaigns, fund raising, issuing a call for the state convention, selecting temporary convention officers, fixing the time for the party primary, defining "party member" for purposes of deciding who is eligible to participate in the party's primary, filling vacancies in the party slate of candidates for an election, canvassing, and certifying the results of party primary contests.

Because all state committees have some control over the selection of party delegates to the national convention, and indirectly over the selection of the state delegation to the convention, control of the state committee may be of considerable interest to those who are lining up delegates behind a particular candidate for that party's presidential nomination.

County Committees

Whoever holds the top post on a county committee may be a notable political power. Not a few such committee heads have cut a deep notch for themselves in the party structure using the county committee as their base of operations. Carmine De Sapio (New York County, i.e. Manhattan Island) and Jake Arvey

(Cook County, i.e. Chicago) are two examples that come readily to mind. The influence of these men extended far beyond the boundaries of their respective counties, though the formal base of their authority within the party was one county.

The county committee usually consists of the precinct committee members in that county, and normally its main concern is with the election of county officers. Its formal tie with the state committee usually arises from the fact that whoever heads the county committee also serves as a member of the state committee. The precinct committee members, in turn, may be elected within their precincts in a party primary, chosen by party convention or caucus, or in some cases selected by higher officers in the party—a legislative district leader, for instance. There are perhaps better than 100,000 precinct committee posts of each party in this country. This is the lowest-ranking party office, the first step up the ladder of party officialdom.

General Characteristics of Party Organization

The Dispersal of Power. The American political party has often been described as a loose confederation of state and local parties, and this description continues to be an accurate one. Formal connections do exist between every level of the organization, but these connections scarcely establish a tightly organized, hierarchical structure in which commands issue from the top and pass through intermediate levels down to the lowest rung of the organizational ladder. Quite the opposite seems to be the case. Power is widely dispersed throughout the party structure, and each unit of the organization enjoys considerable autonomy in the exercise of that power. Nor is this decentralization of power the result of a conscious decision by the national officers. The lowest elements of the organization enjoy a position of autonomy because they are themselves the source of political power. In this regard, it is strikingly characteristic of the structure of the political party that one moves up the ladder not in order to gain the power that the higher position affords; one moves up by virtue of having first successfully built a base of power below. Carmine De Sapio was unquestionably a major figure in Democratic party politics in New York State, if not indeed in the nation, in the 1950s and 1960s. His influence depended upon his position as New York County chairman, a post which in turn depended upon his holding the chairmanship of a legislative district. His defeat in this last constituency removed the base upon which his activities in the higher organizational reaches of the party were built, and led, rather dramatically, to his virtual disappearance from the political scene.[9]

The Effects of Open Membership. There are few important barriers to party membership, and the result of this open membership policy—a policy not merely tolerated but aggressively pursued by the party—is to make the party a broadly based coalition of diverse social interests, a loosely connected coalition of a multitude of population subgroups. The very looseness of the ties that bind individuals to the party is both a strength and a weakness of the organization. If the party is to survive as an institution, it must do battle with a number of competitors for the loyalty of its clientele, most immediately the other major opposition party. An open membership policy helps the party be adaptable to the changing demands of its clientele, present and potential, and sufficiently flexible in its structure and programs to hold together as one great political group the many diverse groups whose support it needs but whose separate group interests seldom if ever coincide exactly. On the other hand, the looseness of the ties that bind individuals to the party are also a potential threat, for loose ties are the more easily broken. The possibility that major defections from the ranks of party supporters will occur represents a constant threat to the stability and coherence of the party organization.

This, then, is how the formal party organization in America is organized. Open in membership, with power diffused and decentralized, stratarchical rather than hierarchical, large in numbers, a loose confederation of diverse social groups whose loyalties may never be completely taken for granted, the political party offers a schedule of services of considerable importance for the orderly management of the political business of society.

Appraising the Party Organization

Is the party organization just described appropriate? effective? responsible? Some are inclined to say yes; others say it definitely is not. Who is right?

Criticism.   For a good many years American students of parties have been in the forefront of critics of American party organizations, finding them weak, splintered, undisciplined, unprogrammatic, and irresponsible—in other words finding them perfectly designed to make it impossible to fulfill their major function of articulating and aggregating citizen interests and translating these into public policy. Parties in general are seen by these critics as playing a major role in the political system, and are sometimes described as being "major agents of public affairs," [10] or as having "created democracy," which is unthinkable "save in terms of parties," [11] or as providing the "major linkage between people and government." [12]

RECOMMENDATIONS FOR CHANGE.   Many changes are recommended to make American parties fulfill their major role effectively: abolition of the seniority rule in Congress, making advancement to power within Congress dependent upon the regularity with which a member of Congress supports policy positions taken by a majority of the party caucus; giving the national committee a stronger voice in the allocation of campaign money, again to reward those who are strongest in their support of party policy positions; making party platforms more precise, stronger, so that citizens may easily know that between the parties they have a genuine choice in programs; letting cabinet members sit in Congress, there to be questioned by members of Congress, so that, once again, party programs may be laid out in full public view, explained, and perhaps defended, and also so that a closer link may be forged between the White House and the majority party in Congress; encouraging the use of closed rather than open primaries, the intention once again being to buttress party control over the crucial nominating process; creating a party council to recommend congressional candidates, screen presidential candidates, and interpret the platform; making the platform binding on all candidates, including state and local ones; and so on and so forth.[13] Except for the first item on the list of recommendations, abolition of the seniority rule, no perceptible movement along the recommended lines has occurred.

Contrasts Between Party Critics and Defenders.

DIFFERENCES OVER PARTY ROLE.   As the foregoing list of criticisms and recommended changes makes clear, critics generally see parties playing a major role in the political system, with primary responsibility for development and implementation of public policy. This is perhaps the clearest point of contrast between critics and defenders, for generally speaking, the party defenders see parties as only one, though admittedly an important, mechanism among many for bringing citizen influence to bear upon the making of public policy. Thus argues Leon Epstein, who has articulated the defense of American parties as well as anyone:

> For the last generation or two, political scientists who specialize in the study of political parties, in the United States and elsewhere, have tended to regard the mass membership, cohesive, and issue-oriented party of Western Europe and especially of Britain as a superior, because more highly developed, form of political life. American specialists, notably of the responsible-party school, have explicitly wanted parties in the United States to develop in a similar way. . . . Whatever might be wrong with the American political system and its policy outputs would be dealt with most effectively by building responsible parties— organized, centralized, and cohesive. Understandably, the party specialists regard their subject or, it might be said, their clients, as the most suitable point of entry for changing the political system. . . . I do not regard parties as so obviously crucial. And I certainly do not exalt them. . . . What I have sought is a middle ground on which parties can be viewed as important but not overwhelmingly important political agencies. After all, they do exist in every modern democracy. But they differ considerably in organization and function from one political culture to another. For example, parties are especially impressive in Britain. They will be observed, as organized entities, actually to govern the country in a way that parties do not in the United States. But that cannot be assumed to make the American political system less effective. It is only the parties as such that may be less effective. Why should they be thought so important that their effectiveness determines the effectiveness of the system? [14]

THE MAJORITARIAN VIEW.   Epstein continues the argument by saying that the existing appraisals of parties are closely related to two distinguishable concepts of democracy. The first is the majoritarian. According to majoritarians, more than half of a community's electorate may be mobilized to support a policy or set of policies, and the majority thus mobilized ought to have the means to enact its policy. The means are to be provided by an organized party. "How else," asks a leading spokesman for the responsible-party school, "can the majority get organized? If democracy means anything at all, it means that the majority has the right to organize for the purpose of taking over the government." [15] The majority-rule position, says Epstein, is especially compatible with (though by no means the exclusive property of) the Marxist view that there exists an industrial working class constituting a majority with distinctively socialist policy preferences juxtaposed against the minority interests of a minority capitalist class.

THE PLURALIST VIEW. The second concept of democracy is pluralist. Here the central idea is that rather than majority versus minority, there are groups of various types and sizes seeking to advance their views. The crucial point here is a denial of the existence of a well-defined majority view. Of course, if such a majority did exist it would, say the pluralists, have a clear right to rule on its own behalf and against the wishes of the minority, even though pluralists do tend to find minority interests legitimate and entitled to constitutional protection.

Critics of the American party organizations, says Epstein, especially those who urge reforms to make the parties more responsible, are inclined to accept the majoritarian view of democracy. They find responsible, programmatic, unified, and cohesive parties better suited to a majoritarian-style democracy. The defenders, such as Epstein himself, are usually explicit in their preference for a pluralist concept of democracy and believe that American-style parties—loose, decentralized, one institution among many—are well suited to a pluralist democracy such as the United States.[16]

DIFFERENT VIEWS OF CHANGE. Critics and defenders are also inclined to diverge in what they see as the effective point of entry toward change. Is change in the structure of parties the avenue to follow to effect changes in the system, including system outputs, as the critics seem to maintain? Or rather, should change in the party structure follow from or perhaps run current with changes in the system, as the defenders seem to believe? One does not, of course, have to accept only one or the other of these two views of change. Both system and party can conceivably change through interaction.

Citizen Impact on Parties.   Earlier chapters have indicated some of the ways in which citizens have changed in recent decades and have measured the impact of those changes upon party structure and operation: The increase in the education level of citizens and the resulting increase in the number of young persons who decline to identify with a party, preferring a posture of independence of party, is a case in point.

Party Impact on Citizens.   There are also indications that party actions have left an impact upon citizens. A case in point: In 1964 and again in 1972 the parties presented clear choices to voters, and voters perceived the policy choices available and responded with a measurable display of policy voting. Admittedly, the most obvious impact of party actions has been the resulting decline in citizen affection and regard for parties—a consequence, apparently, of a failure of parties to meet citizen expectations.

Citizen Appraisals of the Parties.   How about citizens—are they generally critics or defenders? From what we already know about citizen feelings about parties, it seems fair to say that they would like to see parties act more responsibly, at least in the sense of being genuinely concerned about fulfilling campaign promises and demonstrating a capability for acting to further some broader public interest than they now appear to do.

What options do citizens have to make their influence felt? Some options, all limited, do exist. Most fall within the framework of the existing party structure. Electing Independent candidates to public office, as happened in the gubernatorial election in Maine in 1974, is one obvious vehicle. Turning the rascals out, as also happened in the general election of 1974, is another, though perhaps more limited if citizens feel strongly that candidates in both parties are inclined to be rascals. Staying home on election day, which also happened in 1974, is another. Joining up to work within the formal organization as precinct workers and the like is another, though again, this option is a little unreal if parties are seen as not worth working for. Supporting nonparty organizations which may affect the making of public policy is still another. This line of action, though again demonstrably limited in utility, was an option often chosen in the sixties, well illustrated in movements on behalf of the environment, against the war in Vietnam, to protect the consumer, to protect and defend the rights of welfare recipients, to make suffrage a reality for blacks, to gain equal treatment for women, to make gay power acceptable, and to support a host of other causes. The sheer number of such movements and their general effectiveness are themselves perhaps the clearest indications that the citizenry is giving up on parties as vehicles for molding desirable public policy.

In the further development of citizen attitudes toward parties, the actions of the parties themselves will be crucial. The greatest opportunity for change in party organizations lies not in individual citizen initiative but in citizen response to leadership initiative from within the party organization itself. The present trend evidences a decline in citizen regard for parties as effective governing institutions. One indicator of a continuation or a reversal of that trend will be citizen response to the work of the Ninety-fourth Congress, which concludes its life near the end of 1976. Certainly there is no end of problems for Congress to work on. Democrats control a solid majority of seats in both houses of Congress. If citizens perceive that Congress takes less than adequate action on national problems—and any such failure is likely to be immediately reflected in their daily lives—public confidence in parties is certain to decline further, and the trend already running against parties can hardly be expected to reverse.

NOTES

The first quote at the beginning of the chapter is from Daniel Katz and Samuel J. Eldersveld, "The Impact of Local Party Activity upon the Electorate," *Public Opinion Quarterly* 25 (Spring 1961), 1–15. The second is from Joyce Gelb and Marian L. Palley (editors), "Introduction," *The Politics of Social Change* (New York: Holt, Rinehart & Winston, 1971), 1–6.

1. Harold D. Lasswell and Abraham Kaplan, *Power and Society* (New Haven, Conn.: Yale University Press, 1950), 219–220; and especially,

Samuel J. Eldersveld, *Political Parties* (Skokie, Ill.: Rand McNally, 1964), 98–117. Comparable descriptions may also be found in Pendleton Herring, *The Politics of Democracy* (New York: Holt, Rinehart & Winston, 1940), 121; and Elmer E. Schattschneider, *Party Government* (New York: Holt, Rinehart & Winston, 1942), 129–169.

2. James M. Burns, *The Deadlock of Democracy* (Englewood Cliffs, N.J.: Prentice-Hall, 1963), 234–264.

3. Since 1952 the state chairman has been included as a member of the Republican National Committee if in the last election his state (1) cast its electoral votes for the Republican presidential candidate; (2) had a Republican majority in the state's congressional delegation; or (3) had a Republican governor.

4. The best study of the national party committees is Cornelius P. Cotter and Bernard C. Hennessy, *Politics Without Power* (New York: Atherton, 1964); but see also Hugh A. Bone, *Party Committees and National Politics* (Seattle, Wash.: University of Washington Press, 1958), 3–68.

5. In the 1972 campaign a replacement for the Democratic vice-presidential candidate was required when the nominee of the convention, Senator Thomas Eagleton of Missouri, resigned because it was considered politically disadvantageous to run as a vice-presidential candidate a man who was three times in 10 years hospitalized and given shock treatments for "nervous exhaustion." His replacement, though officially chosen by the national committee, was in reality the choice of the presidential nominee, George McGovern, who was equally the one responsible for Eagleton's departure.

6. It was the Democratic National Convention of 1968 that called for the creation of a commission to study the procedures used for selecting delegates to the national convention, a demand which did produce change, most notably an increase in the number of states using a party primary for the selection of convention delegates. And it was the 1972 Democratic convention which called for the creation of a charter commission and an interim national party convention, which met in 1974 in St. Louis and did indeed produce a set of bylaws for the Democratic party.

7. In 1972 the Democratic presidential nominee appointed a woman, Jean Westwood, to chair the national committee, but named Gary Hart as the manager of his campaign. This was something of a departure from tradition, which probably proves no more than that at the level of the national committee, political tradition is especially weak.

8. *The New York Times,* October 2, 1970.

9. Edward N. Costikyan, *Behind Closed Doors* (New York: Harcourt Brace Jovanovich, 1966).

10. Sigmund Neumann, *Modern Political Parties* (Chicago: University of Chicago Press, 1956), 4.

11. Schattschneider, *Party Government,* 1.

12. Avery Leiserson, *Parties and Politics* (New York: Knopf, 1958), 35.

13. American Political Science Association, "Toward a More Responsible Two-Party System," *American Political Science Review* 44 (September 1950 supplement).

14. Leon D. Epstein, *Political Parties in Western Democracies* (New York: Praeger, 1967). Used by permission.

15. Schattschneider, *Party Government* 208.
16. A superb review of the literature on party organization types is provided by William E. Wright, "Comparative Party Models: Rational-Efficient and Party Democracy," in William E. Wright (editor), *A Comparative Study of Party Organization* (Columbus, Ohio: Merrill, 1971), 17–54.

You know how it is here [in the Philippines]. It is not the same as in Great Britain or the United States. We have only private interests, no party loyalties. We change parties when it suits our interests. Everybody does it.

My field work committee is the most important. Its members contact delegates in the precincts. I am much more in touch with party workers than my predecessor. He was from the upper strata of society and found it difficult to converse with all levels of workers.

I am a conservative but I believe the party should reflect the moderate view. . . . Parties can't be run by amateurs any more than schools or businesses. People with no background politically should not dictate top policy at the convention. . . . I was a Republican amateur in 1964 but I wouldn't support Goldwater today. Our leader must reflect majority opinion, namely the views in the middle, because a man is elected to represent this country's beliefs, not to force his own on the country. . . . After the primary we work for the ticket because party unity is the result of both free discussion and being a good loser if necessary.

Republican politicos and political appointees are generally at the conservative end of the spectrum. In general the liberal end is occupied by the media, interest groups, and labor, with Democratic politicos and civil servants occupying the middle of the continuum. One notable exception is system change, where the three sectors most directly involved in politics (political appointees, Democratic and Republican politicos) are those strongly opposing institutional reform.

The Party Actives

There is a considerable range in the amount of effort people put forth on party activity. By virtue of what they do, some people are recognized as party actives, while those who do much less are appropriately thought of as the party rank and file. In chapters 2, 3, and 4 our attention was focused on the latter group. It's time now to move on to look at the actives.

In Chapter 2 we noted that SES (socioeconomic status) was both weak in its relationship to partisanship and strong in its relationship to participation. This chapter pursues the relationship between SES and participation further, by taking a close look at the characteristics and the motivations of those who become active participants in the work of party organizations. There are literally thousands of formal party posts in America established by law, and at least an equal number of slots in campaign organizations which may or may not be closely regulated by law.

Who comes to occupy these posts? What are their characteristics? How do they differ from the rank and file? Why do they become active in the first place? What satisfactions do they find in their work? What keeps them active? Where do they stand on issues? Are they even interested in issues? Are those who participate today like the actives of yesterday? These are among the matters considered in this chapter.

People engage in political party activity by doing many different things. Some do little more than complete a ballot on election day. Others are not interested only in voting; they talk politics. They have opinions and like to share them with others and on occasion try to convert others to their particular point of view. Some do volunteer work for a party or candidate. They will hold a "coffee" for a candidate, hand out campaign literature, register voters, offer their help with the jobs that need to be done on election day, contribute money in support of a party or candidate, help organize a political rally, make addresses to groups on behalf of a party or candidate, and so forth. They may do this occasionally, or they may make such work a full-time occupation as election day approaches. They are among the party actives. They may or may not hold an official position within the party organization. Whether they do or not seems to make little difference in the amount of energy and time they are willing to devote to this kind of activity. Holding a formal post in the party organization does not, we have learned, guarantee that an individual will necessarily work harder or as hard as, or more effectively than, the individual who does not have a position in the formal party organization. Most actives, however, either occupy a defined position within the party or did or will.

Party Actives: Social Characteristics

From a long line of studies have come four leading propositions about the social characteristics of party leaders:

1. Party leaders broadly mirror the ethnic and racial characteristics of the population from which they are drawn.
2. Party leaders enjoy a higher socioeconomic status than the population from which they are drawn.
3. Party leaders of the majority party in a community enjoy a higher socioeconomic status than do party leaders of the minority party, in part because higher status persons in the community are more likely to be found in the ranks of the majority party.
4. Republican party leaders enjoy a higher socioeconomic status than do Democratic party leaders.

Party Leaders as a Reflection of the Electorate. Broadly speaking, political party leaders are a cross section of the American electorate. Both major parties include individuals of different ages, religions, socioeconomic status, and other group characteristics. Differences between Republican and Democratic leaders tend to mirror the differences between Republican and Democratic party identifiers in the electorate. Thus, the ranks of Democratic party leaders generally include more Catholics, Jews, labor union members, Irish, and Poles. Republicans tend to include among their party leaders more Protestants, people whose occupations are managerial, professionals, Germans, English, and people in upper-income brackets.

The structure of the formal party organization parallels electoral subdivisions. Precinct committee members are drawn from within the boundaries of the precinct they represent, county chairmen from within the county they represent, and so forth. One should not, therefore, expect either party to have black or Catholic or wealthy precinct committee members in any precinct where there are few or no blacks, Catholics, or upper-income people. Nor should we be surprised that the ranks of party leaders in a predominantly farming county include many farmers, while the ranks of party leaders in the suburban "bedroom" community of Montgomery County, outside Washington, D.C., include many younger, upwardly mobile professionals. Neither are we surprised that Democratic county chairmen in Oklahoma have a higher socioeconomic status overall than Republican county chairmen: Oklahoma has long been a one-party Democratic state, and the politically ambitious in Oklahoma appreciate that the Democratic party has offered a surer route to local political advancement than the Republican party. The situation is exactly opposite in neighboring Kansas, a one-party Republican state.[1]

The Overlap in Groups Represented by Leaders in Both Parties. Neither group enjoys the exclusive support of any major group within the electorate. Nor does either party deny any major group access to its leadership posts. When the population unit served by the party organization is heterogeneous, the leadership of both parties at that level reflects that heterogeneity. Thus a study of leadership done in Detroit, Michigan, found a significant overlap in the groups represented in the leadership positions of both

Table 6-1 Competitive Recruitment of "Deviant" Social Categories by the Two Political Parties in Detroit, Michigan

Percentages of Republicans from "Democratic" Social Categories		Percentages of Democrats from "Republican" Social Categories	
Catholic	24%	Protestants	44%
Black	16	Business managerial	10
Union members	30	Clerical-sales	17
Irish	6	German	8
Poles	7	English	7
Semi- and unskilled	15	Professionals	16
Income under $4000	15	Income over $10,000	17
		Income over $15,000	7

Source: Samuel J. Eldersveld, *Political Parties: A Behavioral Analysis* (Skokie, Ill.: Rand McNally, 1964). Used by permission.

parties. The measure of this overlap is indicated in the data presented in Table 6-1. This same study revealed that party practices of recruiting leaders from groups normally aligned with the opposition party were not a recent departure. The Republicans studied had not just recently discovered an interest in Catholics, or labor union members, or blacks. Nor had the Democrats suddenly developed a concern for proprietors, Germans, the English, or people with high incomes. Both parties had a long history of attempting to recruit members from among those groups that were usually thought of as supporters of the opposition party. Thus it was found that 50 percent of the union members who held leadership positions in the Republican party had been active in the party for 30 years or more!

Leaders who deviated from the socioeconomic characteristics normally associated with the membership of each party were most often found in closely competitive districts. Apparently the political party is inclined to recruit workers from the ranks of the other party's clientele when such recruitment promises to aid in the development of a base of party strength which will enable the party to remain, or become, competitive with the other party.[2]

Age. Those active in the political party do not generally become leaders until they are in their late thirties or forties, and the

Table 6-2   Age of Party Leaders In Selected Communities

PRECINCT COMMITTEEMEN:
MONTGOMERY COUNTY,
MARYLAND

	Dems.	Reps.
Under 30	2%	9%
31–40	27	36
41–50	38	29
51–65	32	20
Over 65	2	6

PRECINCT COMMITTEEMEN:
KNOX COUNTY, ILLINOIS

	Dems.	Reps.
Under 30	5%	5%
31–40	13	3
41–50	31	22
51–65	49	62
Over 65	3	8

PRECINCT COMMITTEEMEN:
NASSAU COUNTY,
NEW YORK

	Dems.	Reps.
20–39	35%	8%
40–49	46	26
50–59	17	38
60 or over	2	25

PRECINCT COMMITTEEMEN:
MANHATTAN, NEW YORK

	Dems.	Reps.
Under 35	28%	18%
35–54	47	52
55 or over	26	30

COUNTY CHAIRMEN:
NORTH CAROLINA

	Dems.	Reps.
Under 24	7%	9%
25–44	34	39
45–54	33	29
55–64	19	12
65 or over	7	11

COUNTY CHAIRMEN:
OHIO

	Dems.	Reps.
26–35	6%	4%
36–45	26	25
46–55	35	34
56–65	22	18
66 or over	10	18

Source: See footnote 3 of this chapter.

bulk of party leaders are between 35 and 55 years of age. Table 6-2 presents data on the age of party leaders drawn from several studies.[3] The number who are 30 years old or younger seldom exceeds 10 percent of party leaders in a community. Where the proportion is significantly higher than this, and where the proportion of leaders above 60 is correspondingly low, as is the case in Nassau County, New York, it is likely to be a reflection of a pattern of population growth peculiar to the area. Nassau County, on Long Island, is a rapidly growing suburb of New York City. In 1960 the median age of the population of the county was 30.8 years. Within the decade of the sixties, large numbers of upwardly mobile residents of New York City, many of them young professionals, technicians, and business executives, moved into this long-time stronghold of the Republican party, bringing with them their Democratic party loyalties and providing a new source from which Democratic party leaders might be recruited. The impact of this population movement on the newly invigorated Democratic party is apparent in the data on age given in Table 6-2, which indicates that in 1968 35 percent of Democratic party leaders in Nassau County were under 40, in contrast to 8 percent of Republican leaders; while only 2 percent were over 60, in contrast to 25 percent of the Republicans.

DIFFERENCES BETWEEN THE PARTIES.   One might expect Republican leaders to be somewhat older than Democratic leaders, because Republicans are generally thought to be more conservative than Democrats, and aging is often associated with a tendency toward conservatism. The expected difference does appear in the data we have on the age of party leaders, but the difference is not all that great. As indicated in Table 6-2, the percentage of Republicans over 60, for example, is usually greater than the percentage of Democrats in the same age bracket in the same community. Only in the South is the pattern often reversed, a further indication that the age of leaders in a long-established, locally dominant party will tend to be higher than the age of leaders in the minority party.

YOUNG PEOPLE AND THE MINORITY PARTY.   Younger people appear to offer a particularly fertile source for recruitment to the ranks of the minority party in any place where the minority is weak, as is the Republican party in most of the South. The reasons for this are undoubtedly complex. However, two factors in particular probably underlie this fact: youth's mobility and its willingness to challenge the status quo. The young executive who has grown up in a background of midwestern Republicanism and who finds himself transferred by his employer into the heart of Dixie may find it difficult to put aside his loyalty to the Republican party. He is certainly unlikely to share the local man's sense of traditional loyalty to the Democratic party. He is, therefore, ripe for recruitment into the ranks of Republican party actives. Other young people may be persuaded to support the weak minority party because they have not as yet developed strong ties to any party and can be influenced by a plea to join in a movement to reform political institutions, a promise to "fight city hall," an argument for the need to restore an effective two-party system, or perhaps simply by an appeal to help fight the "establishment."

Socioeconomic Status. While party leaders may broadly mirror the characteristics of the people as a whole, their socioeconomic status (SES) is clearly higher. Tables 6-3, 6-4, and 6-5 present, respectively, data on education, income, and occupation drawn from several studies of party leaders.

EDUCATION. At some points, the contrast between the SES of leaders and the population is striking. Look, for example, at

Table 6-3   Education of Party Leaders in Selected Communities

PRECINCT COMMITTEEMEN IN WASHINGTON COUNTY, ILLINOIS

	Dems.	Reps.	County Population
Grade school	54%	52%	71%
High school	29	39	22
Some college	17	9	7

PITTSBURGH PRECINCT COMMITTEEMEN

	Dems.	Reps.	City Population
Grade school	27%	25%	48%
Some high school	21	22	17
Completed high school	30	29	21
Some college	12	11	5
Completed college	6	10	6

NORTH CAROLINA COUNTY CHAIRMEN

	Dems.	Reps.	State Population
Grade school	—%	4%	27%
High school	16	27	47
Trade school	3	15	—
Some college	21	25	7
Completed college	21	17	6
Advanced degree	40	13	—

Source: See footnote 3 of this chapter.

Table 6-4   Income of Party Leaders

DETROIT, MICHIGAN PRECINCT COMMITTEEMEN

	Dems.	Reps.
Under $4000	7%	15%
$4000–$5000	16	10
5000–10000	53	35
Over 10,000	17	35

KNOX COUNTY, ILLINOIS PRECINCT COMMITTEEMEN

	Dems.	Reps.
Under $3000	3%	11%
$3000–$4999	3	11
5000–6999	13	8
7000–9999	36	32
10,000–14,999	28	32
15,000–19,999	8	3
20,000 and over	10	3

NASSAU COUNTY, NEW YORK PRECINCT COMMITTEEMEN

	Dems.	Reps.
$5000–$9999	6%	3%
10,000–14,999	20	18
15,000 or more	74	79

Source: See footnote 3 of this chapter.

Table 6-5   Occupation of Precinct Committeemen and County Chairmen in Selected Communities

MANHATTAN ISLAND (NEW YORK COUNTY)

	Libs.	Dems.	Reps.
Professional	23%	14%	13%
Business executive	9	10	5
Small businessman	23	24	24
Salesman	22	7	11
Skilled worker	21	20	13
Unskilled worker	4	12	15
Public servant	4	5	3
Clerical	0	2	8

Table 6-5 (Cont'd)

	MONTGOMERY COUNTY MARYLAND		KNOX COUNTY ILLINOIS	
	Dems.	Reps.	Dems.	Reps.
Professional	42%	36%	13%	5%
Farmers	0	2	8	16
Managers	8	11	3	3
Clerical	5	5	5	11
Sales	8	9	5	27
Craftsmen	2	2	39	3
Operatives	0	3	10	3
Farm laborers	2	0	0	3
Laborers	7	2	13	0
Students	3	2	0	3
Housewives	20	17	3	5
Retired	3	9	3	5

WASHINGTON COUNTY, ILLINOIS

	Dems.	Reps.
Farmer	21%	39%
Government employee	38	8
Proprietor-official	8	13
Professional	0	4
Sales-clerical	4	0
Laborer	25	35
Other	4	0

	OKLAHOMA		KANSAS		WISCONSIN	
	Dems.	Reps.	Dems.	Reps.	Dems.	Reps.
Farmer-rancher	19%	25%	29%	15%	16%	3%
Businessman	22	20	19	33	17	45
Sales-clerical	10	13	15	6	8	4
Attorney	24	12	14	28	19	30
Other professional	15	18	7	10	6	13
Laborer	2	5	1	4	23	0
Public official	2	0	1	1	2	0
Housewife	2	0	7	1	5	0
Retired	3	3	6	0	3	3
Other	2	2	0	0	0	0

Source: See footnote 3 of this chapter.

the data on education. In all three communities, Washington County, Pittsburgh, and North Carolina, there are more college-educated persons among the leaders than in the population, and fewer persons who report that their education did not go beyond the eighth grade. The data for North Carolina, which shows the greatest contrast, indicates that the higher the level of office (and thus the larger the political unit from which the leaders are drawn) the greater the disparity between the SES of the leader and the SES of the population.

INCOME.   A similar pattern of contrast is evident in the data for income, but what is also evident is that leaders in some communities are obviously better off financially than leaders elsewhere—compare, for example, the income of leaders in Knox County with those in Nassau County. This is also obviously a reflection of a marked contrast in the general income level of these two quite different communities.

OCCUPATION.   What is true of education and income is also true of occupation: Leaders tend to work at higher-status occupations. In the occupation data from these several communities we see both similarity and contrast. The lawyer is everywhere in evidence, less evident in a predominantly farming community like Knox County, Illinois, more evident in urban areas and in upper-level organizational offices.

How different are Republican leaders from Democratic leaders? Within a particular community contrasts do appear and are, from what we recall about differences in the social characteristics of partisans generally, predictable. Yet characteristics of Republican leaders in one place often closely resemble those of Democratic leaders in another place—an indication, clearly, that the critical factor affecting who is recruited for leadership posts may be whether the party is dominant or weak. See, for example, the data for county chairmen in Oklahoma, where Democrats have been dominant for decades, and for county chairmen in neighboring Kansas, where Republicans have been dominant for at least as long. It is also obvious from the occupation data that there is a significant difference from place to place in the number of leaders who earn their living working for government. The overall thrust of these data, along with data from other studies, is to indicate that patronage is not the dominant incentive employed to recruit and hold party workers—a point to which we shall return presently.

Only one more observation needs to be made about the significance of occupation. Not all occupations afford an individual the same opportunity to gain and exercise skills which will prove useful in politics. Herbert Jacob has made the point especially well by distinguishing between what he labels brokerage occupations and nonbrokerage occupations. The first of these includes jobs such as lawyer, general practitioner, journalist, auto dealer, insurance salesman, labor union official, and barber. A brokerage occupation is any occupation which frequently places the practitioner in a bargaining role, where he must deal with outsiders (nonsubordinates) and try to reach a mutually satisfying agreement. Brokerage roles prepare the individual for political participation in many ways. They often allow him time to seek office. They teach him many of the skills a politician needs —the skill of bargaining, the ability to convince, the art of inspiring trust and confidence—and they facilitate the development of contacts, often at the fringe of politics itself. The extensive collection of data on hand does suggest rather strongly that political leaders are likely to come from the ranks of those who occupy brokerage occupations.[4]

Social Characteristics of Public Officeholders.   What is true of organization leaders is, if anything, more true of those who make it to the top—those who win election to public office and thus become major policy makers. In social background, they have long been unrepresentative of the population as a whole. Historically, public offices have been disproportionately filled by upper-status, white, Anglo-Saxon Protestants, many of them from families long active in the conduct of the nation's affairs. Lawyers are frequently in evidence. They usually make up 60 percent of the membership of the houses of Congress, always the entire membership of the U.S. Supreme Court, and most presidents, vice-presidents, and cabinet members have also been lawyers.[5]

A study covering the more than 1,000 individuals who held executive appointments from 1933 through 1965 reported that 39 percent had gone to private schools, certainly not a typical American experience. The total for the Department of State was

60 percent. Twenty-nine percent of these same 1,000 individuals who held executive appointments were lawyers and 24 percent businessmen.[6] Obviously the situation in the executive branch is not greatly different from that in Congress.

Even in a developing society, where the demand for new leadership is urgent, or in a society in which the barriers to wider participation have suddenly been lowered, the individual who works his way into public office is likely to be unrepresentative in important respects of the population as a whole. Whether the society in question is Turkish,[7] Ceylonese,[8] or Indian,[9] or that of a small town in Mississippi where blacks are in a clear majority and have recently gained control of all major local offices, the pattern is the same. In Mississippi towns, for example, black candidates for public office, both winners and losers, have largely been older, upper-income individuals, with considerable formal education and white-collar occupations.[10] By and large the new black officials are not those who were involved early in the civil rights movement of the sixties (those who were, interestingly, are more often found among the losers than the winners), nor do all of them have a strong commitment either to rapid social change or to black separatism. However, these new officeholders do take what would generally be considered a liberal position on many policy questions. While, therefore, they are hardly typical of people in the community on the score of social characteristics, they are most likely closer to blacks in the community on matters of policy than the white officeholders they replaced.

Defining Their Jobs

How do party leaders define their jobs? When they are asked about this they usually mention one of two kinds of activities.

Party-Building Functions Some leaders are oriented toward building the party organization itself. Such a leader believes an important part of his job is to keep in touch with party people, encourage individuals to be active in the party, keep records, and generally participate with other leaders and activists in doing whatever needs to be done to keep the party strong or make it stronger.

Campaign-Oriented Functions. Other leaders are oriented toward campaigns. Such a leader often mentions activities such as raising campaign funds, recruiting candidates to run for office, preparing voter lists, helping citizens to register and vote, canvassing an election district, and in general tending to those things which are vital ingredients in the interparty battle.

These two lines of activity are reported frequently in studies of party leadership, but the studies differ in their report of the frequency with which each line of activity is mentioned. A study of Oklahoma county chairmen indicated that one in every five chairmen was campaign oriented, and that leaders in both parties were likely to be more organization minded in counties where their party was dominant and more campaign oriented where the other party was dominant. Opposite results were reported in a study of precinct committee members in Pima County (Tucson), Arizona. In that study, four of every five committee members defined their job in terms of a campaign-related function. An even higher proportion thought campaign-related functions were *the most important functions* they performed. Even different results were reported in a study of leadership in Detroit, where one out of five leaders thought their job required them to offer a service to their constituency in the area of social welfare. That same study, incidentally, elicited no fewer than 71 different definitions of the functions of party leaders.[11]

In light of the differences in job definitions revealed in the findings of these and other studies, one must be cautious in generalizing about the functions of party leaders.[12] What one can say is that the sheer variety evident in the answers party leaders give indicates that there is no hard-and-fast job description for such positions as precinct, ward, district, and county leaders. The "welfare promoter" role apparently important to a sizable number of leaders in Detroit is not a function being performed by precinct committee members in Pima County, Arizona, but there is no rule to say that precinct committee members in either community have inappropriately defined their jobs. In defining their jobs, party leaders react to particular elements in the politics of their community as they see them, and again, there is no rule to say that they ought to be doing things differently, or doing different things.

Recruitment and Incentives

By and large, party leaders initially come to work for the party
under their own motivational steam. Their first contact with the
party may be a social event—perhaps a fund-raising event for a
particular candidate, or a campaign rally. The contact may be
made through a friend, a fellow union member, a co-worker,
a member of the family, or through an interested relative already
active in the ranks of the party. It is unlikely to be the result of a
formal solicitation by a distant (and unknown) officer of the
party. In short, party activists are likely to be self-starters who
find the impetus to take up party work in their personal associations.[13]

The Initial Impetus to Get Involved. The easiest way to ferret
out the reasons why party leaders get involved with party politics
is simply to ask them to recall how they came to decide to do
something more in politics than just vote. In response to that
question, leaders generally cite four reasons: (1) Someone asked
them to get involved, usually someone close, such as a relative or
a good friend. (2) They became concerned with policy matters.
For example, they came to feel that the country was going to
the dogs, that such-and-such an officeholder (presidents get mentioned a lot) was doing a terrible (or excellent) job, or they
were concerned with the development of some policy of special
interest to them personally. (3) Some particular campaign or
candidate caught their attention. The candidacies of Eisenhower
and John Kennedy are frequently mentioned. (4) It was merely
a developing interest in politics that made them active. In this
regard they often speak of how exciting campaigns are and how
much fun campaigns and politicking can be.[14]

Advancement to Leadership. Once an individual is active in
party work, the decision to seek or to accept party office—even
so lowly an office as precinct committee member—is frequently
the result of precise and definite encouragement of party leaders.
The road to party office is thus a two-stage affairs. First comes
the decision to participate in the affairs of the party, a decision
made upon the initiative of the individual himself. Later comes
the stage of advancing into the ranks of party leadership, a

move normally taken with the active encouragement of party
leaders.[15]

Those who serve in the higher levels of the party organization are seldom newcomers to party work, and they are much
more likely than those in the lower levels to report having worked
for the party for a long time. Time and experience are needed to
move up the party ladder. Nonetheless, at every level we find
some leaders who are new to the party scene, and therefore we
have no hesitation in describing the party organization in the
United States as a grassroots organization.

The Rise of the Amateur Activist. Is a position in the local
party organization a stepping-stone to higher elective office?
The evidence is scanty but what there is of it indicates that it is
not. Few elected officials come from a subordinate position in
party organization.[16] When they do seek elective office, local
party leaders normally run for local offices. Sometimes they may
run for a seat in the state legislature, but that office itself may be
very much a "local" office in practice, if the officeholder chooses
to regard it as primarily an opportunity for him to serve the folks
in his local constituency. But on the whole, party leaders seldom
have a desire to run for elective office.[17]

THE AMATEUR AND PROFESSIONAL: A DEFINITION. A recent line of studies, beginning with James Q. Wilson's study of
reform clubs in three American cities, employs a model of party
activism which distinguishes between the "amateur" and the
"professional" politician. Wilson describes the amateur and the
professional this way:

> It is not his liberalism, or his age, education, or class that sets
> the new politician apart and makes him worth studying. Rather,
> it is his outlook on politics, and the style of politics he prac-
> tices. . . . Although no single word is completely satisfactory,
> the word I will use in this study is "amateur."
>
> By amateur is not meant a dabbler, a dilettante, or an inept
> practitioner of some special skill; many amateur Democrats have
> a highly sophisticated understanding of practical politics and
> have proved their skills in the only way that matters—by win-
> ning at the polls. Similarly, a good many undoubted profes-
> sionals—by which word I mean all non-amateurs—are hope-

lessly incompetent and have proved themselves so in the only way that matters.

An amateur is one who finds politics *intrinsically* interesting because it expresses a concept of the public interest. The amateur politician sees the political world more in terms of ideas and principles than in terms of persons. Politics is the determination of public policy, and public policy ought to be set deliberately rather than as the accidental by-product of a struggle for personal and party advantage. . . . . The amateur takes the outcome of politics—the determination of policies and the choice of officials—seriously, in the sense that he feels a direct concern for what he thinks are the ends which these policies serve and the qualities these officials possess. . . .

The professional, on the other hand—even the "professional" who practices politics as a hobby rather than as a vocation—is preoccupied with the outcome of politics in terms of winning or losing. Politics, to him, consists of concrete questions and specific persons who must be dealt with in a manner that will "keep everybody happy" and thus minimize the possibility of defeat at the next election. . . .

The principal reward of politics to the amateur is the sense of having satisfied a felt obligation to "participate," and this satisfaction is greater the higher the value the amateur can attach to the ends which the outcomes of politics serve. The principal reward of the professional is to be found in the extrinsic satisfactions of participation—power, income, status, or the fun of the game. The ideal amateur has a "natural" response to politics; he sees each battle as a "crisis," and each victory as a triumph and each loss as a defeat for a cause. The professional trends, by contrast, to develop a certain detachment toward politics and a certain immunity to its excitement and its outcomes.[18]

The amateurs that Wilson studied were all Democrats. and liberal. But studies done since Wilson's indicate that the amateur as such is independent of ideology. The amateur Democrat is likely to be liberal in policy attitudes, but the amateur Republican is likely to be quite conservative: [19] What chiefly distinguishes amateurs in both parties are the incentives that bring them to work for the party and keep them active.

THE INCENTIVES MOTIVATING AMATEURS AND PROFESSIONALS. In an early work on organizations, Clark and Wilson distinguished three kinds of incentives: (1) *Purposive incentives,* which derive

from the stated ends and suprapersonal goals of an organization
—the procedures and public policy program of a political party,
for example. (2) *Solidary [sic] incentives,* such as socializing,
congeniality, sense of group membership and identification, fun
and conviviality, and so on. (3) *Material incentives* that are directed toward tangible personal gain—patronage, social mobility,
political careers, for example.[20] It is the overriding appeal of the
first of these incentives that distinguishes the amateur politician.
Solidary and material incentives may also have some appeal to
the amateur, but they take second place to purposive incentives
as a stimulus of the amateur's participation. Professionals, on the
other hand, are primarily attracted by material and solidary incentives, with solidary more important these days, because the
supply of material incentives available to the party is not as
plentiful as it used to be. What distinguishes the amateur from
the professional, therefore, is not a total lack of interest in any
kind of incentive; it is rather a question of combination, intensity,
and degree.

The different ratings which the amateur and the professional
give to incentives is nicely illustrated by a study of delegates to
the Republican National Convention of 1972.[21] The delegates
were asked to rate the importance of a set of incentives for remaining active in the Republican party. The ratings given by two
groups, classified as strong amateurs and strong professionals, is
reported in Table 6-6. The differences are striking: 40 percent
of the strong professionals rate material incentives important,
compared with 18 percent of the amateurs. Sixty-two percent
of the amateurs, on the other hand, consider purposive incentives
important, compared with only 37 percent of the professionals.

The incentives which amateurs say encouraged them
initially to take up party activity are not always identical to the
incentives they say sustain their party activity. Purposive incentives remain important, but when amateurs are asked what
they would miss most if they had to give up party work tomorrow—a line of inquiry designed to identify sustaining incentives—they often mention incentives that fall in the solidary
category. Obviously, some amateurs gradually discover that party
work can be rewarding for many different reasons. They can
come to appreciate being on the inside of things, knowing what
goes on, being a leader, participating in the fun and excitement of

campaigns. And while their concern with performance of a public duty or commitment to an issue may not diminish, newly discovered rewards of party service may help keep them active.

Amateurs are not necessarily purists. The word *purist* is applied to the party active who is so concerned with principle that he prefers to see his party nominate a candidate who is "right" even if it is clear that the candidate cannot win.[22] Amateurs can be as interested in winning elections as the next person. It is winning elections, after all, that is commonly thought to be one of the best ways for concerned citizens to bring about a change in the direction of public policy. Yet a point may come when the amateur feels obliged to draw a line on compromising his principles, and the decision may not be an easy one to make. The difficulty McCarthy supporters had bringing themselves to

Table 6-6   Activist Style and Incentives for Maintenance of Party Activism: 1972 Republican Convention Delegates

Incentive Categories	Strong Amateurs ($N = 109$)	Strong Professionals ($N = 110$)
MATERIAL		
Important	23%	40%
Fairly Important	27	33
Not Important	50	27
SOLIDARY		
Important	24%	43%
Fairly Important	40	38
Not Important	36	19
PURPOSIVE		
Important	62%	37%
Fairly Important	27	43
Not Important	11	20

Source: Thomas Roback, "Amateurs and Professionals Among 1972 Republican National Convention Delegates," a paper prepared for delivery at the 1973 annual meeting of the American Political Science Association, Table 7, p. 17, modified. Used by permission.

support the Democratic presidential candidate, Humphrey, in 1968 is an instance that comes immediately to mind.

FACTORS ENCOURAGING AMATEURISM.   Amateurs may be found in different locales. Neither urban, suburban, nor rural communities have a monopoly on their services.[23] However, the relative affluence of a community does seem to encourage the amateur style.[24] Conway and Feigert, among others, discovered this in their study of wealthy, suburban Montgomery County, Maryland, peopled by well-educated professionals and white-collar workers, and Knox County, Illinois, a poor agricultural and industrial community. There were many more amateurs in the ranks of both parties in Montgomery County than in Knox County. Material rewards for party service have little appeal to the wealthier, better-educated amateur. He may well appreciate them if they are available, but they are not crucial in his decision to take up party work. Low-salaried jobs at city hall or the county courthouse, which 30 years ago were valued rewards for party service, have little appeal today to the salaried executive or professional who frequently appears in the ranks of the amateur.

Amateurs are also more in evidence when parties in a community are closely competitive. A long-dominant party has little reason to encourage activity by amateurs. They are often bent on changing things, and their concern with issues may easily lead to divisive battles, bickering, intraparty feuding and bad feelings. A weak minority party is more likely to be receptive to suggestions for change and to welcome support from amatuers whose rewards come from a sense of having participated in a worthwhile public venture.[25]

The amateur is relatively new upon the American party scene, whereas the professional clearly dominates in the studies of party leaders active in the 1920s and 1930s. There are signs that the number of amateurs is definitely increasing.[26] Why? The sustained increase in the educational and income levels of the whole of the population, the decrease in the availability of patronage as a source of rewards for party work, and perhaps above all the evolution of an issue-oriented politics which has characterized the last decade, all contribute to the presence of amateurs. These developments parallel the growth of extraparty organizations, the rapid rise in the number of persons (particularly college-educated youth) calling themselves Independents, and the very clear preference of reformers, amateurs, and insurgents to take a particular interest in campaign organizations.

IMPLICATIONS FOR THE FUTURE OF PARTIES.   These several concurrent developments suggest some rather clear directions for the future of formal party organizations, that is, they suggest a further weakening of them and a further fragmentation of electoral coalitions which have been in existence since the 1930's. The new amateur tends to think of himself as rather more liberal than the population as a whole and very much concerned with issues rather than with either candidates or parties *as such*. His motivations are purposive rather than material, rather decidedly so. He is inclined to attach himself to an extraparty organization or to a particular candidate precisely because he then finds himself associated with other persons who appear to believe as strongly as he does about some issues. He is inclined to reject the regular party organization precisely to the extent that he finds that existing party groups fail to take a position on those issues in which he himself is interested.

The existence of persons who criticize the major parties for not taking clear stands on issues is nothing new. What is new is the sheer number of such persons who are concerned with issues, the strength of their commitments, and their willingness to bypass existing party organizations in the pursuit of strategies and candidates they believe offer the best hope of converting their commitments into public policy.[27] To this end they have joined in forming consumers organizations, antiwar protest groups, neighborhood associations designed to combat segregation in housing, associations concerned with the protection of the environment, and so forth. And it was largely the talent and work of youthful amateurs that enabled James Longley of Maine to run as an Independent in 1974 and defeat both the Republican and Democratic candidates for the office of Governor.

Regular party organizations are likely to be at their strongest when broad national consensus exists on questions of public policy and when trust in political institutions is high. Under those circumstances, the higher-SES persons who come to hold party leadership positions find their task of leadership relatively unencumbered by particularistic demands from the rank and file. But the seventies are not such a time. The consensus on national policy which was so well and easily demonstrated in studies during the 1950s and 1960s is being eroded, very slowly perhaps, but eroded nonetheless. These are hard times for party leaders, and one thing only is clear: Party organizations will either change or they will atrophy, as their function of providing a channel for the expression of citizen interest is displaced by other, smaller, but more issue-cohesive organizations which find it more effective to exert pressure from the outside than to try to work from the inside. The reforms adopted by the Democrats for the 1972 presidential selection process—of which, more later—represent a nice example of the changes that can help party organizations survive. These reforms attempt to guarantee the representation in the process of persons—blacks, youth, women—who have been conspicuously absent in earlier years. Another example is the Twenty-sixth Amendment, which, if nothing else, served to eliminate the frustrated cry of youth that those old enough to fight should be considered old enough to vote not to fight. So too the passage of the 1965 Voting Rights Act, which facilitated the registration of blacks and thus had a dramatic impact upon the politics of the South, and the 1970 Elections Act, which by setting 30 days as the maximum permissible residence requirement for voting also went far toward eliminating the single most important institutional barrier to political participation. Party organizations have a history of being able to adapt to changing circumstances. Their ability to adapt to the pressure of a new issue consciousness among voters, however, is not guaranteed.

Issue Conflict and Consensus Among Party Leaders and Followers

In their political activity, political leaders differ from the party rank and file. Just the fact that they take part in party affairs makes them a small minority of the electorate. Most citizens do not participate beyond the act of voting on election day.[28] This has been a constant fact of political life in America that has gone unchanged over at least three decades. Studies of participation—from a pioneering study done in 1952 to studies of each presidential election through 1972—indicate that for something like 90 percent of the electorate, voting is the sole act of participation in politics. Roughly 2 percent of all voters say they belong to a political club or organization, 5 percent say they help out in campaigns, and 7 percent say they attend political rallies and such. Merely by participating in party organizational affairs, therefore, the party activist sets himself apart from the great majority of citizens.[29]

There is also evidence that the party activist differs from the rank and file in political beliefs, that discernible differences exist between the beliefs of Republican and Democratic party activists, and that over the course of the last decade or so these differences have become sharper.

A Seminal Study of Beliefs. The beginning of our understanding of these things comes from a seminal study of the beliefs of party leaders and followers done by Herbert McClosky in 1958,[30] using a sample of delegates to the national conventions of the two major political parties to represent party leaders, and a sample of adult voters in the nation to represent followers. Respondents in the two surveys were asked about their attitudes toward 24 specific issues, which fell into five broad policy areas: public ownership, government regulation of the economy, equalitarianism and human welfare, tax policy, and foreign policy.

CONTRASTS BETWEEN DEMOCRATIC AND REPUBLICAN LEADERS. Democratic and Republican leaders were found to diverge sharply on many issues, and the differences noted conformed to the popular image of the Democratic party as the more "progressive" party and the Republican as the more "conservative" of the two parties.[31] They were farthest apart in their attitudes on public ownership of natural resources. They were also far apart on the question of government regulation of business, to which the Republicans were overwhelmingly opposed, and on farm price supports, which the Republicans wanted to reduce. They were divided on federal aid to education, slum clearance and public housing, social security and minimum wages. Democrats were in favor of increasing support of these activities, while Republicans wanted less. They were sharply divided on tax policy, the Republicans being far more eager than the Democrats to cut taxes on corporate and private wealth, and less willing to reduce taxes on lower-income groups. The two groups of leaders were least divided on foreign policy, but even here a difference was observed. Twice as many Democrats as Republicans wanted to see the United States make more use of international agencies such as the United Nations and military alliances like NATO, while many more Republicans than Democrats favored a reduction in American commitments abroad.

SIMILARITIES BETWEEN THE FOLLOWERS OF BOTH PARTIES. Rank-and-file members of the two parties were *far less divided* than were party leaders. Whereas leaders differed significantly on 23 of the 24 issues examined, the followers differed significantly on only 5. Furthermore, the magnitude of the differences among followers was much smaller than among leaders. The issues upon which followers disagreed were bread-and-butter issues: restrictions on credit, farm supports, segregation, and corporate and business taxes. They disagreed least on foreign policy.

In short, not only did party leaders disagree more sharply than their followers, but the level of consensus among followers was very high. The views of the Republican rank and file were, on the whole, closer to those of the Democratic leaders than to those of the Republican leaders—a finding of great interest, one that goes far to explain why the 1964 presidential election turned out the way it did.[32]

A 1968 Follow-up Study of Leaders. A decade after McClosky, a follow-up study was done with a sample of delegates to the Democratic and Republican national conventions of 1968. One objective was to determine whether the two parties were still as ideologically dissimilar as McClosky had found them a decade earlier. So many things had happened on the American party scene since the 1950s that no one could be sure that what McClosky had found would be true of the delegates who assembled in Miami Beach and Chicago in 1968.

CONFIRMATION OF INTERPARTY IDEOLOGICAL DIFFERENCES. McClosky had described Democratic convention delegates as liberal, that is, "more progressively oriented toward social reform and experimentation"; and Republican delegates as more conservative, that is, "subscribing in greater measure to symbols of individualism, laissez-faire, and natural independence." The 1968 results indicated that McClosky's earlier description was still accurate. On eight of nine issues designed to measure conservatism or liberalism, Democrats were significantly more liberal than Republicans. On the ninth item—an agree/disagree item dealing with the Vietnam War—the difference between the two groups of delegates was slight; and moreover, a higher proportion of Republican than Democratic delegates gave the "dovish" or liberal response.[33] In 1968 the differences between Republican and Democratic delegates was also sharper on issues of domestic policy than they were on issues of foreign policy, another finding consistent with McClosky's study.

CONTRASTS IN INTRAPARTY CONSENSUS. In 1968 Democratic degelates revealed *much less* consensus on issues among themselves—less intraparty agreement—than did Republicans. Both groups of delegates showed the largest measure of intraparty agreement in their responses to the same item: "One has a moral responsibility to disobey a law he believes is unjust." Eighty-three percent of the Democrats and 96 percent of the Republicans disagreed. On the remaining eight items, Democrats achieved consensus [34] on only one, an item which said, "The U.S. should give help to foreign countries even if they are not as much against Communism as we are." Republicans, on the other hand, achieved consensus on five of the remaining eight items. Three of these involved law and order (Republicans displayed a more punitive orientation), while the other two involved school integration (Republicans were almost unanimously opposed to it)[35] and communism (Republicans were not ready to say it had changed much). Thus the overall image of the leaders of the parties was of a conservative, homogeneous Republican leadership and a generally more liberal but more fragmented Democratic leadership.

The 1968 study also noted an absence of any relationship between interparty differences and intraparty consensus. One might expect that leaders within each party would agree most among themselves on those items upon which leaders of the two parties disagree most sharply. Such was not the case in 1956, nor was it the case in 1968. Parties are not necessarily unified on those issues that most clearly distinguish them from the opposing party. This characteristic is consistent with a widely accepted view that because both parties must court the same votes —those of a broad middle class—if they are to win, American parties must minimize serious conflict between them and can therefore afford to be cohesive and homogeneous in belief only on issues upon which the two of them are not all that far apart.

PARTY MEMBERSHIP AS AN INFLUENCE UPON LEADER ATTITUDES. Finally, the 1968 study also revealed that membership in the party itself is a significant source of consensus for leaders within each of the parties. In the earlier study, McClosky said: The parties must be considered not merely as spokesmen for other interest groups but as reference groups in their own right helping to formulate, to sustain, and to speak for a recognized point of view." [36] In many population groups a correlation has been found between education, income, region, and religion on the one hand, and beliefs on the other. In the case of the 1968 convention delegates, party differences remained even after these crucial background variables were controlled for. The 1968 study reaffirms that for party leaders, the political party functions as a reference group that exerts an important independent influence on their beliefs. [37]

Leader and Follower Attitudes in the 1970s. A considerable number of studies have followed up the inquiry begun by McClosky, and each in turn has observed the same marked differences in the beliefs of leaders of the two major parties. [38] County chairmen nationwide, for example, show even greater differences in policy attitudes than did the convention delegates of 1956, 1968, and 1972. [39] The scope of these later studies has been extended to newer issues, and the findings show substantial disagreement between Democratic and Republican leaders' attitudes on such issues as the unionization of public officials, the right of police, firemen, and teachers to strike, and capital punishment; and virtually no disagreement in attitudes on some other issues, such as no-fault insurance and abortion reform. [40] That Republican and Democratic leaders, however defined, do reveal a clear disparity in attitudes toward many major public issues does not, therefore, appear to be a subject of controversy at this time.

The beliefs of party followers, however, are a different matter entirely—not unexpectedly, considering, for one thing,

that already commented-upon tendency for voters in the 1970s
to be more policy-aware than voters of the fifties and even of
the sixties. For another, differences in the beliefs of followers
of the two parties may well be minimal when party identification,
a measurable *attitude,* is used as the criterion by which *follower*
is defined; but differences in beliefs do appear when a *behavior*
criterion, voting, is used to distinguish one set of party followers
from the other.[41] In the South, for example, many white voters
have indicated a willingness to support Republican candidates
even while they continue to call themselves Democrats. They
themselves may well be aware of the discrepancy between their
voting behavior and their self-declared party identification, noting
that they think of themselves as "Jefferson Democrats," or
"Southern Democrats," or by saying that they are simply waiting
for the too liberal national party to return someday to practices
consistent with its original principles.

None of this is at all surprising. Those who vote, by that
act alone distinguish themselves from those who might vote but
choose not to. And studies of turnout tell us that those who vote
generally show a greater interest in, concern with, and awareness
of political events and outcomes than those who do not. This in
itself is sufficient to explain why differences in beliefs between
followers of the two parties are sharper when *follower* is given
a behavioral definition tied to voting than when the groups
compared are the much larger number of people who think of
themselves as being Democrats or Republicans.

NOTES

The first quotation at the beginning of the chapter is from Samuel P. Hunting-
ton, *Political Order in Changing Societies* (New Haven, Conn.: Yale University
Press, 1968), 412. The second is from Samuel Eldersveld, *Political Parties*
(Skokie, Ill.: Rand McNally, 1964), 382. The third is from Thomas Roback,
"Amateurs and Professionals Among 1972 Republican National Convention
Delegates," a paper prepared for delivery at the 1973 meeting of the American
Political Science Association, New Orleans, La., September 1973, p. 21. The
fourth is from R. Wayne Parsons and Allen H. Barton, "Social Background and
Policy Attitudes of American Leaders," a paper prepared for delivery at the
1974 annual meeting of the American Political Science Association, Chicago,
September 1974, p. 13.

1. Samuel C. Patterson, "Characteristics of Party Leaders," *Western Political Quarterly* 16 (June 1963), 332–352; see also William J. Crotty, "The Social Attributes of Party Organizational Activists in a Transitional Political System," *Western Political Quarterly* 20 (September 1967), 669–681; Lewis Bowman and G. R. Boynton, "Activities and Role Definitions of Grassroots Party Officials," *Journal of Politics* 28 (February 1966), 121–140; and Donald M. Freeman, "Party Leadership in a Developing Area: The Case of Pima County, Arizona," a paper prepared for delivery at the 1968 annual meeting of the Rocky Mountain Social Science Association, Denver, Colorado.

2. Samuel Eldersveld, *Political Parties: A Behavioral Analysis* (Skokie, Ill.: Rand McNally, 1964).

3. In Tables 6-2, 6-3, 6-4, and 6-5, the data for Montgomery County, Maryland, and for Knox County, Illinois, come from Margaret Conway and Frank B. Feigert, "Motivation, Incentive Systems, and the Political Party Organization," *American Political Science Review* 62 (December 1968), 1159–1173. Data for Pittsburgh come from William J. Keefe and William C. Seyler, "Precinct Politicians in Pittsburgh," *Social Science* 35 (January 1960), 26–32. Data for Manhattan, New York, come from Robert S. Hirschfield and others, "A Profile of Political Activists in Manhattan," *Western Political Quarterly* 15 (September 1962), 489–506. Data for county chairmen in North Carolina come from Crotty, "The Social Attributes of Party Organizational Activists." Data for county chairmen in Ohio come from Thomas A. Flinn and Frederick M. Wirt, "Local Party Leaders: Groups of Like-Minded Men," *Midwest Journal of Political Science* 9 (February 1965), 77–98. Data for Washington County, Illinois, come from Philip Althoff and Samuel C. Patterson, "Political Activism in a Rural County," *Midwest Journal of Political Science* 10 (February 1966), 39–51. Data for Detroit, Michigan, come from Samuel J. Eldersveld, *Political Parties*. Data for Nassau County, New York, come from Dennis S. Ippolito, "Political Perspectives of Suburban Party Leaders," *Social Science Quarterly* 49 (March 1969), 800–815. Data for Oklahoma and Kansas and Wisconsin come from Patterson, "Characteristics of Party Leaders." All data for tables 6-2, 6-3, 6-4, and 6-5 reprinted by permission.

4. Herbert Jacob, "Initial Recruitment of Elected Officials in the United States: A Model," *Journal of Politics* 24 (November 1962), 703–716.

5. In a study of the background of members of the U.S. Senate between 1947 and 1957, Donald Matthews found that 84 percent had attended college (at a time when only 14 percent of the population had done so) and that 53 percent had been to law school. The senators came from middle- and upper-status families. There were no representatives of any blue-collar occupations, only one woman, and no blacks. See his *U.S. Senators and Their World* (Chapel Hill, N.C.: University of North Carolina Press, 1966).

6. David T. Stanley and others, *Men Who Govern* (Washington, D.C.: Brookings, 1966).

7. Frederick W. Frey, *The Turkish Political Elite* (Cambridge, Mass.: M.I.T. Press, 1965).

8. Marshall Singer, *The Emerging Elite: A Study of Political Leadership in Ceylon* (Cambridge, Mass.: M.I.T. Press, 1964).

9. Myron Weiner, *Party Building in a New Nation: The Indian National Congress* (Chicago: University of Chicago Press, 1967), and George Rosen,

Democracy and Economic Change in India (Berkeley, Calif.: University of California Press, 1967).

10. Lester A. Salamon, "Leadership and Modernization: The Emerging Black Political Elite in the American South," *Journal of Politics* 35 (August 1973), 615–646.

11. The Oklahoma results are given in Patterson, "Characteristics of Party Leaders." The Pima County results are in Freeman, "Party Leadership in a Developing Area: The Case of Pima County, Arizona." The Detroit results are in Eldersveld, *Political Parties.*

12. Other studies worth noting include Philip Althoff and Samuel C. Patterson, "Political Activism in a Rural County"; Phillips Cutright, "Activities of Precinct Committeemen in Partisan and Nonpartisan Communities," *Western Political Quarterly* 17 (March 1964), 93–108; Phillips Cutright and Peter H. Rossi, "Party Organization in Primary Elections," *American Journal of Sociology* 64 (November 1958), 262–269; Gerald Pomper, "New Jersey County Chairmen," *Western Political Quarterly* 18 (March 1965), 186–197; James E. Titus, "Kansas Governors: A Resume of Political Leadership," *Western Political Quarterly* 17 (June 1964), 356–370; Joseph A. Schlesinger, "Political Party Organization," in James G. March (editor), *Handbook of Organizations* (Skokie, Ill.: Rand McNally, 1965), 764–801; James A. Mitchener, *Report of the County Chairman* (New York: Random House, 1961); Daniel Katz and Samuel J. Eldersveld, "The Impact of Local Party Activity upon the Electorate," *Public Opinion Quarterly* 25 (Spring 1961), 1–24; Richard T. Frost, "Stability and Change in Local Politics," *Public Opinion Quarterly* 25 (Summer 1961), 221–235; Phillips Cutright and Peter H. Rossi, "Grass Roots Politicians and the Vote," *American Sociological Review* 23 (April 1958), 171–179; and for a look at how leaders look at the public, see Roberta Sigel and H. Paul Friesema, "Urban Community Leaders' Knowledge of Public Opinion," *Western Political Quarterly* 18 (December 1965), 881–895.

13. Eldersveld, *Political Parties.* Robert H. Salisbury "The Urban Party Organization Member," *Public Opinion Quarterly* 29 (Winter 1965–1966), 550–564.

14. Eldersveld, *Political Parties,* 122–134. Lewis Bowman and G. R. Boynton, "Recruitment Patterns Among Local Party Officials: A Model and Some Preliminary Findings in Selected Locales," *American Political Science Review* 60 (September 1966), 673–674.

15. Eldersveld, *Political Parties,* 122–134. Bowman and Boynton, "Recruitment Patterns Among Local Party Officials."

16. Eldersveld, *Political Parties.* See also Avery Leiserson, *Parties and Politics: An Institutional and Behavioral Approach* (New York: Knopf, 1958).

17. Patterson, "Characteristics of Party Leaders," reports that in Oklahoma more than 40 percent of the county chairmen interviewed said they had not run for public office and did not intend to run. Similar results were reported for county chairmen in Kansas and Wisconsin. It is apparent that these leaders do not regard elective office as the preferred or only way to satisfy their political ambitions.

18. James Q. Wilson, *The Amateur Democrat* (Chicago: University of Chicago Press, 1962), 2–4. Used by permission.

19. Thomas Roback, "Amateurs and Professionals Among 1972 Republican National Convention Delegates," a paper prepared for delivery at the 1973 annual meeting of the American Political Science Association, New Or-

leans, La., September 1973. For contrasts and similarities among the motivations reported by two elites within the Republican party in 1964 in California see Edmond Constantini and Kenneth H. Craik, "Competing Elites Within a Political Party: A Study of Republican Leadership," *Western Political Quarterly* 22 (December 1969), 879–903.

20. Peter B. Clark and James Q. Wilson, "Incentive Systems: A Theory of Organizations," *Administrative Science Quarterly* 6 (September 1961), 129–166.

21. Roback, 1973 American Political Science Association paper.

22. Aaron B. Wildavsky, "The Goldwater Phenomenon: Purists, Politicians, and the Two-Party System," *Review of Politics* 27 (July 1965), 386–413. And see especially De Felice's paper prepared for the 1973 meeting of the American Political Science Association.

23. Peter R. Cluck, "Research Note: Incentives and the Maintenance of Political Styles in Different Locales," *Western Political Quarterly* 25 (December 1972), 753–760. And see Ronald J. Busch, "Party Structure: The Case of Cleveland Ward Leaders," a paper prepared for delivery at the 1973 annual meeting of the American Political Science Association, New Orleans, La., September 1973.

24. Conway and Feigert, "Motivation, Incentive Systems, and the Political Party Organization." And by the same authors, "Motivations and Task Performance Among Party Precinct Workers," a paper prepared for delivery at the 1973 annual meeting of the American Political Science Association, New Orleans, La., September 1973.

25. E. Gene De Felice, "Purism vs. Professionalism Among Party Leaders in a Semi-Competitive Party System," a paper prepared for delivery at the 1973 annual meeting of the American Political Science Association, New Orleans, La., September 1973. Dan Nimmo and Robert L. Savage, "The Amateur Democrat Revisited," *Polity* 5 (Winter 1972), 268–276. W. Robert Gump, "The Functions of Patronage in American Party Politics: An Empirical Reappraisal," *Midwest Journal of Political Science* 15 (February 1971), 87–107. One who finds the concept of the amateur politician difficult to operationalize is C. Richard Hofstetter. See his "The Amateur Politician: A Problem in Construct Validation," *Midwest Journal of Political Science* 15 (February 1971), 31–56.

26. Vicki G. Semel, "Ideology and Incentives Among Democratic Amateurs and Professionals," a paper prepared for delivery at the 1973 annual meeting of the American Political Science Association, New Orleans, La., September 1973.

27. Ibid.

28. A new model of political participation applied to several countries is offered by Sidney Verba and others, "The Modes of Participation," *Comparative Political Studies* 6 (July 1973), 235–250. See also Sidney Verba and Norman Nie, *Participation in America: Political Democracy and Social Equality* (New York: Harper & Row, 1972).

29. Julian L. Woodward and Elmo Roper, "Political Activity of American Citizens," *American Political Science Review* 44 (December 1950), 872–885. William G. Andrews, "American Voting Participation," *Western Political Quarterly* 19 (December 1966), 639–652. John H. Lindquist, "Socio-economic Status and Political Participation," *Western Political Quarterly* 17 (December 1964), 608–614. Austin Ranney and Leon D. Epstein, "The Two Electorates: Voters and Non-voters in a Wisconsin Primary,"

Journal of Politics 28 (August 1966), 598–616. Angus Campbell and others, *The Voter Decides* (New York: Harper & Row, 1954). Angus Campbell and others, *The American Voter* (New York: Wiley, 1960). James A. Robinson and William H. Standing, "Some Correlates of Voter Participation: The Case of Indiana," *Journal of Politics* 22 (February 1960), 96–111.

30. Herbert McClosky and others, "Issue Conflict and Consensus Among Party Leaders and Followers," *American Political Science Review* 54 (June 1960), 406–429. See also McClosky's "Consensus and Ideology in American Politics," American Political Science Review 58 (June 1964), 361–379; Lloyd A. Free and Hadley Cantril, *The Political Beliefs of Americans: A Study of Public Opinion* (New Brunswick, N.J.: Rutgers University Press, 1968); Lester W. Milbrath, "Latent Origins of Liberalism-Conservatism and Party Identification: A Research Note," *Journal of Politics* 24 (November 1962), 679–688.

31. Similar conclusions are offered by Eldersveld, *Political Parties,* 183–219; by David B. Truman, "The State Delegations and the Structure of Party Voting in the United States House of Representatives," *American Political Science Review* 50 (December 1956), 1023–1045; and by Malcolm Jewell, "Party Voting in American State Legislatures," *American Political Science Review* 49 (September 1955), 773–791.

32. McClosky and others, "Issue Conflict and Consensus."

33. The item dealing with the Vietnam War was worded this way: "Vietnam is historically and geographically an Asian country and should be allowed to develop autonomously within the Asian sphere of power." Sixty-four percent of the Democratic delegates agreed with the item, as did 71 percent of the Republican delegates.

34. Soule and Clarke define *consensus* as "agreement by at least 75 percent of the group." John W. Soule and James W. Clarke, "Issue Conflict and Consensus: A Comparative Study of Democratic and Republican Delegates to the 1968 National Conventions," *Journal of Politics* 33 (February 1971), 72–91.

35. We should note that a majority of *both* Democratic and Republican delegates opposed busing—67 percent of the Democrats and 90 percent of the Republicans.

36. McClosky and others, "Issue Conflict and Consensus," 427.

37. Soule and Clarke, "Issue Conflict and Consensus," 89.

38. The report for 1972 comes from Roback's paper prepared for delivery to the 1974 meeting of the American Political Science Association.

39. William R. Shaffer and others, "Mass and Political Elite Beliefs About the Policies of the Regime," a paper prepared for delivery at the 1973 annual meeting of the American Political Science Association, New Orleans, La., September 1973.

40. Everett Carll Ladd, Jr., and Charles D. Hadley, "Party Definition and Differentiation," *Public Opinion Quarterly* 37 (Spring 1973), 21–34. Gerald M. Pomper, "Toward A More Responsible Two-Party System? What, Again?" *Journal of Politics* 33 (November 1971), 916–940. Sidney Verba and Norman Nie, *Participation in America* (New York: Harper & Row, 1972), especially part 3.

Part Three

Party in Elections

Party organizations can no longer control the selection of their candidates, for nominations through primaries are now virtually universal in the United States.

So when people speak of political power they often are referring to the power to endorse. And they're right, so far as they go. For real power is the power to elect. Insofar as endorsement helps insure election, it remains the central tool of party power. This, of course, depends in turn on how the people view the party at any given time, on whom they deem to be in charge. The endorsement of a political party is only of value when the voters regard that party's leadership structure as being legitimate, when they think the party truly represents its rank-and-file roots. The public's perception in these matters is almost unerringly keen.

The nomination process is obviously one of the points at which parties can be studied most advantageously if for no other reason than that the nomination is one of the most innately characteristic pieces of business transacted by the party. A party must make nominations if it is to be regarded as a party at all.

The most important effect of the primary in the recent past in Massachusetts has been to dissipate the strength of the leaderless, majority Democratic Party in bloody intramural conflicts while the cohesive Republican Party has held its troops in order for the battle of the general election.

Nominating Candidates

In Part 1 we looked at the citizen, in Part 2 at party leaders. Here we look at elections. Elections are one area where citizens and leaders meet, where leaders as candidates and organizers court voters, and where voters get a chance to render judgment on the quality of leadership and make a choice of leaders for some part of the future.

We are ultimately heading toward an understanding of the impact which parties have upon the making and substance of public policy. That is the concern of Part 4. The best opportunity to shape policy, to ride off in new directions (either forward or backward) is enjoyed by those public officials who hold elective public office. Who gets to run for public office? Normally it is candidates who have been nominated to run by their parties. When election day rolls around, the voter usually finds that his choice is limited to a choice between two candidates, one Republican and one Democrat. There may be others on the ballot, but as a rule only the major party candidates stand a decent chance of actually winning.

American parties use a variety of devices in the nomination of candidates, but the most common and distinctive is the direct primary election. The primary is thought both to maximize the opportunity for popular participation in the nomination process and also to weaken control over the selection of candidates for public office. It is a unique American invention, and its impact

both upon the style of the party battle and upon the
strength of the parties themselves has been considerable.
What it is, where it comes from, how it works, what
impact it has had upon the parties, what political forces
it encourages and discourages, and what alternatives
to it exist, are among the subjects taken up in this chapter.

Nothing distinguishes American political parties from parties in
other countries better than does the role which the mass electorate
is allowed in nominating candidates to run for public office. Mass
participation by voters who often have but the slightest notions
of party commitments or ideology, and have indeed little involvement in politics generally, in the selection of party candidates for
public office, is the hallmark of nominating procedures in
America. The institution that more than any other guarantees this
measure of popular participation is the direct primary election.

It was not always this way. Nor indeed are nominations for
all public offices today made by the direct primary route. Nomination by party convention is still used in this country. However,
the bulk of offices are occupied by individuals who got into office
because they were first successful in winning a primary election.
Even the presidency—candidates for which are nominated by the
national conventions of the two parties—is not untouched by the
influence of primaries, for in recent years the two parties have
found it difficult to resist giving their nominations to the candidates who perform best in the state presidential primaries. The
condition of our political parties today may be the product of
many diverse influences, but none of these influences has had a
greater impact than the American invention known as the direct
primary election.[1]

By *direct primary election*—or simply *primary,* to give it its
more common name—we mean an election in which the electorate chooses who will be the candidates to run for offices under
a party label.

Marcy Tweed, the celebrated boss of New York's Tammany
Hall in the nineteenth century, once said: "I don't care who does
the electing just so I can do the nominating." With that remark,
he paid respectful tribute to the importance of the selection of
party candidates for public office, a process that is of great interest to party leaders at any time. No party can honestly be happy

with a process that produces a losing candidate to run under its label, or a candidate whose image is not the image the party wants to convey of itself to the mass electorate. It is easy to understand, therefore, the consternation with which the Democratic party of Ohio faced its discovery that the candidate nominated in its primary to run for congressman-at-large in 1962 was an avowed segregationist.[2] The positions a candidate takes on issues become to some degree the positions of the party, for candidates are among the most visible spokesmen for the party. Party leaders, therefore, must exercise some control over the crucial nominating process or accept the risk that candidates will be nominated who can do damage to the party.

Quite apart from being a means of avoiding trouble, party influence over nominations also adds to the strength of the party organization itself. The ability to offer the faithful activists the reward of the party's nomination for elective public office (or even the opportunity for activists to share in the decision of who among their members shall be given the party's nomination) can be a powerful tool in recruiting and holding party activists. This tool is unavailable when party leaders exercise little or no control over the processes by which its candidates for elective office are chosen. When party influence over nominations is absent or negligible, it constitutes an open invitation for nonparty groups, including self-seeking individuals with little in mind except to use public office for their own personal advantage, to exert influence over the selection of candidates. The manner in which party candidates are nominated is, therefore, a matter of major importance for any party. It can promote the party's welfare or its demise. In its impact for the party, it is seldom neutral.

Development of the Primary

The primary became a prominent feature in American party politics only in this century. First used in Crawford County, Pennsylvania, in the 1830s, then in the South in the 1880s, it became a major element in the program of the Progressive movement and won acceptance in states where Progressive ideas were most readily accepted, mainly in the West. By 1917 it was accepted as the common method of nominating candidates by all but a handful of states. By 1968 it was used by all states for nominating candidates for at least some offices, and 40 states were using it to nominate candidates for all state offices.

The Primary as a Response to One-Party Politics.   That the primary should have been invented and so quickly adopted by states at a time when one-party systems flourished was scarcely a coincidence. The primary was designed in reaction to unwanted characteristics of one-party politics. Through the latter half of the nineteenth century, the party convention was the prevailing mode of nominating candidates. It was used at all levels, from the ward on up. When the Civil War reduced Republican parties in the South and Democratic parties in many states of the North to mere shadows, it made shadows also of general election contests. The outcome of such elections was thereafter determined not by genuine interparty competition on the day of the general election, for that no longer existed, but by the inner processes of the dominant party within the state. Thereafter, the electorate was left with little function except to ratify the choice of candidate made by the leadership of the dominant party. Actual electoral choice, in short, was transferred from the voters using the ballot box on election day into the hands of the delegates to the convention of the dominant party. In effect, that transfer of power made oligarchical what before had been a democratic election process. This situation might have remained unchallenged longer than it did, had it not been for the fact that party leadership in that era had acquired a reputation for being corrupt and self-serving. This was the era of the muckraker, and muckrakers frequently told more than they knew about the evil ways of party bosses and machines. This combination of circumstances fostered the movement to return the selection of public officials back to the hands of the people, where it more properly belonged. The device chosen to accomplish this end was the party primary.

Considerations in Developing a Primary System.   The variations possible in primary elections are suggested by the following list of questions upon which any state must reach a decision in working out its primary process. Will parties be required (or merely permitted) by law, under all (or merely some) circumstances, to use the primary to nominate candidates? Will the primary be applied to all offices, or merely some, and in the latter case, to which offices? Who among the electorate will be eligible to participate in party primaries? What latitude, if any, will be left party leaders to endorse candidates in advance of the party primary, or to otherwise attempt to bring party influence to bear on the selection of candidates in the primary? Will a plurality of votes be recognized as sufficient to win a primary election, or will a winner be declared only if he secures a majority of votes in the primary?

In light of the variations possible, it is better to think of the primary as an idea, rather than an institution of clearly specified dimensions. As it appears on the American scene today, it takes many different forms. Clearly, one of its strengths is its adaptability. Party leaders have not always taken kindly to the primary and in defense have responded with inventions of their own, designed to mitigate some of its effects. That party leaders should feel obliged to take such action is itself a tribute to the impact a primary may have upon the political party.

Types of Primaries: Who May Vote?

Party primaries come in one of two principal forms, the form depending upon who among the electorate is eligible to participate. If the only requirement for voting in a primary is that the voter must be legally qualified to vote, and the voter is therefore free to choose which primary he wishes to participate in, then the primary is said to be *open*. If, on the other hand, only voters who are members of a particular party may vote in that party's primary, then the primary is said to be *closed*. How is membership determined? In some closed primary states, the individual must indicate membership in a party when registering to vote. At the polls on primary day the voter receives the primary ballot of the party in which he or she is registered. In the other closed primary states, the individual need not indicate a party membership until the day of the primary itself. The voter does so either by requesting the ballot of one party, or by receiving the primary ballots of all parties and making a choice among the parties in the privacy of the polling booth. Presently, 43 states use the closed primary. Nine use the open. The state of Washington uses a special form of the open primary known as the *wide-open* or *blanket* or *jungle primary*.[3] Here the voter receives only one primary ballot, on which all the candidates, regardless of party labels, are grouped together according to the offices to which they seek their party's nomination. The voter is thus free to cross party lines and vote in more than one party's primary, voting for one of the Democratic candidates running for one office, and for one of the Republican candidates running for a second office, and so on through the list of candidates.

Party leaders generally prefer the closed primary. Its presumed value is that it restricts access to the primary to those who are members of the party, while the open primary leaves the party doors open to anyone who chooses to wander in at the time of nominating candidates. In practice, however, the distinction between the open and closed primary is not always that great. Where voters are allowed to wait until primary day to decide which party they are a member of, it is obvious that the closed primary is scarcely more "closed" to nonmembers of the party than is the "open."

Crossing-Over in Open Primaries. Party leaders also charge that the open primary encourages crossing-over—voting in the primary of one party by persons who are supporters of the opposition party. Undoubtedly some crossing-over does occur, though the evidence for it is hard to come by, and its effects upon the outcome of a primary are equally difficult to measure. What party leaders fear, of course, is that voters from the opposition party will cross over solely for the purpose of supporting the weakest primary contender and thus ultimately make it easier for the opposition candidate to win in the general election.

People who vote in primary elections tend to be the more politically involved. Under certain circumstances, voting in the primary election of the opposition party may appear attractive. Voters may find the other party's primary offers candidates they like better than the candidates running in their own party's primary. Or theirs may be the minority party in the state, and its candidates may stand little chance of winning in the general election. In this case, a vote in the primary of the dominant party may offer the only real chance to affect the choice of who will hold public office. Or a voter may gradually have acquired a habit of voting in the general election for candidates of one party, though he retains his registration in the party with which he has long identified. This situation seems most likely to occur in states that are moving in the direction of developing genuine two-party competition. Arizona offers dozens of examples of precincts where the ratio of Democratic to Republican registrations is two to one or better, and where participation in the Democratic primary is much higher than in the Republican, but where the vote for Democratic candidates in the general election ranges between only 30 and 40 percent of the Democratic turnout. Table 7–1 offers data on registration and voter turnout in the general election from four such precincts in Maricopa County, Arizona.

Who May Run in a Primary?

Self-Initiated Candidacy. States limit the electorate's access to the primary election ballot only if they use some form of the closed primary. They show much greater variety in the rules governing the candidate's access to the ballot.

Generally a candidate may have his name appear on the ballot by filing with the appropriate state authority a petition signed by a number of registered voters. The number required may be expressed either as an absolute number or as a certain percentage of the votes cast for a specified elective office in the

Table 7-1 Party Registration and Election Behavior in Four Precincts in Maricopa County, Arizona, 1966 General Election

| | Registration | | Turnout in General Election | | | Vote for Democratic Candidate for Governor | |
| | | | | | | Total | As % of Democratic Turnout |
Precinct	Dem	Rep	Dem	Rep	Total	Total	Turnout
Arlington	159	56	81	39	120	32	39.5%
Buckeye 1	678	298	498	223	721	205	41.1
Palo Verde	106	81	79	64	143	30	37.9
Tonopah	73	25	44	15	59	17	38.6

last general election. The number required is rarely so high that candidates find this requirement a hardship. In some states, not even this is required. A candidate merely appears before the appropriate state authority, declares himself a candidate, pays a small filing fee, and that is that: He is an official candidate.

CROSS-FILING. Until 1959 California gave candidates maximum access to the primary ballot through its provisions for "cross-filing." Here, candidates were permitted to run for nomination in more than one party's primary. Former Governor, later Chief Justice, Earl Warren, was among those who won both the Republican and Democratic primary nominations for governor and hence entered the general election with himself as his principal opponent! Under this system, 84 percent of all candidates for seats in the California Senate won the nominations of both parties between 1940 and 1952. In 1952, the law was changed to require a candidate to state his party affiliation opposite his name on the ballot. One result of the change was immediate: The number of candidates who won nomination from *both* parties declined to less than 25 percent. As this might suggest, cross-filing undoubtedly works to the advantage of the majority party. Its candidates are likely to be better known and to be incumbents, which gives them an edge over their opponents. By giving candidates of the dominant party access to the nominating process of the minority party, cross-filing makes the minority party's task of recruiting and gaining visibility for its own candidates that much more difficult.[4]

Somewhat similar to cross-filing in its results is the practice in New York whereby a candidate can be nominated by more than one party. This makes it possible for the Liberal party to choose whether to nominate candidates of its own or of one of the other major parties.

Party Endorsement: The Pre-Primary Convention. A candidate's access to the ballot is most strictly controlled in states that use some form of the preprimary convention. Among the states that use or once used the preprimary convention are New Mexico, Utah, Colorado, Rhode Island, Nebraska, Minnesota, South Dakota, and Massachusetts. Intended to provide party leadership with a measure of control over the party's primary, a party convention held before the primary election endorses one or more candidates seeking the party's nomination for each office. In Utah the names of the two candidates receiving the most convention votes are placed on the primary ballot. Thus, the number of primary contestants for an office can never be more than two, since candidates have their names included on the party's primary ballot only if they receive convention endorsement. In Colorado a candidate is included on the primary ballot if he receives at least 20 percent of the convention vote. Rhode Island permits the state central committee (or the town committee, in the case of local offices) to endorse candidates for statewide office and Congress, and the names of endorsed candidates are listed first on the ballot with an asterisk to indicate the endorsement. Other candidates win a place on the ballot only by petition.

Massachusetts first passed a preprimary convention law in 1932, repealed it in 1937, and then brought it back again in 1953.[5] Other states which have used the preprimary convention for varying lengths of time include Nebraska, New Mexico, South Dakota, and Minnesota. The fact that about as many states have tried and discarded the convention as have tried and kept it, indicates that its appeal is limited. From these experiences it appears that the preprimary convention is most likely to be adopted in a competitive two-party state where each party stands a chance of winning public offices and where, hence, the leadership feels a particular need both to reduce intraparty squabbling and maintain party discipline. Conversely, it is least likely to be used in one-party areas, where open competition among candidates in the primary of the dominant party is the normal route to public office.

The Challenge Primary.   A slightly different blend of party and popular influences on the nomination of candidates was provided by a 1955 law which established the *challenge primary* in Connecticut, the last state to adopt the primary in any form. The party continues to select its candidates in convention, as it always has, but the 1955 law provides an avenue by which the convention's decision may be taken on appeal to the voters. Under the law, nominees of the convention stand as the party nominees, without having to fight a primary battle, unless a second contender for a particular office secures sufficient signatures on a petition to require the candidate nominated by the convention to meet him in a primary.[6] New York adopted a similar law in 1967.

Other Forms of Party Endorsement.   The intent of the prepri-mary convention may also be realized by informal party arrange-ments which have no statutory basis. Notable here are the prac-tices of the California Democratic Council, formed in 1953 for the purpose of endorsing candidates in advance of the Demo-cratic party primary. It achieved its most notable success in 1958, when every Democratic candidate it endorsed won nomi-nation, and all but one (the Democratic candidate for secretary of state) was successful in the general election. A large measure of the council's success can be attributed to its effectiveness as a campaign organization. At that time, it sat at the apex of a pyramid of Democratic clubs whose middle-class party activists constituted a major campaign resource for candidates endorsed by the council. Subsequently, the council suffered damage both in its stature and effectiveness, as a result of differences within the organization's leadership on matters of policy, notably over American involvement in Vietnam. By 1968 it could no longer be said that the council was acting as an unofficial spokesman for the Democratic party of California.[7]

The Run-Off Primary.   In any primary contest in which three or more candidates compete for the same office, it is possible, and not uncommon, for the winning candidate to secure less than a majority of the vote. Several southern states provide that when this happens, the two opponents who secure the highest number of votes shall compete against each other a second time in a primary appropriately called a "run-off primary," which is held, when needed, two or three weeks after the first primary. The run-off is designed to insure that the party's nominee for a public office win the nomination by not less than a majority of votes cast, a matter of particular concern to southern states, where winning the nomination of the dominant party has long been tantamount to final election to office.

Voter Participation in Primaries

What has the widespread adoption of the primary meant to the voter and to the political parties themselves?

It is impossible to present a neat summary of the influence of the primary on nominations. Its impact has been uneven, reflecting in part the many versions of it that have been adopted. The evidence of the several decades in which the primary has been the dominant method of nominating candidates indicates that the primary has not substituted the will of the people for the will of party activists, at least not entirely. It has rather changed the ground rules governing nominations and has forced the party activists to find new ways of coping with the changed circumstances.

Early advocates of the primary expected that given the opportunity, the electorate would move forward eagerly to take over the nominating of candidates. In the past seven decades, the electorate has not behaved exactly as the primary advocates expected. More voters now participate in nominations than did under the old convention system, but it is at least equally significant that overall participation in primaries is generally lower than it is in the general election.[8]

The Predominance of Party Activists. Those who vote in primaries are most often the party activists—a source of the continuing influence of the party upon nominations made in primaries.[9] The identity of the primary voter is important. What it means is that under the primary, nominations are being made not by a group of voters representative of the electorate as a whole nor even necessarily representative of the whole of a party's membership. They are being made by party activists, who, as was earlier established, are the most concerned, most involved, most partisan, and most ideological of the party's members. Thus, candidates in a primary are competing for the favor of an electorate that is quite different from the electorate which the victor will face in the general election. The campaign strategy that will bring succcess in a primary may be inappropriate in a general election. In a primary, certain groups within the party membership—rural conservatives, urban ethnic groups, organized labor, a well-disciplined party faction—may exercise influence considerably greater than they can bring to bear upon the general election. If their influence in the primary is decisive, the primary winner may in fact be a poor candidate for a party to offer the voters in the general election. On the other hand, the tendency for the electorate to leave the primaries to the party activists often offers a chance for the party to maintain some of its influence over nomination of candidates who will bear the party label. When party leaders assert their influence, either formally (as through pre-primary conventions) or informally (by distributing to party workers a strictly "unofficial" list of "party"-endorsed candidates), their influence on the outcome of the primary can be of major importance.

Primary Voters in the South.   The observation that primaries generally attract fewer voters than general elections is not accurate when speaking of elections in the South. Voter turnout in the primary of the dominant party in southern states is higher than in the general election. This is not unexpected. In demonstrating their preference for voting in the primary of the clearly dominant party, southern voters merely illustrate an often-verified law of politics which declares that voters will vote where they believe their votes count most. Since the outcome of the Democratic primary usually determines not just who the Democratic nominees for various state and local offices will be, but guarantees their victory in the general election, the Democratic party primary has become not only a method of nominating candidates; it has, practically speaking, become the general election.

Parties as such scarcely exist in much of the Democratic South. Competition for office does exist, but it expresses itself through factions that compete under the capacious umbrella of the Democratic primary. It is doubtful, however, that factions, when they exist, do all of their competing in public. In a state like Virginia, where two major factions within the dominant Democratic party have displayed the ability to persist through time, the number of entrants into the primary is lower than in the multifactional states of Mississippi and Florida. If divisions within the ranks of a major faction of the Virginia Democratic party are permitted to spill over into the primary, the major faction knows it runs the risk of defeat at the hands of a numerically smaller faction that remains united in the primary behind its candidates. In Virginia (and in other states where a similar pattern of bifactionalism is evident) the factional leadership must, for its own protection, do some weeding out, by designating candidates in advance of the primary.[10] In doing this, factional leaders exercise an influence over nominations similar to that exercised when party leaders in two-party states officially or unofficially endorse particular candidates before the primary. Where this happens, the choice among candidates available to primary voters has been narrowed by the prior choices made by factional leaders.[11]

Candidate Participation in Primaries

Quite as striking as the low voter turnout in primary elections is the low candidate turnout. Instances in which 50 to 75 percent of primary contests—for seats in the state legislature, for example—go uncontested, are not rare. Obviously, candidates as well as voters avoid primaries. That, however, is not the whole story. Candidates may shy away from many primaries, but they press forward eagerly into others. In other words, some primaries are minimally competitive, while others are alive with competition.[12]

How Party Dominance and Primary Competition are Related. When is competition likely to occur and why? Most important, apparently, is the relative position of the parties. Competition is most often found in the primaries of the dominant party, the party most likely to win the subsequent general election. Candidates, like voters, prefer to put their efforts where they are most likely to bring results. Southern states provide the clearest examples of this pattern of candidate preference, but the same pattern is evident in more competitive states.[13]

In competitive states, each party has its pockets of strength, its "safe" electoral districts, where the candidates of one party not only win the general election far more often than do candidates of the other party, but usually do so by a wide margin. In other electoral districts the two parties are likely to be more evenly competitive. The number of candidates who enter primaries does not appear to be affected by the probable outcome of the election; that is, the number does not appear to depend upon whether the electoral district is safe or competitive. However, in safe districts more candidates are attracted to the primary of the party that is dominant in that district. Furthermore, in safe districts two other interesting patterns of competition also appear.

First, candidates of the party that is dominant statewide are more willing to take risks than are candidates of the party that is the minority party statewide. To put this more precisely:

Candidates of the party that is dominant statewide enter their party's primary in districts that are safe for the minority party statewide, more often than candidates of the minority party statewide enter their party's primary in districts that are safe for the dominant party statewide. The second pattern suggests that the minority party statewide is likely to be less successful in preventing a contest from developing in primaries within its safe districts than is the dominant party statewide in preventing contests in the primaries of its safe districts. To put this more precisely: Primaries of the minority party statewide are more frequently contested in districts that are safe for the minority party than are primaries of the dominant party statewide held in districts that are safe for the dominant party. These two patterns provide an interesting contrast between the behavior of the dominant and minority parties. The party that is dominant statewide appears to be aggressive in its competition with the minority party, less inclined than the minority party to avoid contests where the chances of victory are slim. It is better able than the minority party to avoid contests in the primaries of its safe districts. And finally, it enjoys the opportunity (more than it offers it) of profiting from the competition that occurs in the primaries of the opposition party in districts that are regarded as safe for the minority party.[14]

Primary Competition and Urbanization.   Primary competition is also associated with urbanization. Despite occasional indications that no strong relationship exists,[15] the bulk of the evidence supports a finding that competitive party primaries are positively associated with urbanization.[16] Why this should be is not precisely clear. Perhaps nonurban areas are less subject to political commotion. Perhaps it reflects a greater likelihood that officeholders will be elected on an "at large" basis in metropolitan areas, or perhaps the heterogeneity of urban areas, out of which may spring a greater variety of interests and associations and a more vigorous politics. Perhaps it may only be that parties tend to be better organized in cities. Perhaps the explanation lies in part in all of these conditions. Whatever the explanation, competition in primaries is far more often found in urban than in rural communities.

The Advantages of Incumbency.   Is the incumbent officeholder running again? If he is, chances are that he or she will not be challenged in the primary. Incumbency offers decided advantages in a primary. It provides status of a kind, and a chance to use the office to build support with major groups within the constituency. It also provides an opportunity to build a name, and in the primary, where name identification has often been crucial, having the well-known name is no mean advantage.

The Party Convention as an Alternative to the Primary

Widespread use of the primary does not mean that party leaders have accepted the primary with grace or favor. They have shown considerable inventiveness in designing techniques for maintaining a certain measure of party influence in nominating candidates —surely an indication that they are not prepared to accept the primary without reservation.

State Conventions: the Connecticut Example. Some states, like Connecticut, continue to nominate candidates for most offices by party conventions. They have resisted the primary without suffering any large-scale protest from voters claiming they have been denied rights which voters in most other states enjoy. How may we account for this? An important clue is provided by Duane Lockard, a long-time observer of Connecticut politics who says:

> Why such protracted and successful resistance? Connecticut is not immune to political innovation. Although it may be known as "The Land of Steady Habits," it has nonetheless adopted an imposing array of progressive legislation, particularly in matters of labor law and social welfare. Still, matters of party concern are different—at least in Connecticut. For Connecticut parties are different from those of most other states; they are strong, centralized, and highly competitive with each other. The character of Connecticut party leadership—the power it has and the generally responsible manner in which it uses its power—constitutes the main reason why advocates of the primary have made so little progress in Connecticut.[17]

The phrase "generally responsible manner" may cover a lot of ground, but at least it suggests that the competitive parties of Connecticut have performed in a fashion that has prevented the development of any major insurgency among the electorate against the party system as it exists in Connecticut. It reminds us that the primary came upon the country at a particular moment in time to meet widely recognized abuses in the convention system. It had behind it the force of a great and general reform movement. Connecticut's convention system is not currently charged with major abuses, or with being a tool of special interests, or of ignoring the wishes of the people, or of being under the control of bosses or in the hands of corrupt petty grafters. As for the Progressive movement, its strength has long since ebbed away. Let us also recall what should by now be obvious: the choice of a process to nominate candidates is not strictly limited to a choice between the party-controlled convention and the popularly controlled primary. All nominating processes in America now display a mixture of party and popular control, even those in Connecticut and New York, both of which have installed the challenge primary. Lockard also reminds us that in Connecticut the two parties are highly competitive. Voters do have a choice and the opportunity to express that choice in a meaningful way at the general election. That alone probably goes far to explain why Connecticut has successfully resisted the party primary.

National Conventions. Two other uses made of the party convention must also be noted. Both parties nominate their presidential and vice-presidential candidates by party convention. These two conventions are undoubtedly the best known of all party conventions. They have been at their task now for a century. From time to time there is talk of adopting a national primary to allow the people to choose their party's candidates for the two highest offices in the country, but there is no evidence of widespread support for that idea.[18] To some extent, the primary has already made inroads on the territory of the national conventions. At this time, better than 60 percent of the delegates to each of the national conventions come from states where the delegates are chosen in party primaries. In several states, voters have the opportunity not only to choose delegates but also to indicate the person they would like to see receive their party's nomination for president. States vary in the extent to which they oblige delegates to support the winner of this presidential preference poll. Oregon requires delegates to support the winner of the preference poll at least through the first convention ballot, unless released by the candidate himself before that time. A fuller explanation of the complexities of nominating presidential candidates appears in a later chapter.[19]

Finally, party conventions are also used by very weak, very small parties. The typical primary law in a southern state requires that a political party nominate its candidates by party primary if it obtains a certain percentage of the vote cast in the previous general election. Any political party that obtains less than that has the option of deciding whether it will nominate its candidates in a primary or by convention. This provision is designed to make it possible for small, minor parties to maintain their existence and be recognized in the eyes of the law as bona fide parties, without being put to the expense of a party primary at frequent intervals. Among the major beneficiaries of this have been the Republican party organizations in the South, which, until very recently, nominated all their candidates for office by convention or by a vote of the central committee.

The Primary and Its Critics

The primary election as an instrument of popular government is now firmly engrafted upon American politics. Controversial when it was first advocated by reform-minded legislators early in this century, it remains no less controversial some seventy years later.

The main argument advanced by those who defend it hinges upon the fact that the primary affords rank-and-file voters a chance to participate in the crucial nominating stage and that, by being yet another instance of a means for assuring popular participation in politics, and therefore being democratic, it is easily approved. In support of this central line of thought, it is argued that the primary (1) creates a healthy voter interest in nominations, (2) allows (where write-in votes are permitted) a groundswell of popular support to develop for a candidate who might otherwise be overlooked, (3) is a testing ground for candidates, some of whom prove themselves and some of whom are proved wanting, (4) provides a valuable arena for the airing and development of issues, (5) makes it difficult for special interests or party bosses to ignore the broader public interest in the choice of candidates, and (5), notably in one-party areas—of which there are many in the country—guarantees that the vote can be meaningful, a guarantee that could not be made if all that were allowed the people at large was to ratify in the general election the choice of candidates made earlier by a party elite.[20]

The widespread acceptance of the primary election in this century has by no means stilled the critics. On one important point they and the primary's defenders are agreed: The primary does afford voters at large the chance to be influential in the nominating of candidates. And that, for the critics, is a large part of the problem with the primary! The critics say the primary denies party leaders adequate control over the nominating process and thereby works against the interest of party responsibility. Parties are weak, they argue, and hence too often unable to deliver what they promise in the way of government programs because the crucial nominating process is not actually within their hands. The primary system allows candidates to win and wear the party's label who need pay no attention to party leaders or party programs. The absence of any substantial control over nominations also makes the party's role of recruiting people for public service more difficult, because those who enter the party ranks in the expectation of being able to exercise an influence on public policy through party channels soon discover that that influence can be reduced by the election to office of persons who owe no allegiance whatever to the party organization. The primary system, further, allows fly-by-night operators to win nomination for reasons that ought not to be factors in the selection of candidates. Often cited here as a case in point is the nomination in the Democratic primary of a clerk in a razor blade factory who three times won election to the post of treasurer of the Commonwealth of Massachusetts, apparently only because his name was John F. (for Francis, not Fitzgerald) Kennedy. Critics of the primary complain further that the primary system too often offers an easy target for manipulation by groups that have none but their own special interests to promote: newspapers, utilities, mining and oil men, and other groups with either easy access to the media or a sizable treasury are often cited here.[21]

Unquestionably there is a large element of truth in this bundle of criticism, even if the charges do not equally apply to all primaries. Much of this criticism grows out of the evident

fact that the primary has not worked exactly the way the reformers who advocated it thought it would. It has not served to
eliminate party influence from the nominating process entirely;
nor has it served to place nominations squarely in the hands of
the electorate at large. It has produced instead a situation of
shared power, in which the balance now shifts in the direction of
increased influence by party leaders and activists and at another
time in the direction of greater influence by the electorate at
large. The exact balance that will be achieved at any given
moment is hardly predictable. Indeed, in politics there is nothing
less predictable than the outcome of a party primary. In the
past seven decades, the political parties have learned to adjust to
the presence of the primary, even if at times they have found it
difficult to live with. Today, for better or worse, the primary is an
integral part of the American scene. If the past gives a clue to
the future, the primary will remain no less a part of the American scene than political parties themselves, and the process of
mutual accommodation and adjustment between the needs of the
party organization and popular participation in nominations will
continue.

NOTES

The first quote at the beginning of the chapter is from Gerald M. Pomper,
"Party Functions and Party Failures: The Party Institution," in Gerald M.
Pomper and others, *The Performance of American Government: Checks and
Minuses* (New York: Free Press, 1972), 106. The second quote is from David
Lebedoff, *Ward Number Six* (New York: Scribner, 1972), 83–84. The third is
from Elmer E. Schattschneider, *Party Government* (New York: Holt, Rinehart
& Winston, 1942), 100. The fourth is from Edgar Litt, *The Political Cultures
of Massachusetts* (Cambridge, Mass.: M.I.T. Press, 1965), 110.

1. On the early development of the party primary, see Charles E. Merriam
   and Louise Overacker, *Primary Elections* (Chicago: University of Chicago
   Press, 1928). There is no single work which picks up where Merriam and
   Overacker left off, but see V. O. Key, Jr., *American State Politics* (New
   York: Knopf, 1956).
2. This incident is reported in Fred I. Greenstein, *The American Party System
   and the American People,* 2nd ed. (Englewood Cliffs, N.J.: Prentice-Hall,
   1963), 67.

3. See Daniel M. Ogden, Jr., "The Blanket Primary and Party Regularity in Washington," *Pacific Northwest Quarterly* 39 (1948), 33–38.

4. On cross-filing in California see Winston W. Crouch and others, *California Government and Politics,* 3rd ed. (Englewood Cliffs, N.J.: Prentice-Hall, 1964), 60–64; Gordon E. Baker and Bernard Teitelbaum, "An End to Cross-Filing," *National Civic Review* 48 (1959), 286–291; Evelyn Hazen, *Cross-Filing in Primary Elections* (Berkeley, Calif.: University of California Bureau of Public Administration, 1951); and Robert J. Pitchell, "The Electoral System and Voting Behavior: The Case of California's Cross-Filing," *Western Political Quarterly* 12 (June 1959), 459–484.

5. For a discussion of Massachusetts' pre-primary convention, see Murray B. Levin, *The Compleat Politician: Political Strategy in Massachusetts* (Indianapolis, Ind.: Bobbs-Merrill, 1962), 34–46.

6. On the Connecticut law, see especially Duane Lockard's *Connecticut's Challenge Primary: A Study in Legislative Politics* (New York: Holt, Rinehart & Winston, 1959).

7. On the California Democratic Council, see Crouch and others, *California Government and Politics,* 80–82; James Q. Wilson, *The Amateur Politician: Club Politics in Three Cities* (Chicago: University of Chicago Press, 1966); and Francis Carney, *The Rise of the Democratic Clubs in California* (New York: Holt, Rinehart & Winston, 1956).

8. V. O. Key, Jr., *American State Politics* (New York: Knopf, 1956), 134–140.

9. Austin Ranney and Leon D. Epstein, "The Two Electorates: Voters and Non-Voters in a Wisconsin Primary," *Journal of Politics* 28 (August 1966), 598–616.

10. On Virginia, see V. O. Key, Jr., *Southern Politics in State and Nation* (New York: Knopf, 1949), 19–35. Other studies which consider the part played by party leaders in primary nominations are Peter H. Rossi and Phillips Cutright, "The Impact of Party Organization in an Industrial Setting," in Morris Janowitz (editor), *Community Political Systems* (New York: Free Press, 1961), 81–116; Frank J. Sorauf, *Party and Representation* (New York: Atherton, 1963), 95–120; Phillips Cutright and Peter H. Rossi, "Party Organization in Primary Elections," *American Journal of Sociology* 64 (August 1958), 262–269; Frank J. Sorauf, "Extra-Legal Political Parties in Wisconsin," *American Political Science Review* 48 (September 1954), 692–704; Lester G. Seligman, "Party Recruitment and the Party Structure: A Case History," *American Political Science Review* 55 (March 1961), 77–86; and Leon D. Epstein, *Politics in Wisconsin* (Madison, Wis.: University of Wisconsin Press, 1958), 90–97.

11. For a more recent reading on Virginia, see Philip L. Martin and others, "Republican Grassroot Leadership in Virginia and West Virginia: Continuity and Change, 1966 to 1970," in *Politics 74,* Tinsley E. Yarbrough and others (editors) (Greenville, N.C.: East Carolina University Publications, 1974), 1–26.

12. Kirk H. Porter, "The Deserted Primary in Iowa," *American Political Science Review* 39 (December 1945), 732–740; on Wisconsin, see Epstein, *Politics in Wisconsin,* 199; on Pennsylvania, see Sorauf, *Party and Representation,* 111; and for several non-Southern states, see Key, *American State Politics,* 178.

13. William H. Standing and James A. Robinson, "Inter-Party Competition and Primary Contesting: The Case of Indiana," *American Political Science Review* 52 (December 1958), 1066–1077.

14. Ibid.
15. David Gold and John R. Schmidhauser, "Urbanization and Party Competition: The Case of Iowa," *Midwest Journal of Political Science* 4 (February 1960), 62–75.
16. Key, *American State Politics,* 230–246; Phillips Cutright, "Urbanization and Competitive Party Politics," *Journal of Politics* 25 (August 1963), 552–564; and Heinz Eulau, "The Ecological Bases of Party Systems: The Case of Ohio," *Midwest Journal of Political Science* 1 (February 1957), 125–135.
17. Lockard, *Connecticut's Challenge Primary,* 1.
18. James W. Davis, *Presidential Primaries: Road to the White House* (New York: Crowell Collier Macmillan, 1967), 261–273.
19. See Chapter 9.
20. Davis, *Presidential Primaries,* in his chapter 10 surveys the pros and cons of presidential primaries.
21. These criticisms appear, among other places, in The National Municipal League, *A Model Direct Primary Election System* (New York: National Municipal League, 1951), 14–18.

The candidate [John Lindsay] toured synagogues with such regularity that he was a more familiar sight than fountain pens at a Bar Mitzvah.

Until the moment of truth, a candidate does not know whether he is the bullfighter or the bull.

If you're lucky, even your broom will shoot straight.

It is true that an occasional candidate can win a particularly difficult race by employing interesting and unique campaign strategies. But it is also true that the largest percentage of contested seats are decided with little regard for campaign styles or political tactics.

The political significance of low participation becomes apparent when we consider that nonvoters are disproportionately concentrated among the rural poor, the urban slum dwellers, the welfare recipients, the underemployed, the young, the elderly, the low-income and nonunion workers and the racial minorities. The entire voting process is dominated by middle-class styles and conditions which tend to discourage lower-class participation.

Elections give people a chance to express discontents and enthusiasms, to enjoy a sense of involvement. This is participation in a ritual act, however; only in a minor degree is it participation in policy formation. Like all ritual, whether in primitive or modern societies, elections draw attention to common social ties and to the importance and apparent reasonableness of accepting the public policies that are adopted.

Election Campaigns

One election campaign looks very much like any other. At heart, they are all efforts at persuasive communication in which candidates are those making the effort to persuade while those to be persuaded are the electorate. The things that are done in one campaign bear close resemblance to those done in another, a sign surely of broad agreement among those who participate in campaigns on what kinds of efforts offer the best chance of producing the desired payoff. What is the payoff? Winning on election day. A campaign manager in California once put it rather well when he said that in politics, winning may not be everything, but losing is nothing. Yet candidates do lose. Understanding why *some* campaigns succeed while the others do not is what most of this chapter is about.

Who participates in elections and who does not? How different are they? How numerous? About participation, much is known. It is a subject of considerable interest and importance. Nonparticipation, on the other hand, receives much less attention, even from those who consider themselves close students of politics. Yet consider: Even though turnout in presidential elections is usually higher than for other elections, the number of people who did *not* vote in the 1968 election was greater by far than the number who voted for the winning candidate. When the ranks of the nonparticipants become that numerous, the subject of nonparticipation is one that must engage our concern.

Talking politics and voting are the two forms of political activity in which the greatest number of citizens engage. Of these, voting is by far the more important, because indirectly, through the choosing of policy makers, it can leave an impact upon the substance of public policy. But can elections command that policy must take a particular direction? The common view is that they cannot. Why this is so is briefly considered in the concluding section of the chapter.

At the operating level of any election campaign, there is only one immediate objective: to see that enough people go to the polls on election day to produce a victory for a candidate (or a defeat for his opponent), or a victory or defeat for an issue being put to a vote.

Campaigns may help to realize other objectives, and these can be important. A campaign may educate both the candidate and the voter. It can provide a valuable chance to define new issues or clarify old ones. It can, and often does, provide a test of the effectiveness of a party organization, perhaps even to the point of exposing that organization as weak and splintered. It is a time for doing some political recruitment, for registering new voters, reinforcing the loyalties of partisans, and rounding up new actives and candidates. However, regardless of the value of realizing these goals, they still remain secondary to the all-important objective of winning.

Major Features of Campaigns

Who Participates? People get involved in a campaign for many different reasons, and their reasons for wanting an election victory may be equally as varied. Some may realize that a victory is the only guarantee that they will continue to hold their government job or, much to the same point, retain their influence in the halls of government. Some work out of a personal loyalty to a candidate or an intense commitment to an issue.

Even the most casual look at the ranks of campaign workers in recent elections indicates that the number of workers who are there out of loyalty to a candidate and/or concern with an issue has increased dramatically, with consequences for the political system that are not easily measured. And a number of persons work hours on end out of a sense of party duty or because they are enjoying a love affair with politics: The frantic busyness and hoopla make campaigns the most infectious of all pleasant contagions.

Yet millions of Americans—by far the greatest portion of the electorate—largely limit their participation in the campaign to going to the polls to cast ballots on election day, perhaps having first attended to getting their names listed on the roster of eligible voters, if the laws of the state require periodic registration. Periodic surveys of electoral involvement indicate that the number of voters who actually participate in campaigns beyond the point of voting varies little from one election to the next and is never more than a small percentage of the whole of the electorate. Data from surveys made in the presidential election years of 1960 through 1972 are given in Table 8–1.

The Impact of Campaigns. There are essentially two ways to win an election: A candidate can be successful in garnering enough support to his or her side to produce the votes needed to win on election day. Or, to exactly the same end, the candidate

Table 8-1 Campaign Activities in 1960, 1964, 1968, and 1972

Question	1960	1964	1968	1972
Do you belong to any political club or organization?	3%	4%	3%	4%
Did you give any money or buy tickets or anything to help the campaign for one of the parties of candidates?	11	11	11	10
Did you go to any political meetings rallies, dinners, or things like that?	8	8	14	10
Did you do any other work for one of the parties or candidates?	5	5	5	6

Source: Center for Political Studies, University of Michigan.

may succeed in discouraging the potential supporters of the opponent, so that they fail to turn out in sufficient numbers to give the opponent the victory. Either strategy will succeed, and since the strategies are not mutually exclusive, a combination of the two may also be employed. Certain factors—one being the ratio of party identifiers within a community—may dictate the choice of one strategic emphasis over the other.

Whichever strategy is chosen, it is abundantly clear from past elections that no matter how massive are the efforts made in a campaign, the campaign itself is likely to have a limited impact upon the decisions made on election day by millions of voters. That is because one of the givens with which campaign strategies must reckon is that many voters, including those most strongly identified with a party, make up their minds how they will cast their ballots long before election day comes around.[1] Data on the time by which voters reported having made up their minds in the presidential elections of 1960 through 1972 are given in Table 8–2.

How Competitive Are Elections?   Public offices in many areas in the country are correctly judged to be securely in the hands of one party or the other, in large part because by far the largest portion of the electorate in a given area identifies with one party rather than with the other.

The office of governor generally falls into the competitive category, especially in the Western states, and the tide of party fortunes can change quickly. Success in the general elections of 1969 put the Republicans in control of 32 governorships, their best showing since the 1920s. In the succeeding five years that situation changed drastically. After the returns from state elections were counted in November, 1974, the Democrats found themselves in control of 38 governorships, more than they had controlled since the previous peak of Democratic success in the Depression year of 1938.

Statehouses present a different story in part because so many of them until very recently were severely malapportioned. In the past decade that condition has altered a little and the chance to be genuinely competitive—which reapportionment decisions have offered minority parties in several states—has led to an increase in the frequency of minority party challenges in races for the state legislature.

Table 8-2   Distribution of Democratic and Republican Votes for
              for President According to Time of Decision, 1960–1972

Decided	1960	1964	1968	1972
Before conventions	30%	40%	33%	43%
During conventions	30	25	22	17
After conventions	36	33	38	35
Don't remember	4	3	7	4

Source: Center for Political Studies, University of Michigan.

The presidency may be judged to be openly competitive.
Each party may look at the record provided in Table 8–3 and
properly conclude that in any upcoming election, that grand
prize of American politics is up for grabs. In the postwar period,
Republican candidates have won the presidency four times,
while the Democrats have won it three. Three of these seven
elections, the elections of 1956, 1964, and 1972, deserve to be
called landslides, but in three others, 1948, 1960, and 1968,
the winning candidate was actually the choice of only a minority
of voters.

A similar judgment cannot easily be made about most
other offices in America. Take Congress for example. In 1972,
as in all congressional elections in the past several decades, all
435 members of the House of Representatives were required to
run for election if they wanted to remain in Congress. And as in
previous elections, better than 80 percent of those 435 members
did not have any real fear that they would lose.

Table 8-3   Outcome of Presidential Elections
              1948–1972

Year	Candidate	Party	Popular Vote
1948	Truman	Democrat	49.6%
1952	Eisenhower	Republican	55.1
1956	Eisenhower	Republican	57.4
1960	Kennedy	Democrat	49.7
1964	Johnson	Democrat	61.1
1968	Nixon	Republican	43.4
1972	Nixon	Republican	60.8

The facts of the matter are that in 1972:

Forty-two seats in the House were not even contested. The candidates nominated by one of the two major political parties enjoyed a free ride. Forty of these seats were won by incumbents and two by nonincumbents. Imagine a seat in the House of Representatives so safe for one party that its candidate *can be a newcomer and yet run unopposed!*

Nine seats were contested, but the opposition was provided by a demonstrably weak Independent or third party candidate.

Three hundred and thirteen other incumbents ran for election and won, most of them by a comfortable margin, winning 66 percent or better of the popular vote.

Twelve incumbents were defeated. Two of these were defeated in newly created districts which pitted one incumbent from the 1971–1972 session against another. One of the incumbents had to lose.

In 27 districts, no incumbent was running, but the victor was of the *same* party as the previous incumbent. In 16 districts, no incumbent was running, and the winner was of a *different* party from the previous incumbent.

And finally, 16 contests were held for new seats—seats which were created as a result of the reapportionment of congressional seats required following the taking of the 1970 census.

From this 1972 data it is possible to make a rough estimate of the number of seats in the House that are safe for one party or the other, and the number that are marginal. If we count as safe only those in which (1) the nominee of one of the parties ran unopposed or against clearly weak opposition, or in which (2) the winner obtained 66 percent or more of the popular vote (roughly a two-to-one victory over his opponent), then the number of safe seats in the House turns out to be 206. If we categorize as competitive any seats in which the winning candidate's share of the popular vote was 55 percent or less, the number of competitive seats is 62. Finally, if we categorize the other 167 seats in the House—those in which the winning candidate's share of the vote was between 55 and 66 percent—as leaning toward one party or the other, the result is that presented in

Table 8-4   Outcome of Elections to House of Representatives, 1972

Competitive Status	New Seats	No Con-test	Weak Oppo-sition	Incum-bent Re-elected	New Mem-bers	Incum-bent De-feated
Safe Democratic	2	35	8	83	3	1
Leaning Democratic	3	—	—	76	5	2
Competitive	4	—	—	31	20	7
Leaning Republican	6	—	—	62	11	2
Safe Republican	1	7	1	61	4	—

Table 8-4. Nearly half the seats in the House can be described as safe for one party or the other. About one-seventh of them appear to be competitive. Clearly, the kind of competition that characterizes contests for the presidency are the exception when it comes to Congress.[2]

How does one secure a majority of votes for one candidate on election day? The answer is simple: by making sure the voters who favor that candidate go to the polls on election day in greater numbers than do the voters who favor his opponent. A successful campaign strategy must, therefore, be designed to accomplish these two things: *identify the candidate's supporters, and then in some fashion get these supporters to the polls in sufficient numbers to insure his election.* It is a task that is seldom without serious problems, as witnessed by the fact that in any election year normally about one-half of the strategies designed with these ends in mind must lose! It is perhaps the calculation that the chances of developing a successful campaign strategy are not often better than fifty-fifty, that discourages candidates from believing they can afford to relax, do nothing on behalf of their own candidacy, and still win the election hands down. Always lurking in the shadows offstage is the rival candidates, the undeveloped issue, or—most galling to the candidate—public apathy, which by keeping supporters at home allows the opponent to win by default. Every candidate, therefore, develops at least some line of campaign strategy which he hopes will realize the object of the campaign: his election to public office.

The Appeal to Party. A political campaign is an effort in persuasion. But exactly who is to be persuaded? And how is it to be done? A number of considerations enter into the equation. Are we talking about a primary or a general election?

ITS LIMITED USE IN PRIMARIES. Primaries are often free-for-alls in which appeals to party (which might be serviceable in a general election) have limited utility, precisely because all the candidates running claim allegiance to the same party. Thus, characteristically, candidates in a primary tend to stress their own special virtues—integrity, commitment, general reputation, civic interest, familiarity with public affairs, and the like. When possible, they may also try to garner support by taking a popular stand upon issues that either separate them from their primary opponents or are of known concern to those who are most likely to vote in the primary, or both.

ITS USE IN GENERAL ELECTIONS. On the other hand, a campaign for a general election is likely to require a different emphasis. When the party strength in the district is overwhelmingly in the candidate's favor, he may properly rely upon strong appeals to party. His opponent is most likely to stress the virtue of "voting the man, not the party." So much is obvious. Appeals to party loyalty certainly have been at the heart of a great many successful campaigns.

POSSIBLE DISADVANTAGES. But party is not always enough. It may even backfire, if the party has become identifiable with a demonstrably unpopular issue or a candidate. Such was the case with literally hundreds of Republican candidates for state and national office in 1964, who found it was no easy task to run as a Republican when the none-too-popular Barry Goldwater was at the head of the Republican ticket.[3] A few candidates, but only a few, found that an advantage: *Their* supporters liked Goldwater, and there were enough of them in the district to provide a margin of victory. A much more common problem faced by candidates is what to do when they discover that even the most loyal partisans are out of sorts with the party because it has come to be identified with the side of an issue which they cannot bring themselves to support. This is a problem not only for candidates, but for voters. Such was the problem posed by the Vietnam War in 1968. Since the early 1960s, blacks had declared themselves, both by word and vote, to be strong supporters of the national Democratic party, because it had come to be identified through the decade of the 1960s with a strong pro-civil rights stand. Yet blacks were among the most severely critical of the Vietnam War, a war that was being waged under the leadership of a Democratic president and vice-president who gave every appearance of being more inclined to continue the war than to end it. In the end, the appeal of party proved stronger than disapproval of the war, and few blacks chose to give their support to Republican candidates. Given the deep interest blacks have in the matter of civil rights, that in itself is not as surprising as that turnout among blacks remained as high as it did.[4] For one convenient way the voter may handle the problem of reconciling two contradictory influences upon his vote is not to vote at all. That is an outcome never appreciated by any candidate of the majority party who suffers a defeat because his campaign failed in its mission of turning a natural majority among the electorate into a margin of victory on election day.

Nor are appeals to party likely to be that valuable anytime the proportion of Independents to party identifiers is high, as it is today. Indeed, a too-loud proclamation of a candidate's party associations may well prove counterproductive if it convinces any sizable number of Independents that they will receive a warmer welcome from the other side.

The appeal to party does have its uses, the greatest being its service in reinforcing party loyalties—in reassuring those who identify with the party that continuing to support it at the polls still makes sense. The appeal to party is most likely to prove counterproductive if it is done so stridently that it discourages support from those who call themselves Independents, or if it is done at a time when partisans are troubled by some stand the party has taken on issues.

The Trouble with Issues.   Issues, more often than party, are what usually give candidates the worst headache. There is no end of irony in this, because the evidence from a multitude of election studies indicates, first, that elections rarely provide a clear policy referendum (though the 1972 presidential election appears as a clear exception); second, that voters through their collective decisionmaking in elections do not prescribe specific governmental action; and third, that the crucial decisions on policy are made not by the elector but by the elected. Nonetheless, candidates in any election are expected to say something about "the issues." So the question must always be faced: How should the candidate handle issues?

If the issue (or issues) has been defined, and if the electorate's feelings toward it can be gauged, the candidate's decision may be a hard one to make, but at least the choices are clear. He may find, best of all possible worlds, that the position he would be inclined to take on the issue in any event is precisely that favored by the larger portion of the electorate. Such has been the experience of southern white candidates on the subject of civil rights for decades.

WHEN CANDIDATE AND VOTERS DISAGREE. If, on the other hand, he learns that his own inclinations mirror those of only a minority, and particularly if he discovers that his own preferences differ from the preferences of his partisans, then he may move in either of two directions. He may adjust his thinking to follow the crowd, in effect, a not unreasonable course for a public servant to take. Or instead, he may choose to make his disagreement with the majority known. This latter course is not necessarily either brash or foolhardy. If he comes across as an independent person, capable of thinking for himself, honest in making his views known, persuasive in argument, and knowledgeable about the subject, the result may be to shift attention from the issue to the admirable qualities of the candidate himself. One of the most notable examples of a candidate's turning an issue to his advantage was the success John F. Kennedy had in turning the "religious issue," his being a Roman Catholic, to his advantage, by making it seem as though those who opposed him wanted to use a man's own religion as the sole test of his fitness to be president. There can never be any guarantee that such an approach will work, and most candidates faced with such a problem are likely to follow the course of avoidance, rather than confrontation.

WHEN ISSUES DO NOT EMERGE. But suppose no issue has emerged? And suppose the appeal to party must be limited, perhaps because the number of Independents is so large? That is the tough one. For what is left except the appeal of the candidate himself . . . and the real possibility that the election is engaging so little of the electorate's concern that turnout will be low and the outcome will hinge upon such unpredictable events as some other contest, or even the weather. That is not an uncommon situation. Even in presidential elections, fully half the electorate say after the election that they could not recall any one issue that struck them as important. And not a few candidates have been told by their pollsters that the people they surveyed reported that the most important current issue was taxes, or schools, or big government, or the economy, or prices—but that even this "big" issue was mentioned by only 5 or 7 percent of the sample interviewed. These are the times that try the ingenuity, to say nothing of the patience, of the candidate and his organization.

The Nonparticipating

All campaigns are intended to maximize turnout—not necessarily turnout across the board, but certainly the turnout of each candidate's own supporters. But what of those millions of adults who never participate in elections? Gallup estimates their number at not less than 40 million. In the presidential election of 1968, more adults over the age of 18 *did not vote* for president (47 million in all) than voted for the winning candidate (32 million). *Forty or more million people is a large number of people.* It would be a serious mistake to understate its conceivable impact. As E. E. Schattschneider put it, those who *do* participate in elections

> are at the mercy of the rest of the nation which would swamp all existing political alignments if it chose to do so. The whole balance of power in the political system could be overturned by a massive invasion of the political system, and nothing tangible protects the system against the flood. All that is necessary to

produce the most painless revolution in history, the first revolution ever legalized and legitimized in advance, is to have a
sufficient number of people do something not much more
difficult than to walk across the street on election day.[5]

The Two Categories of Nonparticipants.   Who are these people?
By far the largest number of nonparticipants share characteristics
which we have noted earlier: They have a low level of political
interest and efficacy, they are young rather than old (though
some are both old and infirm), they have little in the way of
formal education, and are more likely to be Independent or
apolitical than Democrats or Republicans. But among the nonparticipants we also find some—an increasing number probably
—who are not at all well pictured by that listing of characteristics. They may be young, some of them, and they may think of
themselves as Independents rather than as Democrats or Republicans, but they score high on political interest and information, they have a concern with social issues, they have gone to
college or are going to college, and their background is middle
or upper-middle class.[6]

Thus, there are two distinguishable categories of nonparticipants. Why do they not participate? Numerous reasons could
be advanced, but two deserve special mention.

Reasons for Nonparticipation.

THE REGISTRATION SYSTEM.   The first is a notable feature
of American electoral arrangements: the registration system in
use across the country. This alone places a formidable barrier
in the way of anyone who is concerned to increase political participation, especially among the poor. On this score, America
offers a striking contrast to other Western industrial nations. Elsewhere, the job of preparing a list of eligible voters is seen as a
responsibility of the government. In America, the burden is
placed squarely on the shoulders of the citizen.

At the very least, registration requires time and information.
Where do I go to register? Can I get there by bus or subway?
Can someone register for me? Can I do it by mail? What ques-
tions will I have to answer? Must I bring documents with me?
Can I do it sometime other than during working hours? Will a

registration booth be set up in my shopping center? When does the registration period end? What happens if I move? Am I still registered if I marry and choose to change my name? How do I establish residence? (Every state requires residence in the state for a period of time before one may register to vote; almost all require, as well, residence within a voting district.) Is there any point in registering when I know I am going to be several states away from home in November or whenever the election is? If I registered once before, do I have to do it again? Do I have to vote in every election in order to stay registered?

Even if one is encouraged to find the time and acquire the information it takes to complete registration, there is still the hazard of embarrassment or fear. The Mexican American or Indian whose command of English is weak, or the southern black whose acquaintance with the ways of the sheriff and his deputies comes firsthand, are only two examples of those whose reluctance to face a bureaucrat to register is not hard to understand.[7]

In every election year, it is easy to find campaign organizations committed to mounting a registration drive. The fear is always that on election day the number of one's supporters registered will be less than the number registered for the last election. The hope is always that the number can be increased substantially before the period of registration ends. The results are often disappointing, even when the effort is well conceived, closely organized, and supported with adequate resources. In 1967, to give just one illustration, a local chapter of the Congress of Racial Equality (CORE) in Cleveland, supported by a $25,000 grant for voter education from the Ford Foundation, undertook a campaign to register voters in three wards of the city. CORE used leaflets, neighborhood canvassers, sound trucks, baby-sitters, and transportation to and from the Office of the Board of Elections; the drive was well advertised in the press and on television and at booths set up at shopping centers; and when the results were in, they showed a net gain in new registrations of 1,147, at a cost of roughly $20 per registrant! [8]

ALIENATION. The second major reason for nonparticipation, alienation, is part institutional, part sociopsychological.

Distinctive family lifestyles make a contribution: The Indian whose immediate daily concern is with tribal matters; the Mexican American woman whose culture encourages leaving politics in the hands of men; the migrant workers, always moving, unconnected; the southern black, sharing with his brothers a history of being deliberately, effectively excluded from the rights of participation—all are likely candidates for the ranks of the nonparticipating. For others, nonparticipation is the product of experience. Students discovering that years of protest have left little permanent impact upon "the system"; black youths learning firsthand that fire in the streets is a surer way to get "the man" than any amount of balloting; the coal miner with black lung and no job; the high school graduate with a job, but angry over busing and taxes—all may share a common disenchantment and sense of disillusion with the electoral process.

The Impact of Nonparticipation. Does this nonparticipation make a difference? Most certainly it does. It has already made its impact felt upon the present structure of the political parties. Because the nonparticipants possess the characteristics observed, their nonparticipation leaves the electoral process in the hands of an active electorate that displays much greater homogeneity of social characteristics and political interests than would be the case if the nonparticipants were mobilized. And while iffy history is always risky, particularly when one is making estimates of future possibilities, it is essential to note that those who are most likely *not* to participate in elections have the very characteristics of those who are among the strongest supporters of left-of-center parties in other countries. If American politics is emphatically centrist in character and lacking in ideological content, it is in part because class lines are not especially sharply drawn. It is in part because both major parties have succeeded in attracting as supporters at least some people from all strata of the society.[9] And it is in part because millions of Americans who might, in pursuit of their interests, provide a major source of cleavage, are not in fact participating.

Can any issue, any event, any leader, provide a focal point for mobilizing such diverse groups as Indians, college-educated youths, long-haired brick layers, urban blacks? That is a question for later consideration. For the moment all that we need say is that if mobilization of the presently nonparticipating were accomplished, the shock to the parties and the political system might be profound.

The Common Paraphernalia of American Election Campaigns

Senator Abraham Ribicoff of Connecticut says there are only two sound rules for campaigning. The first is Do what has worked before, and the other is Try everything. The evidence of past campaigns suggests that there are a good many believers in Ribicoff's laws. Furthermore, there also appears to be a widespread acceptance—an almost automatic acceptance—of the idea that there are certain jobs that must be attended to in *any* campaign if the campaign is to have any chance of success. These jobs include, but are by no means limited to, establishing a headquarters, conducting a registration drive, surveying public opinion; preparing campaign materials, including (and sometimes especially) materials for television; tailoring campaign appeals and actions to special groups; scheduling the candidate's time; raising money; and managing a "get-out-the-vote" drive on election day.[10]

Headquarters.   If the candidate is running for a seat in the state legislature, or for circuit clerk, headquarters is likely to be the kitchen or living room of his home. If he is running for Congress or governor, headquarters is likely to be a storefront somewhere downtown, and indeed there may be several branch headquarters. Simple or elaborate, one or many, the point of having a headquarters is to enable people to know that there is some one place where contact may be made with the candidate, someplace, hopefully, where the conduct of the campaign will be directed.

Conducting a Registration Drive.   In a well-designed campaign, someone is going to know how people have voted in previous elections, perhaps not only for the office the candidate is running for but for other offices as well. Variations in registration rates and turnout do occur. Any candidate who does not know that, knows nothing about elections. One year a precinct may have 1,800 registered voters. They may all be Democrats (or Republicans), and they may have a history of voting for the same candidates. Yet two years later, three months before the next election, registration may have dropped to 300. Obviously, if the candidate thinks of these people as probable supporters, it is decidedly in his interest to see that a registration drive is undertaken (and also, let it be noted, to see that an active get-out-the-vote drive is scheduled for election day, because it is in precincts that show the greatest variation in registration rates that people are also least likely to get themselves to the polls on election day).

The point of a registration drive is to register as eligible voters people who are though to be a given candidate's likely supporters. A decision to undertake a registration drive therefore assumes that (1) the candidate can identify likely supporters, and (2) the number voters who can be registered as a result of the drive and thus be able to cast a ballot on election day can make a difference in the outcome of an election.

IDENTIFYING SUPPORTERS. Identifying a candidate's potential supporters is not usually all that difficult. A listing of how people voted in previous elections will quickly show that some precinct went heavily for the candidates of one party in earlier elections, while some supported candidates of the other major party, while still other precincts were fairly evenly divided. A check of the number of registered voters in each precinct will usually indicate where registration efforts promise the greatest payoff.

If the candidate has never run for office before, this much information may be all that can be obtained and may be enough to indicate where registration efforts should be made. If, on the other hand, he is an incumbent, his targeting of precincts can be even more carefully done, because he has the advantage of knowing not just how well precincts have supported candidates of his party before, but exactly how well they have supported *him*.

COSTS AND RISKS OF A DRIVE. Registration drives are never cheap. They involve considerable expenditure of resources— more often the human resources of energy, time, and patience than hard cash. The payoff in terms of increased registrations may be slight, considering the amount of resources spent. They are one of the high-risk ventures of any campaign. Nor do they offer any guarantee whatever of making a contribution to electoral success. Resources spent on a registration drive must be considered unwisely spent if turnout on election day is lower than hoped for or (even worse, but less likely) if newly registered voters choose to vote the "wrong" way.

Surveying public opinion.   Surveys of public opinion designed to find out what is on the mind of the voter may be of two kinds. The first is a professionally taken survey of a sample of the whole of a population. The other is a survey of all or many members of a segment of a population, such as all or most of the people living in a precinct.[11]

SURVEYING A TARGET PRECINCT.   The latter kind of survey can easily be done by volunteer members of the campaign staff. Such a survey can provide enormously useful information about, say, the people living in a target precinct, a precinct that is thought to provide major support for the candidate. What issues are the voters upset about? Do they know the candidate? Are they strongly partisan? Would they be willing to help out in the campaign? Do they need a ride to the polls on election day? Do they need to get an absentee ballot? If a registration drive within target precincts is undertaken, a survey of this kind can be a useful adjunct to the drive itself. The only danger in relying too reavily on information provided from such a survey about issues, the parties, and the candidates is that those who gather such information may be inclined to hear what they want to hear and may report back to campaign headquarters that the candidate is well known and liked, that enthusiasm for the campaign is high, that turnout is definitely going to be up over the previous election, and that the candidate can't possibly lose—when that may not be the case at all.[12]

SAMPLING A POPULATION.   A professionally conducted survey of a sample of the population—if it is properly done— should provide reliable estimates of the feelings of the population. It can provide information about how the candidate and his party are perceived—and what issues, if any, are visible. Such a survey may be most useful if it pinpoints important differences between the campaigns of rival candidates, telling the candidate not only how his own campaign is going but how his competitor's campaign is perceived. This kind of survey produces an information base which can be of great assistance in the evaluation of possible campaign strategies. It may prove especially valuable if its results strongly suggest where the always-scarce resources of a campaign may most wisely be spent.[13]

PROBLEMS WITH SURVEYS.   Like anything else in a campaign, surveys are not a guarantee of success. In fact, they can be dispiriting if they indicate, as they may, that a campaign has little chance of success. Further, survey taking is an extremely technical business, not something for either amateurs or incompetents. Yet even among survey outfits that claim to be professional, the methods employed are often questionable. In addition, surveys, to be valuable, must be thoughtfully constructed not only to meet well-recognized standards of proper survey design, but also to meet the needs of the campaign. A survey that does not meet this dual requirement probably represents campaign money unwisely spent. But who will know? Few candidates are at all expert in survey design. Worse, candidates do not know what questions need to be asked in order that the information supplied by the survey may be used to maximum advantage in the campaign.

For all the problems associated with professional surveys—their high cost, their inconsistent reliability, their clearly limited value if the thrust of the design is off course—surveys have come into their own in the last 20 years. They are a staple of any campaign for major office. Literally millions of dollars are spent in a presidential election year on surveys. They provide a measurement of public opinion at a given moment in time, and they can be valuable not only as a help in deciding what should be done during a campaign but also taken after an election, as an aid in finding out what went wrong during a campaign, so that, hopefully, whatever mistakes were made can be avoided in the future.

Campaign Materials.   Buttons, bumper strips, billboards, flyers, posters on a stick on a front lawn, signs in a window, tie clasps, rings, campaign hats, and all those television spots for months before election day—these are an established part of the communications effort of American election campaigns. They are the best evidence that a campaign is underway. They constitute a major drain on campaign resources.

Do they accomplish anything? Probably very little, if one judges the value of any campaign effort by the favorable impact it may have upon voters. In fact, reports from postelection surveys indicate that few voters are consciously aware of this kind of campaign material—with the exception of television materials. The greatest value of such materials is in providing reinforcement of the preferences and loyalty of those already favorably disposed to a campaign.[14] There is something to be said about the reassuring value for a voter in seeing how many more bumper strips there are favorable to his candidate than there are advertising his opponent.[15] But anyone in a campaign headquarters will tell you that a lot of buttons either end up in the hands of those far too young to vote or are carefully stashed away by those whose hobby is to collect them.

Materials prepared for the media, especially those prepared for television, are a somewhat different matter. A great deal is known about who watches television, how many hours each day, during what time periods, and what kind of programs they prefer. If spots for the Democratic candidate for president appear immediately before and after the evening news on CBS far more often than do spots for the Republican candidate, it is likely because media studies over several years have shown that many who watch that show are inclined to be Democratic partisans. Similarly, if Republican candidates for major office place far more political advertisements in your local newspaper than do Democrats, it may not be merely the result of superior Republican resources; it may instead be because media studies have also observed a political bias among the readership of daily newspapers that tends to favor Republicans over Democrats.

But what is to be said? There is considerable range both in the imagination and skill brought to the preparation of media materials, whether they are supposed to entertain, sell bathtub cleanser, or promote a political candidate. Television time is especially expensive. As much as 60 percent of the total funds of a major campaign may go to this side of the campaign effort.

And as is true of survey research, in this area there are both experts and bunglers.

A man sits at a desk, stolid, a flag on the right of him, a flag on the left of him, unsmiling, talking about the need for a new procedure for assessing commercial, business, and residential property, and unimproved lands, the need for a consolidation of stage agencies, and more autonomy for local taxing authorities. Will anyone listen besides his mother? Yet when a president of the United States addresses the nation in just such a setting in the Oval Office, people *do* watch.

A 10-second spot shows the sweep second hand of a stopwatch counting down the seconds from 10 to 1, while a voice in the background says: "Can you name three good things that Gerald Ford has done while he has been in office? . . . Two? . . . One? . . ." Too clever by far? Likely to irritate Republicans, making them even more ardent in their support of the Republican candidate? Or is it both funny (and thus good television sport), as well as comforting to Democrats? A spot like this will hardly succeed in doing anything except give the Republican candidate advertising time he has not had to pay for, unless you are correct in your hunch that most people will freeze when faced with the demand to supply three positive statements about *any* subject in what seems like a very short time, especially when the ticking sound of the stopwatch arrests their attention.

An incumbent president running for reelection for a second term and his wife visit the home of four people referred to as Mom, Dad, Sis, and Junior. The message of the advertisement—illustrated by references to the two cars in the garage, the new dishwasher, clothes dryer, and freezer, Dad's higher paycheck, the vacations they have taken, the cabin on the lake, the new piano, and the bikes for Sis and Junior—is that times are much, much better now than they were four years ago. At the conclusion, the president and his wife join hands, face the camera, and sing "God Bless America." Is this a bit much? Hard to take? Perhaps so, for the television audience of the 1970s, but this proved to be by far the most successful piece of campaign advertising produced for television in 1956 in support of the candidacy of incumbent President Dwight D. Eisenhower.

As with almost all campaign materials, media material is prepared with the reachable supporter in mind. Studies of opinion formation have consistently told us since the 1930s that partisans pay heed to messages that are intended to reinforce the opinions they are already predisposed to hold. They are much less likely to give attention to appeals which are designed to shake their beliefs. The weaker the partisan, the less attention he is inclined to pay to any political communications.

This observed behavior makes it difficult to be overly concerned with the possibility that—as is sometimes argued [16]—with just enough money, just enough cleverness, and enough media time available for purchase, almost any candidate can be sold to the voter. The argument might be taken a little more seriously if it were being made about soap, or cold remedies, or laundry detergents. But unlike the consumer of commodities, the consumer of political advertising brings to it a well-developed set of political biases. He knows even before the advertisement begins what he is prepared to hear and believe. His partisanship and his recall of events give him an independent reference point for evaluating what he is told by the advertisement. Any media entrepeneur who sets out to market a candidate exactly as he might a toothpaste will, if he is at all observant, soon learn that the sales pitch that works when the commodity is toothpaste does not work nearly so well when the product is political.[17]

Appeals to Special Groups.   A candidate from a farm district is going to spend some time talking with farmers. Fall election campaigns come at a time when annual fairs are held, and the candidate will certainly spend time there because that is where a significant number of his constituents are going to be. A candidate in a district in which there are a large number of labor union members is going to spend some time shaking hands at the factory gates (or the mine entrance) when the shift changes. Both will probably respond to the request they receive from the League of Women Voters asking them to provide a statement about themselves and their stand on issues which will be published in a League "newspaper" a few weeks before election day.

WHAT CAN GROUPS GIVE THE CANDIDATE?   There are literally tens of thousands of special groups in America. Some of them are actively courted by candidates because they are able to provide him with three resources vital to a campaign: (1) money, always a usable commodity, (2) manpower, useful in such tedious and time-consuming projects as voter registration, and (3) an endorsement by group leaders which provides for group members as indication that the candidate has been found worthy of their support.[18]

POLITICALLY PROMINENT GROUPS.   Not all groups stand at the same proximity to politics. Some have little or no interest in politics. (It is difficult to see what a candidate might say in a letter to all members of a philatelic society after he said that he had always loved stamp collecting.) Others have acquired a well-developed sense of group identity and have been able to relate that to political action. Among those that are noted for having an interest in politics we must include:

1. Business groups, especially those concerned with government contracts; those concerned with taxation (e.g., the petroleum industry, the savings and loan association, and the dairy industry); and those regulated by government, including truckers and utilities.
2. Labor unions, notably the United Auto Workers, the United Steel Workers, the Ladies Garment Workers Union, the Machinists, and the Teamsters.
3. Groups of government employees, such as the National Federation of Postal Clerks.
4. Medical and health groups, notably the American Medical Association.
5. Veterans groups, such as the American Legion and the Veterans of Foreign Wars.
6. Farm groups, notably the National Farmers Union and the Farm Bureau.

Groups are not equally prominent in all constituencies. The Farm Bureau is rarely a strong influence within urban areas; unions are seldom a measurable influence except within urban areas; while veterans groups are found almost everywhere. Groups are no different from individuals when it comes to elections. They would rather back a winner than a loser. Thus the record of group action shows that incumbents and sure winners have a better chance of receiving group support than either the newcomer or the candidate who is running in a close race. Nor are groups equally hospitable to all candidates. Unions are generally more receptive to appeals for support from Democrats, while business groups are a little more inclined to tender support to Republicans. In this respect, groups merely mirror the dominant political preferences of their individual members.[19]

Raising Money.   The amount of money spent on campaigns for major offices has increased dramatically in the past 20 years. There are few men or women in the country anymore who can afford the burden of financing a major campaign from their own pockets.[20]

Where does the money come from? Typically, the largest share comes from those who can afford to contribute amounts of $500 or more. Substantial amounts are also contributed by organized interest groups. A donation to the Nixon campaign of more than $900,000 by the political arm of the Associated Milk Producers Association in 1972 attracted public attention, criticism, and criminal prosecution, not because it was so large, but because it was not made until 10 days before the election—and thus invited a reasonable suspicion that Nixon's campaign managers had some reason for wanting the donation concealed from public view until after the election was decided.[21]

NONCASH CONTRIBUTIONS.   How much is spent? We know as little about campaign finance as we know about any other important aspect of campaigns. State laws require campaign receipts and expenditures to be reported. But a campaign finance law probably cannot be devised that will realistically gauge the costs of running a major election campaign. For one thing, the amount of contributions made not in cash, but in kind and services, is always substantial, and these are seldom counted in the calculation of campaign costs reported publicly; contributions of man-hours from the local union hall; the skill of a $45,000-a-year advertising man, "on leave" from his company for six months; company cars loaned for election day to aid in getting voters to the polls; the car loaned by the local automobile agency for a day or for the entire period of the campaign; office space provided free or at a reduced rate; a gasoline credit card loaned for the period of a registration drive; a postage meter volunteered by an optician for the mailing of an appeal directed to his fellow opticians in the state (his proud contribution to the campaign); the food and manpower provided for endless evenings and Saturday mornings in the voter registration drive—the list of such strictly noncash contributions is always long.

DEMANDS FOR REGULATION OF CAMPAIGN FINANCE.   Yet
the demand for some regulation of campaign finance does not
diminish. Why? There is no evidence that money in itself is a
guarantee of an election victory. No one variable, neither money
nor party identification, can always be counted on to provide a
sure victory. There is, however, some indication that if the *difference* between the resources available to two candidates *is great
enough,* then money can make a measurable contribution to the
outcome, especially in a party primary, in favor, of course, of
the candidate who has more. The place of money in elections
continues to bother any number of people. The pattern of campaign solicitation in the Republican presidential campaign of
1972—the laundering of contributions via Mexico City, the
prodigous (and highly successful) efforts made to encourage
large contributions before the effective date of a recently en-
acted law governing campaign finance, and the tendering of
gifts from corporate treasuries in clear violation of the federal
law—is only the latest in a series of episodes that have built up
a demand for change.

What are the concerns of those who continue to press for
change? Among those most often mentioned are:

> Men and groups of wealth may seldom ask (and perhaps
> more rarely receive) any quid pro quo from public
> officials for the contributions they make. However, what
> they do receive is access, a better chance of a hearing
> on any public policy they wish to represent, than the
> man or group who is not numbered among the ranks
> of major campaign contributors.

> The pattern evident in contributions reveals just one more
> example of the extent to which the party system favors
> the incumbent officeholder. An incumbent congressman
> can usually count on receiving *twice* as much in the way
> of campaign contributions as his opponent. "Them that
> hath tend to get even more." As one of the severest
> critics of present campaign financing says, "In Congress
> today, we have neither a Democratic or Republican
> Party. Rather we have an incumbent party which operates
> a monopoly." [22]

> While money may not generally prove critical in the out-
> come of general elections, it has repeatedly caused candi-

dates competing for a nomination to withdraw, even though they enjoyed a substantial measure of public support.[23]

In campaigns for major office, television is a major medium of communication, the major medium of communication between candidate and voter. It is also likely to be the greatest single drain on the campaign treasury. In October 1968, the cost of *one minute* of commercial time for programs such as *Walt Disney, Bonanza, the F.B.I.,* and *Jackie Gleason,* ranged from $57,500 to $60,000. Rates for programs equally popular in 1974 were over $10,000 a minute higher. The candidate who is hurting for money is the candidate most likely to have to limit his use of this now-essential campaign instrument.

And finally, even if there was little publicized evidence of substantial corruption of public men and morals attendant upon the private financing of campaigns in the postwar period, the Watergate scandals definitely served to heighten seldom discussed suspicions that the public interest is not well served by a system which invites the real possibility of corruption.

What Elections Mean

Elections do have consequences. But it is as important to understand what they cannot do as what they can.

An Expression of Confidence or Dissatisfaction. They can be an occasion for an expression of the electorate's confidence in the political system. They can shore up trust. In this regard, successfully using the ballot to throw the rascals out may be an even more reassuring act for voters than using the ballot box to say all seems to be well.

Elections represent a chance to try for change. The election of 52 new Democrats to the House of Representatives in 1974, some of them in districts that had sent a Republican to Congress for decades, was very much a general repudiation of the Republican party, Watergate, and problems in the economy. Elections clearly provide a chance to change leaders. This is the thing they do best, even if the structure of competition between parties within electoral units sometimes limits the possibility of change severely.

Can Elections Give a Policy Mandate? But can they give a mandate? Everything we know about elections and about how those elected view voters and elections tells us the odds are against it. Election outcomes are subject to interpretation. Their results— particularly as they indicate voters' policy preferences—are seldom unambiguous. Leaders may find mandates in election outcomes, but different leaders find different mandates. Elections can have policy consequences, but the connection between what happens on election day and the day of policy decision is indirect, not immediate.

For one thing, the wishes of the voters are not always clear, perhaps not even to voters themselves. Some are moved to act by issues, some by candidates, some by party, and almost all by some combination of the three. But issues differ from one voter to the next, and so do perceptions of candidates and of the parties. What specifically are voters in Miami saying about farm prices? or voters in Oregon saying about rail transport subsidies? or voters in California about postal service? or voters anywhere saying about foreign aid? As Gerald Pomper puts it, "A total popular majority is composed of many policy minorities. Rarely, if ever, is this minority united on all particular issues. The victory of a party cannot be interpreted as endorsement of its total platform." [24]

Furthermore elections in America are decentralized. Constituencies of widely dissimilar social and economic characteristics may each choose a Democrat (or a Republican) for public office, but the chances are slim that the two chosen will have identical attitudes toward all major policy questions. Nor dare we forget that millions of voters take no part in electoral politics. By what course of logic can we say that those who do participate —or more especially those who support the winners—are more representative of the whole of the popular will than those who do not?

Thus, the effect of elections upon policy must be indirect. It is politicians alone, not the voters, who can take the initiative in the design of policy. And it is politicians who ultimately must define and choose among policy alternatives.

NOTES

The first quotation at the beginning of the chapter is from Penn Kimball, *The Disconnected* (New York: Columbia University Press, 1972), 161. The second is from Stimson Bullitt, *To Be A Politician* (Garden City, N.Y.: Doubleday, 1959). The third is an old Slavic proverb. The fourth is from Robert J. Huckshorn and Robert C. Spencer, *The Politics of Defeat* (Amherst, Mass.: University of Massachusetts Press, 1971), 227. The fifth is from Michael Parenti, *Democracy For the Few* (New York: St. Martin, 1974), 158. The last is from Murray Edelman, *The Symbolic Uses of Politics* (Urbana, Ill.: University of Illinois Press, 1964), 3.

1. Philip Converse, "Information Flow and the Stability of Partisan Attitudes," *Public Opinion Quarterly* 26 (Winter 1962), 578–599. An older, pathbreaking study that looked at the time of decision in great detail is Paul F. Lazarsfeld and others, *The People's Choice,* 2nd ed. (New York: Columbia University Press, 1948), especially chapter 6.
2. Warren Lee Kostroski, "Party and Incumbency in Postwar Senate Elections," *American Political Science Review* 67 (December 1973), 1213–1234.
3. There are a great many books and articles written about every presidential election. Those worth reading about the 1964 election are Aage R. Clausen and others "Electoral Myth and Reality: The 1964 Election," *American Political Science Review* 59 (June 1965), 321–332; Bernard Cosman, *Five States for Goldwater* (University, Ala., University of Alabama Press, 1966); Bernard Cosman and Robert J. Huckshorn (editors), *Republican Politics* (New York: Praeger, 1968); John Kessel, *The Goldwater Coalition* (Indianapolis, Ind.: Bobbs-Merrill, 1968); Theodore H. White, *The Making of the President, 1964* (New York: Atheneum, 1965); Milton C. Cummings, Jr., (editor), *The National Election of 1964* (Washington, D.C.: Brookings, 1966); F. Clifton White, *Suite 3505: The Story of the Draft Goldwater Movement* (New York: Arlington House, 1967); and Robert D. Novak, *The Agony of the G.O.P., 1964* (New York: Macmillan, 1965).
4. Philip E. Converse and others, "Continuity and Change in American Politics: Parties and Issues in the 1968 Election," *American Political Science Review* 63 (December 1969), 1083–1105.
5. Elmer E. Schattschneider, *The Semi-Sovereign People* (New York: Holt, Rinehart & Winston, 1960), 98–99.
6. An unusually fine survey of the nonparticipants is provided in Penn Kimball, *The Disconnected* (New York: Columbia University Press, 1972). Also worth examining are Seymour Martin Lipset, *Political Man* (New York: Anchor Books, 1963), especially chapter 6, and Angus Campbell and others, *The American Voter* (New York: Wiley, 1960), especially chapter 5.
7. Stanley Kelley, Jr., and others, "Registration and Voting: Putting First Things First," *American Political Science Review* 61 (June 1967), 359–379.
8. Kimball, *The Disconnected,* 148.
9. Robert Alford, *Party and Society* (Skokie, Ill.: Rand McNally, 1963).
10. There are a great many how-to-do-it books on election campaigning. Those

that bear looking at are John Dean, *The Making of a Black Mayor* (Washington, D.C.: Joint Center for Political Studies, 1973); Edward Schwartzman, *Campaign Craftsmanship: A Professional's Guide to Campaigning for Elective Office* (New York: Universe Books, 1973); Chester G. Atkins, *Getting Elected: A Guide to Winning State and Local Office* (Boston: Houghton Mifflin, 1973); James M. Perry, *The New Politics: The Expanding Technology of Political Manipulation* (New York: Potter, 1968); Frederick Pohl, *Practical Politics* (New York: Ballantine, 1971); Dick Simpson, *Winning Elections: A Handbook in Participatory Politics* (Denver, Colo.: Swallow, 1972); Meyer D. Swing, *The Winning Candidate: How To Defeat Your Political Opponent* (New York: Heinman, 1966).

11. On the construction and uses of opinion surveys, see Dan Nimmo, *The Political Persuaders* (Englewood Cliffs, N.J.: Prentice-Hall, 1970).

12. On the value of canvassing, see a case study of an effort made on behalf of the candidacy of Senator Eugene McCarthy in Minnesota reported in David Lebedoff, *Ward Number Six* (New York: Scribner, 1972). For a comparison, read also the study of a campaign for a seat in the House of Commons reported in Robert T. Holt and John E. Turner, *Political Parties in Action: The Battle of Barons Court* (New York: Free Press, 1968).

13. The balancing of choices in the expenditure of campaign resources is well outlined in Murray Levin's study of Edward Kennedy's campaign for the Senate in 1964, reported in his *Kennedy Campaigning* (Boston: Beacon, 1966).

14. One of the more detailed studies of media and voting is provided by Harold Mendelsohn and Irving Crespi, *Polls, Television and the New Politics* (Dunmore, Pa.: Chandler 1972).

15. The many varieties of campaign materials and an assessment of their probable effectiveness is given in chapter 5 of Schwartzman's *Campaign Craftsmanship*.

16. Two very popular presentations of this argument are Joe McGinnis, *The Selling of the President, 1968* (New York: Trident Press, 1969), and Eugene Wyckoff, *The Image Candidates* (New York: Macmillan, 1968).

17. The literature on media and politics is enormous in quantity. The following may be recommended as giving at least differing viewpoints on its uses: McGinnis, *The Selling of the President, 1968;* Wyckoff, *The Image Candidates;* Mendelsohn and Crespi, *Polls, Television and the New Politics;* Stanley Kelley, *Political Campaigning* (Washington, D.C.: Brookings, 1960); Joy G. Blumler and Denis McQuail, *Television in Politics* (Chicago: University of Chicago Press, 1969); and see a good discussion in chapter 5 of Delmer D. Dunn, *Financing Presidential Campaigns* (Washington, D.C.: Brookings, 1972).

18. See David A. Leuthold, *Electioneering in a Democracy* (New York: Wiley, 1968), chapter 2.

19. Ibid.

20. Among the better works on financing are David Adamany, *Campaign Financing in America* (Belmont, Mass.: Duxbury, 1973); Dunn, *Financing Presidential Campaigns;* Herbert E. Alexander, *Financing the 1964 Election* (Princeton, N.J.: Citizen's Research Foundation, 1966); and the reports on campaign finance that appear from time to time in the *Congressional Quarterly Weekly Report*.

21. Congressional Quarterly, Inc., *Congressional Quarterly Weekly Report,* Issue #11, March 17, 1973.
22. Ibid., quoting a spokesman for Common Cause.
23. Dunn, *Financing Presidential Campaigns,* 12–13.
24. Gerald M. Pomper, *Elections in America* (New York: Dodd, Mead, 1968), 249.

A Presidential campaign may be thought to be the work of a tightly knit organization spread over the entire country and directed by cunning men wise in the ways of managing the multitude. In truth, the campaign orgnization is a jerry-built and make-shift structure manned largely by temporary and volunteer workers who labor long hours amidst confusion and uncertainty.

Political organization is basically a matter of list-keeping. You canvass a state by foot and by phone to find out who is for you, who is against you, and who is uncommitted. Once you have the list, you cross off the ones against you, barrage the uncommitted with pleas and information, and make sure your supporters get to the polls.
Not so long ago, the Party Organization that kept the best list and had the patronage clout to keep the listees in line could deliver an election. Today even Mayor Daley's fabled machine is showing signs of breakdown, and if a candidate wants an organization he can count on, he has to build it himself.

Frank Mankiewicz constantly complained that the reporters never wrote about the issues. They wrote about staff problems and Democratic county chairmen who refused to support McGovern, he said, but never about McGovern's ideas on health care and pollution. Mankiewicz claimed to have answered 10,000 questions in the course of the campaign, only seven of them about a real issue. This was a valid point, but the reporters had a valid problem: They were swamped with prepared texts *but McGovern did not deliver many of these speeches.* On a typical day, the press would receive a statement on anti-trust policy and another on veterans, both of them provocative treatises by McGovern's most eloquent speech writers. But then McGovern would scrap both statements in favor of a new blast at the Administration over the Watergate affair, and the reporters would have to devote all of their space to the Watergate speech. This frustrated the good reporters, but there was nothing they could do about it.

9

Getting Elected President

An American presidential election is a major event. The presidency is the most competitive of all American public offices. Each party may reasonably judge that its candidate for the office has a good chance of winning. Citizens turn out to vote for president more than they do for any other level of office. Scholars and journalists feast on presidential elections, which are among the most carefully studied of all political events. And myth has it that every American mother wants her boy to grow up to be president. But clearly, some boys are not going to make it. Only one American boy can be elected at a time. And that time comes only after 48 revolutions of the moon about the earth have occurred since the last presidential election. Politics, not chance, narrows the field of those who may ultimately succeed rather severely. The constitutional prescription of the electoral college, the crucial importance of the "big" states in determining the outcome of the election, the increasing role of the primary in the nominating process, the mechanics of the national party conventions, the shifts in public attitudes observable over the course of recent elections, events and issues that change from one election to the next, the increasing sophistication of campaign management techniques, the role of money in the campaign—these are part of the political elements that shape the outcome of elections to the highest office in the land. The politics of presidential campaigns is the subject of this chapter.

The Effect of the Electoral College on Campaign Strategy

How does one get to be president of the United States? A good many people would like to know the answer to that. A surefire way to capture that jop would probably be an even more valuable invention than a better mousetrap.

Actually, there is nothing especially mysterious about what it takes. What it takes is a majority of votes in the electoral college.[1] All states operate under the "winner take all" principle in deciding which presidential candidate gets the electoral college vote of that state; that is, they give all their electoral votes to whichever candidate wins the largest number of popular votes in the state. Therefore, the easiest way to get elected president is to secure enough popular support to win the electoral votes of some combination of states whose total electoral vote equals a majority of votes in the electoral college. Within the past century, all men elected president except one, Rutherford Hayes in 1876, have done that. Every candidate for president today tries to repeat their performances.[2]

A person may win only a plurality of the popular vote in the nation and yet win a majority of the votes in the electoral college. This happened in three of the seven elections from 1948 through 1972. It is equally possible for the reverse to happen: for a person to win a majority of the popular vote in the nation but not a majority of the votes in the electoral college. If *no* candidate wins a majority of electoral college votes, then the selection of the president is put in the hands of the House of Representatives, where each state casts one vote, regardless of the number of representatives in the state delegation.

Candidates know how the electoral college works. Its peculiarities figure in the design of their campaign strategy. Delegates to the national conventions also know how it works, and it becomes a factor when they are choosing their party's presidential ticket.

How Electoral Votes Are Apportioned Among States.   The essential features of the electoral college are prescribed in the U.S. Constitution. They may be changed not by political parties, not by an election, nor even by Congress alone. They may be changed only through the complicated procedures which the Constitution itself lays down for passing an amendment to the Constitution. The Constitution says that each state is entitled to a number of electoral college votes equal to the number of its congressional delegation. By the terms of the Twenty-third Amendment, the District of Columbia is entitled to a number of votes in the electoral college equal to the number of members of Congress it would have if it were a state, but not more than the number of electoral college votes given to the least populous state. Beginning with the 1964 election, there were 538 votes in the electoral college, and a majority of 270 was required to elect a president. No state can have fewer than three electoral college votes, since no state can have fewer than three in its congressional delegation, two in the Senate and one in the House of Representatives.

States with the largest populations have the largest congressional delegations, since seats in the House are allocated among the states roughly on the basis of their populations, and these states, therefore, have the largest number of votes in the electoral college. In the 1960s, five states, Alaska, Delaware, Nevada, Vermont, and Wyoming, plus the District of Columbia each had three votes, while New York and California with 43 and 40 votes respectively, had the largest number of votes in the electoral college. As a result of the 1970 census some states, like California, now have even more votes than before, while others, New York included, have fewer. Table 9–1 gives the electoral college vote for each state in 1968 and in 1972.

Importance of the Big Eleven.   The range in the distribution of votes in the electoral college is highly significant. Through the period of the 1968 election the first 12 states listed in Table 9–1 held a majority of the votes in the electoral college. As a result of the 1970 census, a majority of votes can now be put together from the votes of 11 states—the votes of the first 10 states in the list plus the 13 votes of either North Carolina *or* Indiana. Putting it another way, it is impossible to win a majority of the votes in the electoral college without winning the electoral

Table 9-1　Electoral Vote of the 50 States and D.C., 1968 and 1972

Electoral Vote			*Electoral Vote*		
State	1968	1972	State	1968	1972
California	40	45	S. Carolina	8	8
New York	43	41	Colorado	6	7
Pennsylvania	29	27	Kansas	7	7
Illinois	26	26	Mississippi	7	7
Texas	25	26	Arizona	5	6
Ohio	26	25	Arkansas	6	6
Michigan	21	21	Oregon	6	6
Florida	14	17	W. Virginia	7	6
New Jersey	17	17	Nebraska	5	5
Massachusetts	14	14	Hawaii	4	4
Indiana	13	13	Idaho	4	4
North Carolina	13	13	Maine	4	4
Georgia	12	12	Montana	4	4
Missouri	12	12	New Hampshire	4	4
Virginia	12	12	New Mexico	4	4
Wisconsin	12	11	Rhode Island	4	4
Louisiana	10	10	South Dakota	4	4
Maryland	10	10	Utah	4	4
Minnesota	10	10	Alaska	3	3
Tennessee	11	10	Delaware	3	3
Alabama	10	9	D.C.	3	3
Kentucky	9	9	Nevada	3	3
Washington	9	9	North Dakota	4	3
Connecticut	8	8	Vermont	3	3
Iowa	9	8	Wyoming	3	3
Oklahoma	8	8			

votes of at least one of these eleven states. Obviously, what these states are likely to do in a presidential election years is going to figure importantly in any presidential candidate's campaign strategy.

HOW THE BIG STATES VOTE.　How do these states usually vote? Table 9–2 shows how they voted between 1948 and 1972. In these seven elections, one state, Illinois, voted with the winning presidential candidate every time. Five of them voted for the winner six out of seven times. The other six voted with the winner five in seven times. Of the five winners, Lyndon Johnson in 1964 did best, carrying all of them. Dwight Eisenhower in 1952 and 1956 carried all but North Carolina, and Richard

Nixon in 1972 carried all but Massachusetts. In this period, Indiana showed a marked preference for Republican candidates, voting for them six in seven times. The remaining states have split their votes a little more evenly between the two parties.

BIG-STATE INFLUENCE UPON THE CONVENTION'S CHOICE OF CANDIDATES. To the national party convention falls the task of choosing a man who can be elected president, and this means someone who can carry states which among them control a majority of votes in the electoral college. Although it might seem possible to produce this majority from the votes of a great many different combinations of states, parties and candidates have discovered that in fact the number of combinations is generally quite limited. The combination will almost certainly include the votes of some of the big states, not simply because they control many votes but because they tend to be pivotal: Each party may realistically hope that its candidate will carry these states, with the possible exception of Indiana. In the seven elections of the postwar period, the winning candidate has carried at least six of them, and their votes have given him better than half the votes required to produce a majority in the electoral college.

Table 9-2 Party Supported by the Twelve States with the Largest Number of Electoral College Votes in Presidential Elections, 1948–1972

	1948		1952		1956		1960		1964		1968		1972	
	D[w]	R	D	R[w]	D	R[w]	D[w]	R	D[w]	R	D	R[w]	D	R[w]
California	x			x		x		x	x			x		x
New York		x		x		x	x		x		x			x
Pennsylvania		x		x		x	x		x		x			x
Illinois	x			x		x	x		x			x		x
Texas	x			x		x	x		x		x			x
Ohio	x			x		x		x	x			x		x
Michigan		x		x		x	x		x		x			x
Florida	x			x		x		x	x			x		x
New Jersey		x		x		x	x		x			x		x
Massachusetts	x			x		x	x		x		x		x	
Indiana		x		x		x		x	x			x		x
North Carolina	x		x		x		x		x			x		x

[w] Indicates party of the winning candidate that year.

THE IMPORTANCE OF THE CANDIDATE'S HOME STATE.   Further, it is generally accepted that either the presidential or vice-presidential candidate, and preferably both, will come from one of these states, and the assumption is made that he is certain to carry at least his home state.[3] In this century all presidents except one, Harry Truman, have come from large states. Three have come from New York, two from Texas, one from California, two from Massachusetts, and one, Gerald Ford, from Michigan.

The presidential and vice-presidential candidates will not come from the same state. If they did, that would guarantee that one of them would be denied the electoral votes of that state, for the Constitution says that members of the electoral college shall ballot for president and vice-president, "one of whom, at least, shall not be an inhabitant of the same state with themselves." Furthermore, assuming that a nominee is likely to carry his home state, it seems the better part of political wisdom to select the candidates on the ticket from different states, preferably from large pivotal states that have recently displayed a tendency to lean toward the candidates of the opposition party.

The number of electoral votes a state possesses, therefore, becomes one major consideration in deciding what combination of states the party will rely on to provide an election victory. Another major factor is the political history of individual states. Large states tend to be pivotal, but not all are. Ohio is pivotal in voting for president, but Wisconsin (which had 11 votes in 1972) is steadier in its support of Republicans. Generally speaking, the midwestern states favor Republicans, as do the smaller mountain states.

THE SOUTHERN STRATEGY.   In 1964, Barry Goldwater planned to fashion his victory from a combination of the electoral votes of the South (127 votes), two border states that were regarded as pure Goldwater territory, plus Arizona (22 votes total), enough of the Republican-leaning western and midwestern states to produce another 50 or 60 electoral votes, and three large states, California (40 votes), Ohio (26 votes), and Illinois (26 votes). Written off as acceptable losses were all of the states of the Northeast. This "Southern strategy" was not an unreasonable one for a Republican candidate—*any* Republican candidate—to consider.[4] Goldwater's hope for penetrating the

South had ample precedents from the days when Dwight Eisenhower proved that a Republican could make it by that road to the White House.

But Goldwater was no Eisenhower, and 1964 was not exactly 1952. Only McGovern after him was a less popular candidate, and an electorate displaying a hitherto unnoticed concern with the issues which Goldwater was at pains to delineate rejected him overwhelmingly everywhere except in the South, where whites found his issue stands much to their liking.

Presidential Primaries

Before a man gets to worrying whether his campaign strategy will work or not, he must first attend to one major preliminary matter: getting himself nominated by either the Republican or Democratic national party convention. Whether he is successful here depends upon many things, including his stature with the leaders and activists of his own party; his standing with the electorate, past, present, and possible future; as well as upon the mechanics of the convention itself, particularly the manner in which the delegates to the convention are apportioned among states.

It is fair to say—and convention balloting of the last two decades bears this out [5]—that today's national party convention more often than not serves merely to ratify the results of a nomination process that is largely completed before the convention itself begins. It is before the convention that the candidate must make his greatest efforts to establish his stature, both with party leaders and with the electorate at large. In determining the success of those efforts, his attitude toward the presidential primaries is crucial.[6]

The Number of Primaries.   The number of states having presidential primaries has varied from year to year. Some primaries, like those in New Hampshire and Wisconsin, have been around for decades. Others, like many of those held in 1972, are new on the scene. Still others are on-and-off-again affairs, like the one in Maryland which was held in 1964, dropped for 1968, but which appeared again in 1972. In recent years, about 15 states and the District of Columbia have held primaries, a total sub-

stantially below the 26 states that used the primary at the height
of its popularity during the second decade of this century. In
1972, 22 states and the District of Columbia held primaries.
From the choice made by voters in these primaries came roughly
60 percent of the delegates to the national conventions—a contrast to the roughly 40 percent of convention delegates chosen
by this means in previous years. This increase came about largely
as a response from state legislatures to the demands which the
Democratic National Convention of 1968 made for reform in
the processes by which delegates are chosen.

There are two basic versions of the presidential primary.
The first is the presidential preference poll. This gives the voter
a chance to indicate which candidate he would like to see
receive his party's nomination for president. The second is the
delegate selection primary, in which voters have the chance to
select their party's delegates to the national convention.[7]

States generally are generous in permitting access to the
presidential primary ballot. In a number of states, some public
official—in Oregon it is the secretary of state; in Wisconsin it is
an 11-man committee—is required to include on the presidential
primary ballot the names of all persons who have been publicly
identified in the news media as possible candidates for the
nomination. In other states a man's name may be entered in the
primary by his supporters without his consent being required.
No candidate is compelled to keep his name on the ballot.
Even states where his name may be entered without his consent,
such as Oregon and New Hampshire, provide a means whereby
a candidate can prevent his name from appearing on the ballot.

Write-In Votes.   Access to the ballot is also made easy by the
acceptability of write-in votes. One of the best-remembered
write-in campaigns was that undertaken for Eisenhower in the
Minnesota primary of 1952. It produced better than 100,000
votes—and literally hundreds of spellings of the candidate's
name. Coming as it did hard upon Eisenhower's victory in the
New Hampshire primary, the Minnesota primary results guaranteed the reluctant general status as a major contender for the
Republican nomination.

A write-in campaign can be of particular value to the
candidate who is uncertain of the extent of his popular support.
A write-in campaign requires organization. It takes determined

voters who will go to the polls with the definite intention of writing in their candidate's name in the right spot on the ballot. It is difficult to believe that any candidate's chances can be hurt by a write-in campaign. If his vote total is small (and in a write-in campaign who can say what "small" is) the candidate need say little about the effort. But if it amounts to more than a small percentage of the total vote cast, he can declare he is pleased and impressed with this demonstration of support. He may even claim it constitutes a "victory." On occasion, write-in campaigns do produce an unmistakable victory, as did the campaigns for Eisenhower in Massachusetts in 1952 and for Henry Cabot Lodge in New Hampshire in 1964.[8]

Easy access to the ballot works to the particular advantage of the reluctant candidate, the position of General Eisenhower in 1952 and Henry Cabot Lodge, then ambassador to Vietnam, in 1964. The candidate can adopt a strictly "hands-off" attitude while his supporters actively promote his candidacy. The results may tell much about the measure of support he enjoys, the effectiveness of his supporters as campaign organizers, and the possible strength of his primary opponents, and may help him decide whether his candidacy might be promoted by further competition in primaries.

Why Candidates Find Primaries Attractive.   Primaries are one place where convention votes can be sought. More than half the delegates to the party conventions are now chosen in primaries. No candidate can afford to ignore such a large number of delegates.

WINNING DELEGATE SUPPORT.   A candidate who does well in the primaries goes into the convention with an impressive number of delegates behind him,[9] and some of these delegtaes will be bound legally by the laws of their state to support him through at least the first ballot. If he scores a number of successes, he comes to the convention a political figure to be reckoned with by other candidates and by the convention. Even if he cannot win the nomination, his support and the support of delegates pledged to him may be what is required by another candidate to win.

The search for delegate support in primaries is likely to appeal particularly to the candidate who enjoys little in the way of support within the narrow ranks of party leaders and activists. In 1952, General Eisenhower, who had been kept from active participation in party politics by a lifetime of military service, found himself competing for the Republican nomination against Senator Robert Taft, a man so well admired by Republican party leaders that he enjoyed the title "Mr. Republican." Through the primaries, the General took his case to the rank and file. His impressive showing there made him a serious contender for the nomination and provided him with a hard core of delegate support around which he fashioned his first ballot victory at the Republican convention.[10] Similarly, the New Hampshire primary in 1968 made Senator Eugene McCarthy a serious entrant into the Democratic presidential race and had the added effect of making Robert Kennedy a second candidate for the nomination. Both senators recognized that the rank and file who turned out for the Democratic primaries might be persuaded to feel differently from the party regulars about denying Lyndon Johnson his party's renomination.

Marked success in a primary ordinarily produces more delegate support than merely the number of delegates won in the primary itself. Party leaders are not usually blind to the meaning of primary result. In 1960 one Democratic leader in New York, where delegates were chosen by convention, remarked after Kennedy's victory in the West Virginia primary, "We had better get on the bandwagon before it runs over us."

DEMONSTRATING VOTE-GETTING ABILITY. Winning delegate support, however, is often a secondary consideration in entering a primary. Primaries can be valuable if they help a candidate acquire a reputation as a vote-getter, and a likely winner for his party if he receives the nomination. Strength among the voters as revealed by public opinion polls has not yet become an established substitute for voter-getting ability which has been put to the test of an actual election.

Hazards of Primary Defeat. Primaries can give a candidate a major defeat as easily as they can give him a major victory. They are seldom equally hospitable to all candidates. Hubert Humphrey, after the West Virginia primary in 1960, was not the first nor the last to remove himself as a candidate after a poor performance in a primary. That same year, Wayne Morse found his candidacy ended when Kennedy defeated him in Morse's home state of Oregon. In 1964, the principal victim on the primary circuit was Nelson Rockefeller, who lost the crucial California primary to frontrunner Barry Goldwater. In 1972, on the Democratic side, the candidate eliminated was Edmund Muskie. The ability to win primaries may not guarantee a candidate his party's nomination, but a failure to win first place in the primaries he enters will almost certainly deny him the nomination. The party cannot afford to nominate someone who cannot win support among the voters of his own party, in primary contests of his own choosing.

Primaries and Issues. Primary contests may raise some campaign issues and put others to rest. In 1960 John Kennedy concluded that he would have to demonstrate by a series of primary victories that his age, lack of experience, and especially his Catholicism did not raise insuperable barriers to his winning the presidency. The New Hampshire primary proved little about any of these issues. Kennedy's victory was attributed to a vote for the "local" boy against token primary opposition. In Wisconsin, Kennedy won all 14 counties in which Catholics constituted 35 percent of the population or more, but lost to Humphrey 37 of the 57 counties in which the Catholic percentage was less than that. How well he might do in largely Protestant areas was still an unanswered question. West Virginia was next. Early polls reported that Humphrey, Kennedy's opponent again, would carry the state with 60 percent of the primary vote. It was a solid Protestant area; fewer than 5 percent of the state's population were Catholic. Organized labor, long a source of Humphrey strength, was strong here. On primary night Kennedy carried West Virginia, with 60 percent of the vote to Humphrey's 40 percent. Since Al Smith's defeat in 1928, it had been an axiom of American party politics that no Catholic could be elected president. After West Virginia, 1960, that axiom began to be questioned seriously for the first time. The issue of Catholicism had been raised and seemingly laid to rest by one candidate's victory in a primary.

Party nominees are not always so fortunate. Some of the issues raised in the New Hampshire primary of 1964 haunted the Republican nominee, Barry Goldwater, to the very end of his general election campaign. Goldwater entered New Hampshire as the favorite on the Republican side. He quickly lost ground. The headline in the *Concord Daily Monitor* reporting on the Senator's first New Hampshire press conference read "Goldwater Sets Goals: End Social Security, Hit Castro." The "end-social-security" theme—not quite a fair summary of Goldwater's position—hurt Goldwater not only in New Hampshire. It followed him through the remaining primaries and became a major weapon used against him by Democrats in the general election, often to the chagrin of Republican leaders, who found many of the Senator's statements embarrassing. Yet the more enthusiastic of the Goldwater partisans found these statements much to their liking and were ready to give them wide currency —an effort which the Democrats did nothing to discourage.[11]

Testing Campaign Style and Organization in a Primary. Primaries give candidates a chance to develop their campaign styles and test the effectiveness of their organizations. In 1960 the succession of Kennedy primary victories produced an enduring image of an invincible Kennedy machine. His only important rival, Humphrey, contributed to that image when he said that in competition with the Kennedys, he was like a "corner grocer competing with a chain store." Theodore White reports that for four years John Kennedy had been traveling the country and had returned from each trip with a survey of the political land and a list of who was who in local politics.[12] This political inventory was just one element in the Kennedy style of organization. The Kennedy primary campaign built upon this four years of experience. It also added to it and made his organization an even greater asset for the later competition with Republican Richard Nixon.

It would be too much to say that the primary route is now an obligatory obstacle course that must be overcome by any aspirant for the presidential nomination of his party, unless he is an incumbent president. But it would not be an exaggeration to say that primaries have begun to play a larger role than ever before in the plans of candidates who seek the nomination. A series of victories may not guarantee a candidate the nomination. But even one or two defeats can deny it to him, as Edmund Muskie discovered on his way to the White House in 1972. Primaries are an important testing device. They weed out candidates. They narrow the list of serious contenders and thus perform a function which once was within the exclusive province of the national convention itself. And because the results are the accumulation of individual choices made by voters, primaries provide voters an opportunity to share in the proceedings of the convention in some fashion besides watching them on television.

The New Party Convention

Changes in the Democratic National Convention. In the use of primaries to assist in nominating presidential candidates, 1972 marked a distinctive break with the past. In 1968, the Democratic National Convention, under pressure from many quarters to begin a reform of its delegate selection processes, called for the establishment of a special committee to make recommendations on the selection of delegates to future conventions.

THE MCGOVERN-FRASER COMMISSION. The commission appointed by the Democratic national chairman was first chaired by Senator George McGovern of South Dakota, and later by Representative Donald Fraser of Minnesota. It produced staff reports, held hearings across the country, and made a set of recommendations which called for all state Democratic parties to take "affirmative steps to encourage . . . representation of minority groups on the national convention delegation in reasonable relationship to the group's presence in the population of the states." In a letter sent to all state party officials in November 1971, Chairman Fraser explained the meaning of the guidelines, saying:

> We believe that state parties should be on notice that whenever the proportion of women, minorities, and young people in a delegation offered for seating in Miami [the site of the 1972 Democratic Convention] is less than the proportion of these groups in the total population, and the delegation is challenged on the ground that [the Guidelines] were not complied with, such a challenge will constitute a prima facie showing of violation of the Guidelines; and the state Democratic Party along with the challenged delegation has the burden of showing that the state party took full and affirmative action . . . to achieve such representation.[13]

Here then was a near-command for a state party to abide by a quota system which demanded representation for minorities, women, and youth in each delegation in rough proportion to their numbers in the population of the state. It is one of the greater ironies that this command came from a commission that itself had so few blacks, women, and youth among its members that it could not possibly have qualified under its own guidelines to be a delegation to the 1972 convention.

EVIDENCE OF CHANGE.   State parties complied, with no little grumbling, but with no little success either. In a number of states, the command which came from the commission could be honored only by persuading the state legislature to make changes in the law. These were soon forthcoming, and one immediate evidence of the new direction was an increase in the number of states that added primaries as a means of providing an opportunity for wider popular participation in nominations.

But the clearest evidence that changes had come was the makeup of the membership of the 1972 Democratic National Convention. Turnover among convention delegates is always high. During the period from 1944 to 1968, approximately two-thirds of the delegates to the national party conventions were new delegates, who had never attended a convention before. Of the remaining third, most had attended only one convention before. In 1972, 9 in 10 of the delegates to the Democratic convention were new delegates. But what was most distinctive about 1972—remarkably so—was the extent to which the membership included persons within the society that had never been conspicuous in delegations to a convention before. This was the great break with the past. The number of young people, blacks, and women in attendance was striking. Most were not the appointees of established party leaders but were chosen in open and democratically run elections and caucuses. Forty percent were women—a figure far higher than for any previous convention, 21 percent were youth, and 15 percent were blacks.[14]

POLITICAL CONSEQUENCES OF CONVENTION CHANGES.   Public opinion polls tell us that with rare exceptions, conventions nominate their most popular candidate for president. Conventions would, therefore, appear to be successful in the matter of representing the wishes of their broader party constituency. What of the 1972 Democratic convention? It produced no winner. That is certain. Its rate of turnover was higher than ever before—evidence that a major party was concerned to enlarge

its support among those in the society who have less. But did
the party, in the course of making that major adjustment, jeo-
pardize its chances of nominating a winner? Alas, the evidence
is sketchy. The 1972 election study indicates that the Republican candidate, Richard Nixon, would have been a formidable
opponent for *any* Democratic candidate; that McGovern did
keep the support of groups that had previously been among the
mainstays of support for Democratic candidates; and finally
that he did notably well in winning the support of some groups,
for example, blacks and young people, whose support for the
Democrats appeared to be wanting or who were inclined to regard both political parties as failures as democratic institutions.[15]
More on this a little later.

The Convention and Its Critics.   The two most important jobs
given the national convention are nominating presidential and
vice-presidential candidates and drafting a party platform. It is
the choice of the candidates that engenders the greatest interest,
both among delegates and among television viewers at home. That
decision seems to be most of what a convention is all about. The
two jobs, of course, are often related. Candidates often run hard
in pursuit of the nomination because they believe they hold opposing policy views from other contenders. Eugene McCarthy's
decision in 1968 to challenge the renomination of an incumbent
president of his own party because of his strong feelings on the
continuation of the war in Vietnam is a case in point, as was
Republican Barry Goldwater's quest for the nomination in
1964, and, to some degree, Senator McGovern's drive for the
nomination in 1972. To these three aspirants—and to many
before them—their fight for the nomination and the making of
the party's platform were all of one piece.

   How the decisions on candidates and platforms are made
does not always satisfy either those who participate or those who
watch from the sidelines. The convention has always had its
critics.[16] At the time of the Democratic convention of 1968, the
criticisms mounted to a crescendo. They covered such simple
matters as the decision to seat insurgent delegations clear at the
back of the convention hall, where, it was hoped, they might
be the more easily ignored by the podium and also be less
within range of the television cameras. They extended to the

much more important matters of the leaders' refusing to seat delegations committed to support candidates who had won a plurality of votes in a primary election.

Some of the criticism was stilled by changes evident in the 1972 Democratic convention. The matter of where in the hall delegations were to sit was easily settled by having these seating decisions made by the drawing of lots. The other, more serious kind of seating problem was less well handled. On the whole, the selection procedures employed within the states in choosing delegates to the 1972 convention were clearly more open and more democratic than were many of the procedures employed in earlier years. In 1968 and before, the entire delegation from a state might be handpicked up one or two party officials. There was nothing even vaguely resembling that in 1972.

Nonetheless, some of the decisions made by the McGovern strategists on the floor of the convention did not square with the democratic objectives in the guidelines prepared by the Mc-Govern-Fraser Commission. It was the carefully husbanded votes of McGovern delegates that invoked the winner-take-all principle in the case of the California delegation (because the delegation was committed to McGovern). McGovern leaders supported the seating of a South Carolina delegation that was challenged by an insurgent group on the ground that it had failed to include adequate representation of women. And the McGovern "reformers" unseated an Illinois delegation that had soundly beaten a rival slate of candidates in an open primary. Fairness and democracy in convention politics often depends on whose ox is being gored.

WHY CRITICISM SEEMS INEVITABLE.   While criticism of the convention has slacked off considerably, it is not likely to disappear. Political institutions are never ideally democratic; they can only be more or less so. In the case of the convention, the most difficult of all questions is the matter of fair representation. Who or what is it that the convention is to represent? How much should the party encourage (or guarantee) participation by elected party leaders? by long-time party workers? by recent enthusiasts? by supporters of the candidate who leads in the public opinion polls? by party voters, registered partisans (whether voters or not), or some even broader constituency?

To encourage participation by party actives is not an unreasonable thing if one conceives of the convention as a *party* meeting. But if this is done, critics will say the convention is being rigged in favor of the status quo and against those who seek to challenge the established party leadership. To leave the convention door wide open to any with the will to come is equally defensible, if instead one conceives of the convention as more of a *public* than a party meeting—as much of a public meeting as the old-fashioned New England town meeting. But this in turn would risk great instability, and uncertainty for the future of the party organization.

The Consequences of Reform.   Since 1968 some important ground rules under which conventions must operate have been changed. How does this affect the major decisions made at the convention?

Any effort to generalize about the choices likely to be made at party conventions must at once take account of one near-certainty: In the choice of a presidential candidate, the convention is much less likely to build to a decision from scratch, so to speak, than to serve to ratify a decision made earlier elsewhere, Yet millions of viewers at home watch television for the hours before that final decision, not at all certain what the outcome will be. Have they been conned? Not always. Coalition building does go on at the convention.[17] The glue can come unstuck from the weaker commitments made by delegates to a candidate, while some delegates may steadfastly refuse to give a commitment. There is, therefore, always a certain amount of uncertainty, although less, probably, than suggested by the extravagant claims of support made by competing candidates. And the ratifying decision is made in full public view.

First-ballot nomination has been the rule, not the exception, since 1948. Will the substantial increase in the number of primaries make it harder or easier for one candidate to tie up enough delegates in primaries to win the nomination? Perhaps not easier. Certainly not harder.[18] With upwards of 60 percent of the delegates now chosen in primaries, it will be more difficult than ever before to take a candidate seriously if he chooses not to compete in at least the major primaries. But if more candidates then ever before enter presidential primaries, are they not likely to split the vote among them and thus guarantee that none of them has a chance of a first-ballot nomination? Probably not. Primary voters in California are likely to

respond to national issues and candidates much the same way as
do primary voters in New York. The appealing candidate in
New York is going to be appealing in California. Primaries do
weed out weaker candidates—often early in the game. They do
little to sap the strength of the frontrunner. More primaries mean
more opportunities to identify the leader, with many consequences, one of which is an increased awareness by voters that
one of the candidates is proving to have substantial appeal to
voters elsewhere.

Presidential Election Campaigns

Any campaign is an exercise in persuasion. It is a case study in
the activation of biases, and, for the candidate, involves persuading those whose biases most closely resemble his own to give him
their vote on election day. A presidential campaign is no exception.[19]

An Overview: 1948–1972.   In some respects the visible mani-
festations of presidential elections have changed little in 25 years.
In some they have. The campaign train of yesterday—last seen
in 1964—may have been replaced by the high-flying jet, but it
may yet return, if the energy crunch is perceived by the voters
as genuine. Television, first used on any scale in 1952, is now
a staple. This is a change of some consequence.[20] Money is spent
as if it were being drawn from a Monopoly game. The budget
for media activities alone is larger by far today than the entire
budget of the 1948 campaign.[21] Two major contenders, Goldwater in 1964 and McGovern in 1972, proved that a significant
amount of campaign funds could be raised in small amounts.
Yet the contributions of "fat cats" still provide a large portion
of the campaign treasury for both parties. No black, no Chicano,
no Indian, no woman has been chosen by a major party for
nomination as a presidential or vice-presidential candidate, but
in 1960 a Catholic did make it all the way to the White House.
The period since 1948 has seen the election of three "minority"
presidents—candidates who won though they captured less than
half the popular vote—and it has seen the election of a Republican four times out of seven, even though the ratio of Democratic

party identifiers to Republican party identifiers has never been less than two to one.

The best showing by a third-party candidate since 1924 occurred in 1968, when George Wallace ran on the ticket of the American Independent Party. His stand on issues won him the support of one voter in seven, reminding us that issues can be as important as party identification in shaping the voter's decision.[22]

Of the 10 candidates offered by the two major parties in these seven elections, 2 in particular—Goldwater and McGovern—were issue candidates. They made every effort to keep policy questions in the forefront of the campaign. Both suffered major defeats. Goldwater carried six states, five of them in the Deep South.[23] McGovern carried only Massachusetts and the District of Columbia.[24] Were voters turned off by issue appeals? Earlier election studies suggested they were. Yet the 1972 election study indicated that issues were a major influence upon the decisions made by voters that year.

Certain significant shifts in citizen attitudes were evident in the period from 1964 to 1972. Trust declined.[25] Belief in the equity of government benefits declined.[26] Feelings of efficacy declined.[27] And so did the number of party identifiers, as the number of Independents increased. Despite these notable changes in attitudes, there was still no indication by 1972 of a marked change in the social bases of the two major parties. However, these attitude changes did reinforce a tendency of voters to perceive the elements of the 1972 campaign rather differently from earlier election years. And what is also clear from the 1972 election study is that the leading factors in the outcome of the election were the choice of candidates and the voters' perception of them in issue terms.

The 1972 Presidential Election. The 1972 election produced a landslide—521 votes in the electoral college, 61.3 percent of the popular vote—for the candidate of the minority party, a candidate moreover preferred by no less than 42 percent of those who claimed an identity with the majority party. Was this not a demonstration of great affection for the candidate if not for his party? (In that same election voters returned a majority of Democrats to both houses of Congress. Presidential coattails were at the cleaners on election day.)[28] Is a landslide victory for an incumbent not a demonstration of voter satisfaction with having things remain just the way they are?[29] Not necessarily. Turnout in 1972 was lower than it had been since 1948. Expressions of distrust of government—as we have already noted—were higher by far than ever before. Reported interest in the election was down.

What was happening here? Some answers can be found in the 1972 election study. Let us look at them and then assess their broader significance for the functioning of political parties.

ELECTORATE MORE LIBERAL THAN IN THE PAST. It was not that the electorate was noticeably more conservative than before. Indeed, on all issues—most notably the issue of Vietnam —the electorate moved to the left between 1968 and 1972. In 1968, Republicans, Democrats, and Independents held roughly the same hawkish attitudes toward the war. By 1972, Democrats and Independents had moved substantially to the left, while Republicans remained about where they were in 1968. Republicans, Democrats, and Independents all moved to the left on the issue of how best to deal with the problem of urban unrest between 1968 and 1972, with Independents making by far the greatest shift. Nixon was perceived as having remained relatively stable in his stand on issues in this period. Indeed he was perceived as being somewhat more hawkish on Vietnam in 1972 than in 1968, a trend opposite to that evident among the electorate.

McGovern on the other hand was the least popular presidential candidate in 20 years. He was only slightly more popular than black congresswoman Shirley Chisholm. The highest-rated Democrat was Senator Edward Kennedy, but his rating was well below that given Nixon. Among whites only, the best-liked Democrat was George Wallace.

As for issues, Democrats generally perceived their party as being to the left of themselves, with McGovern even farther to the left. Nixon was closer to the electorate's issue position on 14 separate issues than was McGovern, and Nixon alone was given a favorable rating by all three distinguishable policy groups within the electorate—by liberals (advocates of social change), by conservatives (advocates of social control), and by those in the middle.

DIFFERENCES BETWEEN McGOVERN AND NIXON SUP-
PORTERS.　There were clear issue differences between Nixon and
McGovern supporters. McGovern supporters were anywhere
from 19 to 41 percent more liberal than Nixon supporters. Even
on the highly skewed issues of busing, amnesty, and the legalization of marijuana—where 86, 72, and 68 percent of the electorate, respectively, took a conservative position—McGovern
supporters were much more liberal than Nixon supporters. Fully
half of McGovern voters exhibited a social-change policy orientation, whereas an equal fraction of Nixon voters displayed a
diametrically opposed social-control orientation. A full 54 percent of McGovern voters called themselves "liberal," whereas
half of Nixon's voters called themselves "conservatives."

THE TWO DEMOCRATIC FACTIONS.　But by far the most
striking difference was that observed between the issue positions
of Democrats who supported McGovern and those who supported
Nixon. *The difference between these two Democratic factions was
greater than the difference between all Democrats and Republicans.* On the other hand, Republicans as a group revealed
a substantial measure of consensus on issues. The extent of the
division between the two Democratic factions is well illustrated
by the position they took on five key issues which proved to have
a close relationship to the vote. The figures are:

	McGovern Democrats	Nixon Democrats
Left	45%	15%
Center	30	33
Right	25	52

What this indicates—a finding of great consequence—is polarization among the Democrats. In 1972, the ranks of Democratic
party identifiers were deeply split *on the matter of issues.* Voters
in 1972 were definitely more likely to vote for the candidate they
perceived as being closer to themselves on the issues than for the
candidate they perceived as being farther away. Thus, even a
voter who took a liberal position on an issue would be likely to
vote for Nixon if he thought of Nixon as being closer to his
own position on issues than was McGovern.

POLICY VOTING IN 1972.   A policy voter has been defined as an individual who casts his ballot for the candidate nearest to him on those issues about which he has expressed an attitude before an election. The ranks of policy voters accordingly exclude individuals who are persuaded by the candidate to take a particular issue position or who rationalize their vote by projecting their own policy preferences onto their preferred candidate. Policy voters have seldom been visible in elections. In 1972, they were around in abundance, especially within the ranks of people calling themselves Democrats.

In short, what the election survey shows is that the electorate —and especially Democrats and Independents—reacted to the political issues of the 1972 election in a highly ideological fashion. Younger people tended to find a meaning for *liberal* and *conservative* with reference to the war, including such questions as withdrawal from Vietnam, reducing military spending, and amnesty; and to a number of cultural issues, including such questions as abortion, equal rights for women, and the legalization of marijuana. Older voters, on the other hand, tended to find a meaning for these two terms with reference to economic issues, such as government health insurance, the obligation of the federal government to provide a good standard of living, and so forth.

PARTY IDENTIFICATION IN 1972.   Is party identification dying as an influence upon voting? Hardly. In 1972, its presence was still indicated. McGovern still received 58 percent of Democratic votes—despite his being the least popular presidential candidate in 20 years, despite being perceived by the voters to be taking a position farther away from them on issues than Nixon, despite being heartily disliked by some Democrats (both Edward Kennedy *and* George Wallace were more popular), and despite his running in an election in which polarization was evident in the ranks of Democrats on a scale never before observed. But in the 1972 election, party identification took second place to issues as the single most important determinant of the vote.[30]

The Role of Presidential Leadership.   Some years ago, in a brilliant study of the presidency, Richard Neustadt considered what he described as the necessary role of the president as teacher to the public. That kind of teaching, he observed, is needed to gain or maintain public approval of policy, but it is no easy job. Why?

> First, it is instruction aimed at students who . . . are habitually inattentive to the teacher: his constituents outside the Washington community. These students grow attentive only when they notice public trouble pressing on their lives. Second, as a consequence he can expect attention from them only when the things he need interpret to his benefit are on their minds for reasons independent of his telling. Third, again in consequence, he teaches less by telling than by doing (or not doing) in the context that his students have established in their minds. And fourth, what he has previously said and done will figure in that context. When the man inside the White House gains attention outside Washington, he finds two other teachers at the podium. Events themselves are there; so are the memories of past performance. Under these conditions presidential teaching is a formidable job. It is not to be confused with advertising.[31]

Students inattentive except when *public trouble presses on their lives*. Students willing to listen only about *things that are already on their minds*. Teaching *less by saying than by doing*. *Two other teachers* at the podium, one of which is *events*.

If Neustadt is correct, then the forces observed at work in the making of the 1972 election suggest the likelihood that public trouble was pressing on the lives of many people (recall the decline in trust and feelings of efficacy, and the polarization among Democrats), that they were ready to listen to teaching on the issues, and that the incumbent president, by his acts, had done a certain amount of effective teaching, and that events during the period before the election had done some teaching of their own.

The findings from the 1972 election study also furnish further reason for repeating what was said earlier about the impact of elections: They cannot themselves directly make policy —they cannot give a mandate—but they can be used to choose leaders whose policy positions matter to the electorate. In turn, what leaders *do,* and that competing "teacher," events, leave their impact upon the voter. Leaders may be chosen because of policies and practices with which they become identified. Then, after being elected, leaders can, by their subsequent acts make other issues, old and new, salient.

NOTES

The opening quotation is from V. O. Key, Jr., *Politics, Parties and Pressure Groups,* 5th ed. (New York: Crowell Collier Macmillan, 1964), 457, 463. The second is from Hunter S. Thompson, *Fear and Loathing: On the Campaign Trail, 1972* (New York: Popular Library, 1973), 173–174. The third is from Timothy Crouse, *The Boys on the Bus:* Riding with the Campaign Press Corps (New York: Ballantine, 1972), 361.

1. See Lucius Wilmerding, Jr., *The Electoral College* (New Brunswick, N.J.: Rutgers University Press, 1958); Judith H. Parris, *The Convention Problem* (Washington, D.C.: Brookings, 1972); and John H. Yunker and Lawrence D. Longley, "The Biases of the Electoral College," in Donald R. Matthews (editor), *Perspectives on Presidential Selection* (Washington, D.C.: Brookings, 1973), 172–203.
2. Eugene Roseboom provides a description of the major features of every presidential election through 1960 in his *A History of Presidential Elections* (New York: Macmillan, 1964).
3. Yet in 1964 the Republican vice-presidential candidate, William Miller, failed to carry his home state of New York; in 1968 Republican vice-presidential candidate Spiro Agnew failed to carry his home state of Maryland; and in 1972 the Democratic presidential candidate, George McGovern, did not carry his home state of South Dakota.
4. On the 1964 election, see especially the following: Aage R. Clausen and others, "Electoral Myth and Reality: The 1964 Election," *American Political Science Review* 59 (June 1965), 321–336; Milton C. Cummings, Jr. (editor), *The National Election of 1964* (Washington, D.C.: Brookings, 1966); John H. Kessel, *The Goldwater Coalition* (Indianapolis, Ind.: Bobbs-Merrill, 1968); Bernard Cosman and Robert J. Huckshorn (editors); *Republican Politics* (New York: Praeger, 1968); Theodore H. White, *The Making of the President, 1964* (New York: Atheneum, 1965); Bernard Cosman, *Five States for Goldwater* (University, Ala.: University of Alabama Press, 1966); Robert D. Novak, *The Agony of the G.O.P., 1964* (New York: Macmillan, 1965).
5. See Nelson W. Polsby and Aaron D. Wildavsky, *Presidential Elections,* 2nd ed. (New York: Scribners, 1968), especially chapter 2.
6. The best available account of presidential primaries through the primaries of 1964 is found in James W. Davis, *Presidential Primaries* (New York: Crowell Collier Macmillan, 1967).
7. Ibid., especially chapter 2.
8. On the usefulness of the primaries in the campaign of Republican Dwight D. Eisenhower for the nomination in 1952, see Davis, *Presidential Primaries,* especially chapters 3 and 4. For a first-rate discussion of the primary competition among Republicans in 1964, including a discussion of the efforts on behalf of Henry Cabot Lodge in New Hampshire, see White, *The Making of the President, 1964,* especially chapters 3 and 4.
9. For a classic account of the mechanics and role of a presidential primary, see Theodore H. White, *The Making of the President, 1960* (New York: Atheneum, 1961), especially chapter 4. A distinctive view of the 1972 primaries worth reading is given in Hunter S. Thompson, *Fear and Loathing:*

On the Campaign Trail '72 (New York: Popular Library, 1973); Thompson covered the 1972 campaign for *Rolling Stone*. See also James P. Zais and John H. Kessel, "A Theory of Presidential Nominations with a 1968 Illustration," in Donald R. Matthews (editor), *Perspectives on Presidential Selection* (Washington, D.C.: Brookings, 1973), 120–142.

10. Dwight D. Eisenhower, *Mandate for Change* (New York: Doubleday, 1963), especially chapter 1.

11. See earlier references to the 1964 presidential election cited in note 4.

12. See White, *The Making of the President, 1960.*

13. See Austin Ranney, "The McGovern-Fraser Commission Reforms and Their Probable Impact in 1972 and Beyond," a paper prepared for delivery at the annual meeting of the Southern Political Science Association, Gatlinburg, Tennessee, November 1971, and Theodore H. White, *The Making of the President, 1972* (New York: Atheneum, 1973), especially chapter 2. See also, for two contrasting perspectives on the Democratic reforms, Judith A. Center, "1972 Democratic Convention Reforms and Party Democracy," *Political Science Quarterly* 89 (June 1974), 325–350; and Jeffrey L. Pressman and Denis G. Sullivan, "Convention Reform and Conventional Wisdom: An Empirical Assessment of Democratic Party Reforms," *Political Science Quarterly* 89 (Fall 1974), 539–562. The quotation is from the report of the McGovern-Fraser Commission published as *Mandate for Reform* by the Democratic National Committee, Washington, D.C., in 1970. A careful assessment of the impact of the reforms upon the national convention of 1972 is given in Denis G. Sullivan and others, *The Politics of Representation: The Democratic Convention 1972* (New York: St. Martin, 1974).

14. Loch K. Johnson and Harlan Hahn, "Delegate Turnover at National Party Conventions, 1944–1968," in Matthews, *Perspectives on Presidential Selection,* 143–171.

15. Arthur H. Miller and others, "A Majority Party in Disarray," as delivered to the American Political Science Association, New Orleans, September 1973.

16. M. Ostrogorski, *Democracy and the Organization of Political Parties,* vol. 2, *The United States,* edited and abridged by Seymour Martin Lipset (New York: Quadrangle Books, 1964), 143; and Dwight D. Eisenhower, "Our National Nominating Conventions are a Disgrace," *Reader's Digest* 89 (July 1966), 76–80.

17. James P. Zais and John H. Kessel, "A Theory of Presidential Nominations, with a 1968 Illustration," in Matthews, *Perspectives on Presidential Selection,* 120–142.

18. But Austin Ranney, "The McGovern-Fraser Commission Reforms," disagrees.

19. On presidential campaigning generally, see Polsby and Wildavsky, *Presidential Elections;* and Karl A. Lamb and Paul A. Smith, *Campaign Decision-Making* (Belmont, Mass.: Wadsworth, 1968).

20. On the role of television, see Stanley Kelley, Jr., *Political Campaigning* (Washington, D.C.: Brookings, 1960); Gene Wyckoff, *The Image Candidates* (New York: Macmillan, 1968); Joe McGinniss, *The Selling of the President, 1968* (New York: Trident Press, 1969); Richard Rose, *Influencing Voters* (New York: St. Martin, 1968); and Gary C. Jacobson, "The Impact of Broadcast Campaigning on Electoral Outcomes," a paper pre-

pared for delivery at the 1974 annual meeting of the American Political Science Association, September 1974.

21. The best recent summary of what is known about financing presidential elections is Delmer D. Dunn, *Financing Presidential Campaigns* (Washington, D.C.: Brookings, 1972).

22. Miller and others, "A Majority Party in Disarray."

23. Bernard Cosman, *Five States for Goldwater.*

24. See White, *The Making of the President, 1972.*

28. On the limited pull of coattails see Warren E. Miller, "Presidential Coattails," *Public Opinion Quarterly* 19 (1955), 353–368.

29. See Bernard Berelson and others, *Voting* (Chicago: University of Chicago Press, 1954), 313–317.

25. In 1964, 22 percent of the population said they could trust the government to do what is right only some of the time. In 1968 the figure was 35 percent. In 1972 it increased to 44 percent. Those individuals most likely to be Democrats—blacks, the relatively poor, the relatively less well educated, Jews, and youth—were those who became less trusting of government between 1968 and 1972.

26. In 1964, 28 percent of the electorate said they thought the government operated in a manner more beneficial to special interests than to the general public. In 1968 the figure rose to 38 percent. In 1972 it had risen again—to 56 percent.

27. In 1964, 60 percent of the electorate disagreed with the following statement, thus indicating feelings of efficacy: "I don't think public officials care much about what people like me think." In 1968 the comparable figure was 53 percent, and in 1972 it was 49 percent.

30. See Miller and others, "A Majority Party in Disarray," as delivered to the American Political Science Association, New Orleans, September 1973.

31. Richard Neustadt, *Presidential Power* (New York: Wiley, 1960), 100. Used by permission.

Part Four

Party in Government

The literature abounds in assumptions concerning the virtues of two-party competition that are difficult to if not impossible to measure, such as that it results in more honest government. However, a central consequence believed to result from two-party competition does lend itself to quantitative analysis. According to most observers, two-party competition almost invariably leads to appeals for the support of lower-income voters because they are so numerous, while other political systems tend to be more oligarchical and less responsive to the needs and desires of the poor. Consequently, it is believed, two-party competition is more likely to lead to subsequent governmental actions addressed to these needs. If this assumption is true, it should be reflected in relative levels of governmental expenditure, particularly for items such as welfare and public education, which are designed to reduce inequalities in the distribution of goods and opportunities.

Recent comparative, quantitative studies of state politics conclude that party competition and other political variables have little or no impact on important state policies such as per pupil expenditure, old age assistance, unemployment compensation, and aid to dependent children. These are rather unexpected and disturbing conclusions. . . .

We have been too simple-minded in our measurement of "politics" and "policy."

Recent empirical investigations have provided scant support for the hypothesis that political participation is integrally related to policy outcomes.

It may not be only "how much" a state has in terms of economic resources, but also "where the resources are," and "who controls them" that trigger political controversies and shape policies.

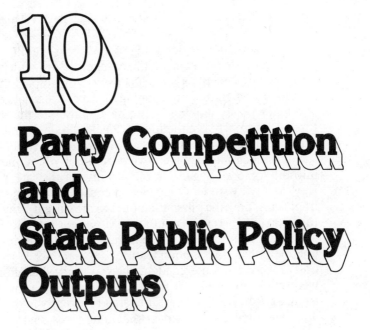

10

Party Competition and State Public Policy Outputs

Earlier chapters noted some important differences between Republicans and Democrats. Chapter 6 added a new twist. It showed that indeed there are differences between Republican and Democratic party leaders, but that sometimes, leaders of one party have much more in common with leaders of the opposite party in another place than they do with leaders of their own party. Data from studies of Kansas and Oklahoma provide a good demonstration of this point. This illustrates the importance of the competitive status of the two major parties within a given community, and the value of distinguishing which is the majority and which is the minority party.

This chapter continues that line of inquiry. It first surveys the various attempts that have been made to measure interparty competition in various locales—a job that one might think would be an uncomplicated business, but which turns out not to be so at all. Literally dozens of ways have been found to measure competition. Here we look at some of the better known of them, and offer still another technique for measuring competition.

The purpose of this section is twofold: (1) First, it seeks to acquaint the reader with a subject (interparty competition and its impact upon public policy) that justifiably continues to engage the attention and interest of a great many people who feel that a two-party or multiparty system is hardly deserving of the label if public policies all look pretty much alike, regardless of which party is in power. In passing, it considers the impact that demands for a fairer apportioning of seats in legislatures and other policy-making bodies have had upon the structure of interparty competition. (2) The second purpose is to use this area of inquiry as an illustration of typical social science inquiry. Here we sketch out where inquiry into the topic all began (in the writings of the late V. O. Key, Jr.), why students were led to consider the subject important, how they first attempted to measure it, why those early efforts were not thought to be entirely satisfactory, what definitional and measurement problems (many unanticipated—a common feature of social science inquiry) were encountered along the way, and what efforts were made to surmount them; and finally, we provide a summary of where we appear to stand currently in our understanding of the impact that interparty competition can have upon public policy. Then too, underlying these two stated objectives is this third, implicit objective: that as a result of this discussion, students may find their own interest engaged and may use what is said here about the substance and methods common to this line of inquiry to explore new directions they believe may extend our understanding of the subject beyond its present bounds.

Anyone who keeps an eye on politics has long observed that there is variety in the politics of the 50 states. One place variety appears is in election returns. Some states seem to be almost solidly in the control of one political party. The states of the South have been like that. Indeed *the Solid South* is only a shorthand phrase useful in summarizing a past tendency of states in that region to elect none but Democrats to all public offices. Other states, like Connecticut and Delaware, are strongly competitive. Here, Republicans and Democrats share control of the statehouse, the legislature, and other elected offices. Such states give their electoral votes for president sometimes to the Republicans, at other times to the Democrats. In still other states, one party has a record of winning most of the time, but the other party—whichever it is—is always there, always competitive, though never quite able to win control of state government.

Why do these differences in competition exist? What is the

best way to measure them? Do they signify anything the student of political parties needs to take note of? It is the search for answers to these and related questions that prompts students of parties to try to categorize states according to the degree of inter-party competition they display.

The Many Ways of Measuring Competition

Many ways of measuring interparty competition have been de-vised. In fact, there are about as many classification schemes as there are classifiers. In part, this abundance reflects the different concerns of those doing the classifying. Some students, chiefly in-terested in *intrastate* competition, concentrate upon the votes cast for state offices only. Others choose a mix of state and national offices. Still others zero in on the variety of factionalism found in state parties. V. O. Key's classic study of southern politics is a notable example.[1] Others use a scheme which demonstrates not only what the *overall* competition has been between the parties, but also demonstrates how frequently (or infrequently) the two parties have *alternated* their control of major office.[2] Still others— Duane Lockard is a good example—classify states according to the dominant characteristics of each state's party organizations, for example their cohesiveness, the strength of the party leader-ship, and so forth.[3]

There is, then, no obvious way to measure interparty com-petition in a given state. Different purposes seemingly demand different devices. Every classification scheme has its distinctive characteristics, which is merely to say that it is limited in its usefulness by the particular methodology undergirding it. The classification scheme has yet to be devised—it probably cannot be—that will highlight all features of state party systems equally well. As analytic tools, all such schemes have their particular limitations which stem from the choices made in the selection of data and concepts. Five choices, which every classifier must face, are particularly significant: the choice of the time span; the selec-tion of offices examined; the choice of which party's votes to count; the decision to measure overall rather than alternating competition; the definition of competition implicit in the scheme.

Choice of Time Span.   Three time periods would appear to be reasonable choices. Some choose the period to date from the time of the Civil War. That cataclysm, like the Great Depression later, rerouted the party loyalties of literally millions of Americans. It not only created solid Democratic states in the South but created entrenched loyalties to the Republican party in the North. The framework for competition thus created persisted relatively intact until the succeeding great event, the depression. What one achieves with such a broad historical perspective is, of course, achieved only at the loss of an appreciation of the impact that particular elections can have upon the broader political landscape. A second time period, to date from the year 1932—a year that may be taken as heralding the beginning of the political impact of the depression—can be justified for the same reasons.

A third period, to date from 1946 or 1948, can also be justified. That period is distinctive in many respects, among which may be mentioned the increasing prosperity, educational attainment, urbanization, and mobility of the population; the growth of the Republican Party in the South; the gradual confrontation with the race problem; the increased salience of issues and candidates; the development of television; and the gradual erosion of party loyalties—all of which developments, one may suspect, have left their impact upon interparty competition. There is no obvious reason why one time period should be absolutely preferred above any other. Campaign managers, for example, usually look no farther back than one or two elections. But it is necessary to appreciate that the choice of a time period is important. Delaware turns up regularly on *any* list of the more competitive states, while Mississippi, all agree, ranks among the least competitive. But the ranking given to a number of western and New England states does differ, depending upon what time period is considered. The lesson is obvious. The patterns of competition over the past century are anything but constant, and one dare not speak of the pattern of competition observed between American parties without carefully specifying the time period about which one speaks.

Overall or Alternating Competition.   Suppose we look at two states, A and B, at four-year intervals over a 32-year period to see which party has controlled one or more of the major offices there. Suppose these results turn up:

State A: D   R   D   R   D   R   D   R
State B: D   D   D   D   R   R   R   R

If we merely count the number of times each party controlled these offices over all of the period, a measure of overall competition, we would have to consider these two states identically competitive. Yet there is much less shifting around in state B. It is more stable. Democrats were in control for the first 16 years, Republicans for the 16 after that. In state A, on the other hand, control of the offices changed party hands every four years. On the score of how often during the period control of offices *changed hands,* a measure of alternating competition, state A is clearly more competitive than state B. None of the 50 states looks exactly like either state A or B in this example, but some states in the Union resemble them. States in the West generally rank high in alternating competition for major offices, though even among the most competitive a change of party control occurs in only about half of the elections. States generally are more competitive in presidential than in gubernatorial elections. Only five states, Wyoming, Colorado, Nevada, Washington, and Connecticut have shown a pattern of alternating competition in races for both offices in this century.[4]

Knowing that one state shows a good deal more alternating competition than another hints at the existence of other things worth looking into. It seems likely that high alternation will be found where any or all of the following are present: large numbers of people who are Independents; high mistrust; rapid population growth; elections in which candidates (rather than parties or issues) are dominant; candidate-centered campaign organizations; a high degree of polarization in either or both of the major parties; marked fluctuations in turnout; marked social cleavage; a distinctive political culture. (The higher rates of alternation observed among western states is attributed to their not having been affected by the Civil War to the extent that other, older states were.[5])

Choice of Offices. There is no agreement on what offices are more likely to provide the better (most accurate and/or revealing) evidence of competition between parties. What choices are made necessarily reflect particular research objectives, quite properly so. Those whose immediate concern is with comparing states usually look at election returns for one or more offices which are everywhere elected on a statewide basis. The offices of president, U. S. senator, and governor are common choices.

Those whose greatest concern is with establishing a connection between interparty competition and state public policy often prefer to look instead at party control of the legislature and governor's chair.

An even more vexing problem is whether to attempt to devise an index of competition that measures competition for just one office or for more than one office at a time.[6] If we go the one-office-at-a-time route and examine competition, say, for the governorship and presidency separately, we quickly find some striking contrasts. Ohio and Wisconsin for example, are about equally competitive across all offices elected on a statewide basis. Yet Ohio is competitive in contests for the governorship, but much less competitive in presidential races, while Wisconsin is exactly the opposite. Arizona is pictured in most classifications as clearly one-party Democratic in statewide races. Yet it has given its votes to the Republican candidate for president six out of seven times in the postwar period. In that same period, states in the South have remained strongly Democratic in elections for state offices, but they have shown an increasing willingness to support Republicans in congressional and presidential races.

Obviously, competition—whether alternating or overall— varies not only from state to state but from office to office within the state. At the least, this tells us to be cautious about ever speaking of interparty competition in a state or among the several states unless we take care to specify which offices are more and which are less competitive. If it turns out that all offices appear to be equally competitive, that in itself may be a notable finding, because such is not usually the case in state politics.

A scheme that assesses the competition evident in races for several different offices by a single measure has one drawback. It obscures (by burying) the range, variety, and details of competition that may be found in individual offices. A campaigner for the president who considered Wisconsin and Ohio similarly competitive, and hence equally worthy of his campaign efforts, would be either naive or just plain stupid. On the other hand, if one's interest is in gaining some appreciation of the totality of competition within a community, a combined measure is valuable.

The Third-Party Problem.   Although Republicans and Democrats stand center stage in most elections, that is not always the case. The Progressives in 1924, the Dixiecrats and the Progressives in 1948, and the American Independent party in 1968 are third parties which have figured importantly in presidential elections. Such a party may be so strong for a time that it completely displaces one of the two parties we usually think of as being *the* major American parties.

Most observers regard Wisconsin as a two-party state. But Leon Epstein, a long-time student of Wisconsin politics disagrees. He regards the period from 1934 to 1944, during which the Progressive party was the second of the two major parties, as something more than just a period of second-party activity under a different party label. He sees this period as a crucial time of *three-party politics,* out of which Wisconsin began in the late 1940s to emerge as a two-party state. Any study therefore, that disguises Progressive party strength, by lumping that party and the Democratic party of an earlier period, together under a broad second-party classification, Epstein regards as a serious distortion of the political forces at work there during the period.[7] However, adding the election victories of the Progressives to the Democrats in Wisconsin to give an overall measure of *second*-party successes can be defended on the ground that party labels are scarcely that important to the dynamics of interparty competition *as such.* Some students argue, as does V. O. Key, that the mere existence of an organized party opposition, regardless of the party *name,* is what gives a party system its most distinctive features. By this reasoning, the classification of Wisconsin as a two-party state is legitimate.[8]

How do we deal with the third-party problem? One way is simply to restrict our attention to competition between the two strongest parties in a place, regardless of what their names happen to be. This is obviously a defensible position. If that is our choice, than it makes sense to ignore the votes given to any *minor* third-party or independent candidates. However, we may well feel nervous if we choose entirely to ignore the votes given a *major* third-party candidate. The appearance of a strong third party suggests that some significant portion of the electorate is dissatisfied with the style of competition between the two major parties, and it may even herald a coming realignment. Its presence may tell us much worth knowing about competition among the parties.

So there are technical problems. And choices to be made. Where does this leave us in our search for what is obviously an elusive phenomenon, but one which a great many people believe is an important area of inquiry? At the very least, it forces us to consider and decide what it is we are trying to measure, and then ask why.

Predicting Margins of Victory and Loss

"He won by a hair." "That was a really close election!" "Soundly defeated." "Landslide." "He never had a chance." "Just wait until next time." Implicit in these popular appraisals of election outcomes is an emphasis not just upon the existence of competition between parties in elections, but upon the closeness of the competition. A measure of interparty competition which fails to take the element of closeness into account is not a very discriminating measure.[9] Further, since competition is normally viewed not at one moment in time, but through time, an adequate representation of interparty competition must consider how much variation there is from one election to the next. Are elections usually close, or only close on occasion? Furthermore, although losing is never literally the same as winning, losers do on occasion receive congratulations for having done better than expected—better than previous candidates, better than others in the same election, or better than expected given the circumstances of the campaign. Similarly, the winning candidate may be considered weak, if he wins by less than some expected margin of victory. How does anyone tell what margin of victory or loss may reasonably be expected?

A Party's Normal Vote.   The solution is not difficult. A party's chance to be a success, its expected share of the vote, its *normal* vote, may be measured simply by seeing how well it has done before.

Suppose the Republican candidate for governor of North Carolina received 41, 43, 47, 46, and 48 votes in the last five elections. (The numbers, of course, are made up and have been kept small to make calculations easier.) In these elections, the Republican candidate received an average of 45 votes. That can be one estimate of the Republican party's normal vote for that office.

Weighted Averages.   One objection any candidate, campaign manager, or close observer of politics may make to this procedure for calculating the normal vote is that it does not take account of what looks like an upward trend in favor of the Republican party, and thus underestimates the party's normal vote *as of this moment*. Campaign people trying to calculate their chances of success this year are inclined to pay greater heed to what happened last year than to what happened years ago. They figure that party loyalties do shift, along with issues, and that the influences which determine the outcome of today's election are more likely to resemble those that operated in more recent elections than those that were at work in elections several years in the past. If we find merit in that argument, as well we may, then our calculation of a party's normal vote should be weighted in a way that will give greater emphasis to the party's comparative strength in recent elections than to its strength several elections back.

All this requires is to count the figures from recent elections more heavily (more often) than the figures from earlier elections. Since we are dealing with five elections we may multiply the figure for the last election by 5, the figure for the election before that by 4, for the election before that by 3, for the election before that by 2, and for the first election in the series by 1. Summing these figures and then dividing, not by 5 but by 15, gives us a weighted average of 46 votes. This weighted average then becomes another estimate of the party's normal vote as of this moment.

Expected Variation. An estimate of the normal vote is a help in knowing how closely competitive parties are. Suppose a candidate receives 45 votes in the next election. This is one vote below the normal vote, but it is three votes below what the candidate won in the last election. Do we say this is an acceptable showing (compared with earlier candidate performances), or do we feel very gloomy? Some measure of how much *variation* has occurred in past elections, and thus can be expected now, may help us decide.[10]

Producing an estimate of expected variation is easy. Using the same data as before, we find the absolute difference between the Republican share of the vote in each pair of elections. There are four pairs and the differences are 2 (41-43), 4 (43-47), 1 (47-46), and 2 (46-48). Sum the four figures (9), and divide by 4. The answer is 2.2. This is our estimate of the normal variation in Republican strength for the office of governor. Since the latest candidate came within one vote of the party's normal vote *and* within the expected variation of 2.2 votes, we may say his was an acceptable showing. If the candidate had won only 44 votes, we would be inclined to say he made a poorer than expected showing, because his share of votes would be below the normal vote and outside the normal variation.

We may also calculate a weighted measure of variation. For these five elections, that turns out to be 2.1 votes. This lower estimate of expected variation obtained using a weighted average —like the higher estimate of the normal vote obtained when a weighted average is used—is appealing because it takes account of the pattern of voting strength evident in the more recent elections.

A Formula for Measuring Interparty Competition.   Once we have calculated each party's normal vote and the expected variation, it is an easy step to calculate a measure of interparty competition (IPC) between the two parties. The following formula will do it quite nicely.

$$IPC = \frac{NV(1)-NV(2)}{V(1)+V(2)} \div 2$$

where

> $NV(1)$ is the estimated normal vote for party 1
> $NV(2)$ is the estimated normal vote for party 2
> $V(1)$ is the expected variation for party 1
> $V(2)$ is the expected variation for party 2

Use of this formula in the examination of election returns should reveal the exact status of competition between the parties through time. In interpreting the figures generated by use of the formula, which provides a quantitative measure of interparty competition, as well as the estimates of the normal vote and variation, the following should be kept in mind:

> High variation across several elections indicates instability and suggests a situation of weak party organization, perhaps a situation in which candidates and candidate organizations play a more prominent role than parties.
> An increase in the size of a minority party's normal vote indicates an increasingly competitive situation.
> A continuous increase in the size of a party's normal vote,

accompanied by a decrease in variation, suggests a consolidation of that party's support and, if it is the minority party, a potential for realignment.

The most highly competitive situation exists not only when the differences between the normal votes of the parties is slight, but perhaps even more importantly, whenever the upper boundary of the expected variation in the normal vote of the minority party is higher than the lower boundary of the expected variation in the normal vote of the majority party. Such a situation would exist, for example, if the normal votes were 46 and 54 for parties A and B respectively, and the expected variations were 3 and 6. In this case, the upper range of the normal vote for A would be 49, while the lower range of the normal vote for B would be 48, a clear indication that no one should be surprised if in the next election, party B, the minority party, won 49 votes, while party A won only 48.

Our Present Understanding of Interparty Competition

Many attempts have been made to uncover the relationship between aspects of politics in the several states, including interparty competition, apportionment, the states' social and economic characteristics, and their public policies. This area of inquiry is thriving. Students of politics have designed more than 100 schemes for measuring interparty competition. With so much talent and effort concentrated on this subject, where do we stand right now? If one thing comes shining through from this multitude of studies, it is that our understanding of the relationships among social, economic, and political characteristics of the states is far from adequate. We have made a good beginning in the direction of understanding, but no more than that. We appreciate, perhaps, better than we did before that state politics is multifaceted and enormously complex and that sorting out the influences that go into the making of state politics and policies is not an easy task. And thanks in part to some imaginative research designs which have struck out in quite new directions, we have come to appreciate the importance of paying attention to the influence of some variables that were not much looked at before. Today we realize that we have probably not identified more than a tiny fraction of the influences that go into the making of state politics and policy. As an illustration of how we have come to this stage in our thinking, let us review briefly two areas of research, both of which have sought to define interparty competition and locate its place and importance in state politics: (1) studies in the impact of interparty competition upon public policy, and (2) studies in the impact of reapportionment upon public policy.

Interparty Competition and Public Policy. In Key's earliest major work, *Southern Politics,* one theme dominates, and that theme is this: One-party politics, southern-style, tends to work for those who have more, and against those who have less. Key saw the degree of party competition as crucial, because it reflects the extent to which politics is organized or unorganized. In his view, party competition produces some semblance of an organized politics, and thus makes it possible for lower-status groups to sort out and distinguish actors and issues and thus to perceive which party is more likely to be helpful in promoting their interests.

In a similar vein, Lockard argued from his study of New England politics that a community with a diverse economy would be more likely to have competitive parties, since the mere diversity of the economic interests would provide a context within which contrasting and competitive parties could flourish.[11]

EARLY FINDINGS. From the work of Key and Lockard emerge several propositions bearing on the relationship between party competition and public policy:

1. In the two-party states, the anxiety over the next election pushes political leaders into serving the interests of the have-less elements of society, thereby putting the party into the countervailing power operation.
2. In one-party states, it is easier for a few powerful interests to manage the government of a state without party interference, since the parties are not representative of the particular elements that might pose opposition to the dominant interest group.

3. Over the long run, the have-nots lose in a disorganized politics. They have no mechanism through which to act, and their wishes find expression in fitful rebellions led by transient demagogues, who gain their confidence but often have neither the technical competence nor the necessary stable base of political power to effectuate a program.

4. A loose factional system lacks the power to carry out sustained programs of social action, which almost always are thought by upper status people to be contrary to their immediate interests. This negative weakness thus redounds to the benefit of those in the upper-income brackets.

5. Weak party cohesion is generally associated with strong pressure politics, and strong party cohesion with weak pressure politics. And party cohesion is a direct function of the degree of competition between political parties; that is, the more marked is interparty competition, the more pronounced is party cohesion.

Though Key's work was published in 1949, it was not until 1963 that a large-scale study was made to determine whether the propositions he advanced were true for *all* states, not just the southern states. The study in question was done by Dawson and Robinson and employed still another classification scheme for interparty competition, which measured three dimensions of competition: (1) the relative strength of each party, as reflected in the popular vote for governor and the percentage of seats held by each party in each house of the state legislature; (2) the percentage of time each party controlled each of the three state institutions; and (3) the precentage of time the parties divided control of these three institutions, one party controlling one of the institutions, and the other party controlling the other two.[12]

COMPETITION AND SOCIAL WELFARE POLICY.   The specific hypothesis the study set out to test was: "The greater the degree of interparty competition within a political system, the more extensive or 'liberal' the social welfare policies a political system will adopt." A *social welfare policy* was defined as any policy or program which directly or indirectly redistributes wealth, that is, whose purpose is to benefit the lower socioeconomic groups at the expense of upper-income groups. Nine such policies were identified, including four revenue and five expenditure policies.

A strong relationship was found to exist between each of the three dimensions of interparty competition and each of the nine public welfare policies. Here, then, was evidence that states with competitive parties tended to adopt more liberal social welfare policies—a finding consistent with the earlier conclusions of Key and Lockard.

Numerous writers have told us that political systems are strongly influenced by economic factors. Could it be shown that competition *and* policies were associated with differences in the economies of the several states? Three economic indices were selected—per capita income, degree of industrialization, and urbanization. A strong relationship was found to exist between per capita income and the nine public welfare policies.

Still unanswered was the question of major concern: Was interparty competition by itself—that is, independent of socio-economic factors—an influence upon the adoption of public welfare policies? The study had shown that wealthier states had more competitive parties *and* more liberal public welfare policies. Did they have more liberal policies merely because they were richer and therefore could afford them, or did the level of competition play a role in shaping these policies? The results of further investigation suggested that wealth influenced or at least was as strongly related to policies as was interparty competition.

The overall conclusion from the study, as Dawson and Robinson themselves put it, was this:

> If the data reported and the operations employed have been measuring what we have presumed them to measure, inter-party competition does not play as influential a role in determining the nature and scope of welfare policies as earlier studies have suggested. The level of public social welfare programs in the American states seems to be more a function of socio-economic factors, especially per capita income.[13]

These findings were something of a surprise, but following Dawson and Robinson a number of other studies appeared and they too concluded that the structure of competition between parties did not by itself have nearly so great an impact upon public policy as it was once thought it did.[14]

OUR PRESENT UNDERSTANDING OF THE RELATIONSHIPS. Then in 1969 came still another study which discovered that a relationship *could be found* between interparty competition and public policies, independent of a state's social and economic characteristics, *but the relationship was much stronger in the case of some policies than it was of others.* It was weak, almost nonexistent, in the case of old age assistance and educational expenditures, but fairly strong in the case of aid to dependent children. This study made by Cnudde and McCrone, reminded us that Key had said that party competition would have an impact in that domain of public policy which was central to the different interests of the "haves" and the "have-less." It also reminded us that we were in danger of misunderstanding the relationship between interparty competition and public policy if we failed to appreciate that not all areas were equally likely to produce a conflict of interests between the haves and those who have less.[15] Studies done after the 1969 study provide additional evidence for the major conclusions offered in that study.[16]

So we came full circle, almost. The essential soundness of the earlier observations of Key and Lockard was upheld, but those observations were qualified now by a need to understand precisely which policies were most likely to be influenced by interparty competition. And still there were questions unanswered. Is the impact of competition upon those policies upon which its impact is greatest the same in every state? Probably not, though even now we do not know. Do states differ in the identity and number of policies that are influenced by competition? Again, probably yes, and again, we do not know for sure. What the work of Dawson and Robinson, Cnudde and McCrone, and others did was to force us to think again about some propositions that had gone untouched by critical thought far too long. Their work did not lead us to reject those propositions outright. Rather it led to their refinement, and thus contributed to a sharper understanding of the place of parties in state politics.

Reapportionment and Public Policy. Similar to the course of the studies mentioned above was the development in studies of the impact of reapportionment upon public policy. In the early 1960s, the U.S. Supreme Court handed down the first in a series of decisions which insisted that the principle of "one man, one vote" must be followed when seats in elective bodies like state legislatures were being allocated among electoral subdivisions.[17] Before the first of these decisions was handed down in 1962,[18] some inequality of voting power existed in every state of the Union. In Vermont, for example, every town was entitled to elect one representative to sit in the lower house of the state legislature, regardless of the number of people who lived there. At that time, the town of Victory had a population of 35. The city of Burlington had a population of 35,000. Each was entitled to *one* representative in the Vermont General Assembly! The existing apportionment schemes, which were soon everywhere under attack, discriminated heavily against people in cities,[19] and against whichever party found its major support there.

Some who considered how things might be in the new days of the reapportioned legislatures did not like what they saw. An editorial writer for the *Phoenix Gazette,* the evening newspaper in Phoenix, Arizona—a city whose delegation to the state legislature later increased greatly under a reapportionment plan—saw it this way:

> The truth is that these changes would put almost the total political power of the nation in the hands of the least educated, least assimilated, social and ethnic groups that reside in the slums and ghettos of the great population complexes such as New York, Chicago, and Philadelphia. This would be done by giving the manipulators of such areas absolute power over state political machines, enabling them to dictate not only state patronage, but national representation also. Most of the big spending, welfare-boosting, centralizing liberals in Congress are elected from such areas.
> This is the stake in the reapportionment struggle.[20]

PRE-REAPPORTIONMENT STUDIES.   In the wake of the Supreme Court decisions, a number of studies undertook to see whether public policy actually was likely to change as malapportionment began to disappear. Early on the scene was Herbert Jacob, who set out to see whether there were marked differences in the kind of public policies adopted by states that at that time had fairly apportioned legislatures and those that did not. He found no real difference between them. He was unwilling to conclude that reapportionment was of no real consequence, but he did warn against exaggerating the impact that reapportionment itself might have upon public policy. As he said: "If malapportionment has a widespread effect on state politics, it is a good deal more subtle than we have hitherto thought." [21]

A later effort by Thomas Dye did find differences in the policies of the 50 states, but these differences could not be related to differences in apportionment alone. To some extent, it was clear that the differences were as much related to differences in the social and economic characteristics of the 50 states as they were to anything else. Harking back to an early study of legislative politics in Illinois, Dye reminded us that legislative control can change and policies remain the same, *if there are few policy differences between those who are taking control and those who are being replaced*. He also noted that many divisions exist in a legislature besides the division between city and country. These include "divisions between parties, between a Governor's supporters and his opponents, between economic interests and organized groups, between liberals and conservatives, between labor and management, between regions of a state, and so forth." [22]

A third study, done by Richard I. Hofferbert,[23] used data from each decade of this century in an attempt to see if individual states had changed much in their characteristics and policies over the course of 50 years. What it revealed was consistency in change. The states of 1960 were not what they had been 50 years earlier. Their social and economic characteristics had undergone major changes. So had their policies. So closely did change in policies follow change in the social and economic environment that there could be no doubt that the closest possible connection existed between that environment and policy. On the other hand, the study found almost no connection between the public policies adopted by states during this period and the level of competition between parties; nor could a relationship be found between these policies and malapportionment.

GEORGIA: A BEFORE-AND-AFTER STUDY. The fourth and last study to be noted here was done by a group of scholars working at the University of Georgia.[24] The Georgia study is different from earlier studies of reapportionment. It is a true "before-and-after" study. It looks at the Georgia legislature before, and then after, it was reapportioned. It differs from the earlier studies, too, because it found that, in Georgia, reapportionment *did* make a difference. After reapportionment, the cities had more representatives. The five urban counties in the Atlanta area had 13 members in the House of Representatives before reapportionment, and 46 after. The income and educational levels of all districts were higher. The number of representatives from counties with large black populations *decreased* (because so many of them were rural), but the number of black representatives went from 0 to 8 in the House and from 0 to 1 in the Senate. The number of Republicans increased from 2 to 23. The average age dropped noticeably. A survey of legislators indicated that those who came to the newly apportioned legislature from urban areas had more liberal attitudes than those from rural areas. After reapportionment, voting along rural-versus-urban lines (which had begun to appear before reapportionment) was very much in evidence.

These several bits of evidence led the authors of the Georgia study to conclude that, *in Georgia at least,* reapportionment did leave an impact and, contrary to the findings of earlier studies, did have policy implications, even if it had to be admitted that that impact was "more subtle than sharp, and less directly shown than inferred." [25]

By way of explaining why reapportionment might have an impact in Georgia when it appeared not to have an impact elsewhere, the study said:

> It is possible that the difference between the Georgia study and most others is simply due to Georgia having been an extreme case of malapportionment. In other words, reapportionment will make a difference for policy but only under exceptional circumstances. . . . Another possibility is that the difference between our findings and others is due to variables besides apportionment; in other words, apportionment systems may really not be that important for policy. When it is discovered that a relationship holds for some states but not others, political scientists should consider the possibility that other, intervening variables explain the difference. The key intervening variable or variables may pertain to properties of Georgia's political system other than apportionment, or to Georgia's political culture.[26]

Current Propositions. Where do we stand right now? The record of how quickly some earlier findings have been applauded, then questioned, then challenged, then qualified, and sometimes rejected, warns us against being too sure that we understand these relationships as well as we ought to. Nonetheless, it does seem possible to offer a few general propositions about these matters and to suggest where we might turn next in order to improve our understanding.

WITHIN-STATE VARIATIONS AND REDISTRIBUTIVE EFFECTS. Particularly in the work of Ira Sharkansky, we find support for the first three propositions, which are:

1. Differences in the public policies of the 50 states are related to differences in their overall social, economic, and political traits, but they are even more closely related to differences in the distribution of these traits within states.

2. The relationship between party competition and level of economic development is strong when it is states we are talking about, but it is not nearly so strong when it is counties we are talking about.

3. As students of comparative state politics, we are far from having assembled an exhaustive, or even adequate, list of the political variables that are worth investigating.[27]

Most of the studies of comparative state politics have had this in common: All have relied upon "averages"—per capita income, per pupil expenditure, per capita old age assistance payment—in the process of measuring relationships among social, economic, and political characteristics of the 50 states. Averages are useful for making broad interstate comparisons, but averages do have limits. An average can tell us how state X rates on some item and how it compares with other states, but it can tell us nothing about how much variation there is on that item *within* state X. Is variation within states important? Almost certainly it is. It may be much less important to know that state X has a slightly higher per capita income and spends a little more on schools than state Y, than it is to know how much variation in income and school expenditures there is within the state. Are there school districts which have a substantial tax base, pay high salaries, and can afford excellent facilities and equipment, while other districts are starved for funds? Or do all districts have roughly the same resources and offer about the same educational product?

Some work has been done along these lines, and the results are enticing. The work of Sharkansky [28] and Dye [29] suggests that within-state variations deserve more attention than they have been given so far. As Sharkansky puts it, "It may not be only "how much" a state has in terms of economic resources, but also "where the resources are," and "who controls them" that trigger political controversies and shape policies." [30]

The same point is apparent in the work of Fry and Winters, [31] who find that political variables have a much stronger relationship to policy than do social and economic variables, when policy variables are defined in terms of their *redistributive effects*. The question of concern to them is not the level of expenditure—not how much money is being spent—but who among various classes of people are receiving the greatest benefit from it, and especially what the ratio of benefit to burden is for different classes of citizens. This line of inquiry is surely one Key would approve.

Most studies have confined themselves to using variables which we can group together under the heading "representative mechanisms." Those most common are measures of interparty competition and malapportionment. The object has been to find the link between these mechanisms and public policies. Studies generally assume that a competitive party situation produces a demand for more welfare services. Yet there is no obvious reason why this should be so. In a competitive situation, it may well be that one party will see substantial advantages to be gained by the advocacy of a *reduction* in taxes and services. Moreover, it is conceivable that the highest levels in the provision of government services may occur where professionalism dominates local government agencies, a situation which may exist whether or not there is party competition. Sharkansky found this true in his study of professionalism and public policy in American counties. [32]

THE IMPORTANCE OF SOCIOECONOMIC DIVERSITY.

4. Party competition is more likely to affect public policies when the socioeconomic environment is diverse than when it is not.

This proposition, advanced by Duane Lockard, for one,

finds a connection between cleavages in the social and economic environment, the structure of political parties, and public policy. It argues that diversity in the socioeconomic environment, cleavages, provides the base upon which party alignments are built. It says that where a correspondence exists between socioeconomic cleavages and party alignments, the substance of public policy is quite likely to be a matter of crucial concern to the contending political parties. Lockard's evidence for this comes from his study of New England politics.[33] His thinking parallels rather closely the ideas of a good many students of comparative politics, including Giovanni Sartori [34] and Maurice Duverger.[35]

> The diversity or the lack of diversity of economic interests in a state tends to be reflected in the prevailing party system and the mode of its operation. In the first place, of course, it is the diversity in part that creates the atmosphere for two-party competition, and the absence of diversity facilitates non-partyism. In the two-party states the anxiety over the next election pushes political leaders into serving the interests of the have-less elements of society, thereby putting the party into the countervailing power operation. Conversely, in the one-party states it is easier for a few powerful interests to manage the government of the state without party interference since the parties are not representative of the particular elements that might pose opposition to the dominant interest groups. The parties do not represent the have-less elements for the simple reason that politically there is no necessity to do so.[36]

INTERPARTY COMPETITION AND POLICIES THAT FAVOR THOSE WHO HAVE LESS.

5. Party competition affects some policies more than others. It tends to have its greatest impact upon policies that are of immediate interest to those who have less.

This proposition merely restates a major finding common to the work of Key, Lockard, Sharkansky, and Hofferbert,[37] Cnudde and McCrone, Broach, and others. It is now one of the best-established propositions bearing upon the relationship between party competition and public policy. It is sometimes said that there cannot be a Republican as opposed to a Democratic way to operate a fire department. It used to be said that there could not be a Republican as opposed to a Democratic way to run a police department, but some people are not so sure about that any more. That in itself reminds us that there are areas of public policy over which the two major parties do not disagree, even though it is conceivable they might. Indeed, the areas of agreement or consensus which characterize the two parties is one of their most distinctive features, as it is also one of the points of contrast between them and parties in other countries, particularly parties in multiple-party systems. It is in part for this reason that the word *subtle* must appear in studies describing the impact of reapportionment upon public policy, and why the authors of the Georgia study felt obliged to observe that reapportionment would likely make a difference in the substance of policy only where the degree of malapportionment was unusually severe.

COMPETITION HAS A BROAD MEANING.

6. Electoral competition is not all there is to party "competition," nor is party "competition" the same as party "organization."

Votes are important. They are a measure of sorts of how effectively parties compete with one another. But using the evidence of how votes are distributed between the parties on election day as if they were the only or best indicator of how effectively parties compete with one another is a trifle indecent. Anyone who looks only to the election returns underestimates both the variety and the intensity of the competition between parties. Parties not only compete with one another for workers and votes, they also compete for talent, influence, dedication, loyalty, prestige, and reputation; and such things as talent and influence and the rest may have little to do with how the body count went last election day.

Lockard is right when he draws our attention to variety in the cohesiveness and leadership of political parties and outlines the impact such differences may have on public policy.[38] So too are Greenstein[39] and Sartori[40] when they observe that there are varieties even of two-party politics. The politics of Connecticut, with its two strong, competitive, broad-based, disciplined, and effective parties are quite different from the politics of Michigan, with its much less well organized and weakly led parties.

What then can we say about party competition in the states? We begin with the observation long made by students of state party politics that there is considerable variety in the politics of the 50 states. It is a mistake to assume that state parties are but little miniatures of the national parties. It is also a mistake to take seriously what every American schoolboy "knows" for certain: that America has a two-party system. By even the most generous standard of measurement, only half the states, or fewer, have two-party systems. By no stretch of the imagination can the American states be offered as proof of America's firm commitment to the virtues and supposed benefits of two-party politics. Insofar as any statement at all can be made about this commitment, it must be said that by their works, manifest in state politics, Americans are committed to two-party politics . . . and one-party politics . . . and weak minority-party politics.

NOTES

The first quotation is from John H. Fenton, *People and Parties in Politics* (Glenview, Ill.: Scott, Foresman, 1966), 32. The second is from Charles F. Cnudde and Donald J. McCrone, "Party Competition and Welfare Policies in the American States," *American Political Science Review* 63 (September 1969), 858–866. The third is from Ira Sharkansky and Richard I. Hofferbert, "Dimensions of State Politics, Economics, and Public Policy," *American Political Science Review* 63 (September, 1969), 867–879. The fourth is from Brian R. Fry, "An Examination of the Relationship Between Selected Electoral Characteristics and State Redistributive Efforts," *American Journal of Political Science* 18 (May 1974), 421–431. The last is from Ira Sharkansky, "Economic Development, Representative Mechanisms, Administrative Professionalism and Public Policies: A Comparative Analysis of Within-State Distributions of Economic and Political Traits," *Journal of Politics* 33 (February 1971), 112–132.

1. V. O. Key, Jr., *Southern Politics in State and Nation* (New York: Knopf, 1949).
2. Joseph A. Schlesinger, "A Two-Dimensional Scheme for Classifying the States According to Degree of Inter-Party Competition," *American Political Science Review* 49 (December 1955), 1120–1128.
3. Duane Lockard, *New England State Politics* (Princeton, N.J.: Princeton University Press, 1959), 320–337. See also his *The Politics of State and Local Government* (New York: Macmillan, 1963), 178–189. A thorough review of the literature on interparty competition is provided in John H. Fenton and Donald W. Chamberlayne, "The Literature Dealing with the Relationships Between Political Processes, Socio-Economic Conditions and Public Policies in the American States," *Polity* 1 (Spring 1969), 388–394.
4. Schlesinger, "A Two-Dimensional Scheme," 1120–1128.
5. Ibid.
6. The better-known studies, which examine various offices, are: Austin Ranney and Willmoore Kendall, *Democracy and the American Party System*

(New York: Harcourt Brace Jovanovich, 1956): president, U.S. senator, governor; Schlesinger, "A Two-Dimensional Scheme": president, governor; Hofferbert (see note 23 for citation): president, U.S. senator, governor; Dawson and Robinson (see note 13 for citation): the percentage of seats won by the predominant party in each house of the state legislature; number of times each party has won the governorship; Eulau (see note 19 for citation): Ohio House of Representatives; Robert J. Golembiewski, "A Taxonomic Approach to State Political Party Strength," *Western Political Quarterly* 11 (September 1958), 494–513: the percentage of seats in the state legislature controlled by the minority party; Lockard, *The Politics of State and Local Government:* many different offices. Pfeiffer (see note 10 for citation): president, U.S. senator, governor, "and any other official elected on a statewide basis"; Broach (see note 16 for citation): same as Pfeiffer; V. O. Key, Jr., *American State Politics* (New York: Knopf, 1956): governor.

7. Leon D. Epstein, *Politics in Wisconsin* (Madison, Wis.: University of Wisconsin Press, 1958), 33–35.

8. On the importance of interparty competition as such, see Key, *Southern Politics,* 299–310.

9. The importance of the perceived closeness of an election as a determinant of turnout is discussed in Angus Campbell and others, *The American Voter* (New York: Wiley, 1960), 90–101.

10. On the concept of the normal vote, see especially Philip E. Converse, "The Concept of the Normal Vote," in Angus Campbell and others, *Elections and the Political Order* (New York: Wiley, 1966), 9–39, and see also William H. Flanigan and Nancy Zingale, "Electoral Competition and Partisan Realignment," a paper prepared for delivery at the annual meeting of the American Political Science Association, New Orleans, La., September 1973, for a discussion of the value of a weighted over an unweighted estimate of the normal vote.

   One way to measure variation is, of course, by calculating the standard deviation. But the standard deviation is incapable of measuring the sequence of observations in measuring the degree of dispersion about the mean. The sequence in which change occurs is also of concern to David G. Pfeiffer, "The Measurement of Inter-Party Competition and Systemic Stability," *American Political Science Review* 61 (June 1967), 457–467.

11. Lockard, *New England State Politics,* especially chapter 12.

12. To arrive at the first of these measures, the following figures were calculated for each state for the period 1938 through 1958: the average percentage of the popular vote for governor received by the dominant party; the average percentage of seats held by the dominant party during each term of the lower house of the state legislature; the average percentage of seats held by the dominant party during each term of the upper house of the state legislature; and the average of the three preceding percentages. States were then ranked according to the last of these figures. This produced a ranking of states from high to low according to the overall measure of interparty competition in each state.

   The second measure of interparty competition was established by calculating the percentage of time each party controlled each of the same three institutions in the period studied, and then calculating the average of these percentages. Using this average, a rank order of states was prepared by ranking those states highest in which the average was closest to 50, and ranking those states lowest in which the average was farthest from 50.

The third measure of interparty competition was calculated by counting the number of times, at two-year intervals, that one party held one of the three institutions, and the other party controlled the other two, and then calculating what percentage this was of the total number of two-year periods. A rank order of states was then prepared, from high to low, according to these percentages, with 100 percent taken as the highest possible measure of this third dimension of interparty competition, and zero percent taken as the lowest. This set of calculations thus produced three rank orders of the states, one for each of the three dimensions of interparty competition.

13. Richard E. Dawson and James A. Robinson, "Inter-Party Competition, Economic Variables, and Welfare Policies in the American States," *Journal of Politics* 25 (May 1963), 265–289. Used by permission.

14. See especially Thomas R. Dye, *Politics, Economics, and the Public* (Skokie, Ill.: Rand McNally, 1966); and an excellent review article, Herbert Jacob and Michael Lipsky, "Outputs, Structure, and Power: An Assessment of Changes in The Study of State and Local Politics," in Richard Hofferbert and Ira Sharkansky (editors), *State and Urban Politics* (Boston: Little, Brown, 1971), 14–40.

15. Charles F. Cnudde and Donald J. McCrone, "Party Competition and Welfare Policies in the American States," *American Political Science Review* 63 (September 1969), 858–866.

16. Glen T. Broach, "Interparty Competition, State Welfare Policies, and Nonlinear Regression," *Journal of Politics* 35 (August 1973), 737–746.

17. A superb analysis of the issues in reapportionment can be found in Robert G. Dixon, Jr., *Democratic Representation* (New York: Oxford University Press, 1968).

18. *Baker* v. *Carr,* 369 U.S. 186 (1962). The other major decisions are *Reynolds* v. *Sims,* 377 U.S. 533 (1964); *Wesberry* v. *Sanders,* 376 U.S. 1 (1964); *Avery* v. *Midland County,* 390 U.S. 474 (1968); and *Hadley* v. *Junior College District,* 25 L. Ed. 2nd. 45 (1970).

19. On reapportionment and rural-urban conflicts, see Gordon E. Baker, *Rural Versus Urban Political Power* (New York: Random House, 1955); Daniel R. Grant and H. C. Nixon, *State and Local Government in America* (Boston: Allyn & Bacon, 1963), 204–205; Malcolm Jewell, *The State Legislature* (New York: Random House, 1962), 30–33; David R. Derge, "Metropolitan and Outstate Alignments in Illinois and Missouri Legislative Delegations," *American Political Science Review* 52 (December 1958), 1051–1065; V. O. Key, Jr., *American State Politics* (New York: Knopf, 1956), 227; Warren Moscow, *Politics in the Empire State* (New York: Knopf, 1948); Winston W. Crouch and others, *California Government and Politics,* 3rd ed. (Englewood Cliffs, N.J.: Prentice-Hall, 1964), chapter 4; Robert J. Golembiewski, "A Taxonomic Approach to State Political Party Strength," *Western Political Quarterly* 11 (September 1958), 494–513; Philips Cutright, "Urbanization and Competitive Party Politics," *Journal of Politics* 25 (August 1963), 552–564; Philip Coulter and Glen Gordon, "Urbanization and Party Competition," *Western Political Quarterly* 21 (June 1968), 274–288; Heinz Eulau, "The Ecological Bases of Party Sys-

tems: The Case of Ohio," *Midwest Journal of Political Science* 1 (February 1957), 125–135; a contrasting study by David Gold and John R. Schmidhauser, "Urbanization and Party Competition: The Case of Iowa," *Midwest Journal of Political Science* 4 (February 1960), 62–75; and on the varieties of urban political systems see Charles E. Gilbert and Christopher Clague, "Electoral Competition and Electoral Systems," *Journal of Politics* 24 (May 1962), 323–349. On the politics of suburbia (and suburbs are by no means all alike, as the first-cited study makes clear), see Frederick M. Wirt, "The Political Sociology of American Suburbia: A Reinterpretation," *Journal of Politics* 27 (August 1965), 647–666; and Robert C. Wood, *Suburbia: Its People and Politics* (Boston: Houghton Mifflin, 1958).

20. *Phoenix Gazette,* August 22, 1964.

21. Herbert Jacob, "The Consequences of Malapportionment: A Note of Caution," *Social Forces* 43 (December 1964), 256–261.

22. Thomas R. Dye, "Malapportionment and Public Policy in the States," *Journal of Politics* 27 (August 1965), 601.

23. Richard I. Hofferbert, "The Relation Between Public Policy and Some Structural and Environmental Variables in the American States," *American Political Science Review* 60 (March 1966), 73–82.

24. Several people participated in this study, including Thomas R. Dye, Frank K. Gibson, Brett W. Hawkins, and Ira Sharkansky. A report on the study may be found in Richard I. Hofferbert and Ira Sharkansky (editors), *State and Urban Politics,* 273–298.

25. Ibid., 296.

26. Ibid., 297–298.

27. Ira Sharkansky, "Economic Development, Representative Mechanisms, Administrative Professionalism and Public Policies: A Comparative Analysis of Within-State Distributions of Economic and Political Traits," *Journal of Politics* 33 (February 1971), 112–132.

28. Ibid.

29. Thomas R. Dye, "Income Equality and American State Politics," *American Political Science Review* 63 (March 1969), 157–162.

30. Sharkansky, "Economic Development, Representative Mechanisms, Administrative Professionalism and Public Policy," 114–115.

31. See Brian R. Fry and Richard F. Winters, "The Politics of Redistribution," *American Political Science Review* 64 (June 1970), 508–22; and Brian R. Fry, "An Examination of the Relationship between Selected Electoral Characteristics and State Redistributive Efforts," *American Journal of Political Science* 18 (May 1974), 421–432.

32. Sharkansky, "Economic Development, Representative Mechanisms," 114–115.

33. Lockard, *New England State Politics,* 336–337.

34. Giovanni Sartori, "The Typology of Party Systems—Proposals for Improvement," in Erik Allardt and Stein Rokkan (editors), *Mass Politics* (New York: Free Press, 1970), 332–352.

35. Maurice Duverger, *Political Parties* (New York: Wiley, 1954), 388.

36. Lockard, *New England State Politics,* 337.

37. Ira Sharkansky and Richard I. Hofferbert, "Dimensions of State Poiltics, Economics, and Public Policy," *American Political Science Review* 63 (September 1969), 867–879.

38. Duane Lockard, *The Politics of State and Local Government* (New York: Macmillan, 1963), 179–189.

39. Fred I. Greenstein, *The American Party System and the American People,* 2nd ed. (Englewood Cliffs, N.J.: Prentice-Hall, 1970), 78–85.

40. Sartori, in *Mass Politics,* 332–352.

"I think it is quite apparent," he [President Eisenhower] told a press conference in 1954, "that I am not very much of a partisan. The times are too serious, I think, to indulge in partisanship to the extreme."

The reason we have suffered governmental stalemate is that we have not used the one instrument available to use for disciplining government to meet our needs. That instrument is the political party.

The ignorance of voters is what makes party government possible.

It is difficult to exaggerate the importance of attention-getting. If a matter is not brought to congressmen's attention, it will not become a subject of legislative action, in statute or otherwise. In an effort to conserve time and handle an impossible job, congressmen often start by assuming implicitly that if a problem is not brought to their attention, then the problem does not exist.

The political leader who thought he was learning about the attitudes of the public by observing the preferences of those activists around him, or the preferences of the citizens who come forward to contact him, or of the citizens who write letters to the press would be receiving an inaccurate impression of the population as a whole.

The Impact of Parties Upon National Policy

Do political parties leave an impact upon the substance of public policy? The previous chapter told us that the impact that parties have upon state policy is both limited and relative, limited because what states pursue in the way of policy is closely related to their wealth, and relative in that it is not equally strong across all areas of public policy. Still, the electorate does have different perceptions of the two major American parties, and these different perceptions relate to what the parties stand for in the way of policy, as well as how different groups within the population will benefit if one party is in charge instead of the other. Issues, we have seen, are becoming a more important factor in the complex process by which voters decide what they are going to do on election day. All this evidence leads us to suspect that indeed parties do influence public policy, and that it does make some difference if one rather than the other of the two major parties is in power.

In this chapter we move to consider the impact of parties upon national policy. The data relied on in the main is the policy made by Congress, the chief lawmaking body in the country. In light of everything that has been said in the previous chapters of this book, the results of the inquiry should provide no surprises.

We are now near the end of our inquiry. In this chapter we want to describe some general features of national public policy in America, to see if any of these features are attributable to the operation of political parties. As a first important step, let us look briefly at what the chief lawmaking body in the country, the United States Congress, has been doing lately. Specifically, let us draw a sketch of the policy output generated by the House of Representatives in 1973, and then, quite briefly, see how this resembles congressional policy of earlier years.

Students of Congress tell us that the important work of Congress is done in committees.[1] That is where bills are given their closest scrutiny, where hearings are held at which interested persons and groups may appear, where the detailed work of molding legislation is attended to. But that is not to say that what is done on the floor of Congress—where all members may participate, not just a handful of committee members—is insignificant. Bills favored by a majority of the members of a committee are sometimes defeated on the floor, though that is rare. They *are* amended on the floor; that happens more often. And they *are* debated. It is what happens during this process of floor debate that interests us.

During a floor debate, a motion may be offered to send a bill back to committee (a motion to recommit a bill), to amend the bill, to amend an amendment, or to bring a halt to further discussion (a motion calling for the previous question or a motion to adjourn). On each motion, the House must take a vote.

If a vote taken is a voice vote, there is no way of telling how each member present votes, or how many members vote, or by what margin the motion carries or is rejected. However, if a vote is recorded, then a record exists which tells us exactly how each member of the House stood with respect to the motion.[2] It is this record that we shall search for an understanding of what the House did and what it refused to do in 1973, and for an appreciation of the influence that political parties have in Congress.

Voting in the House of Representatives: 1973

In 1973 the House of Representatives took a recorded vote on 541 motions. That in itself is remarkable. It is a number greater by far than for any previous year. In 1973 the Democrats were the majority party in the House, a position they have enjoyed during most of the years since the end of World War II. Table 11-1 gives the figures for each Congress, beginning with the Eighty-first, which was elected in 1948 and took office in January 1949, and ending with the Ninety-fourth, which was chosen in the 1974 election. Given what we know about the electorate's partisanship, it is no surprise to discover that the Democrats have controlled both houses of Congress during most of this period. Only once in this period were the Republicans able to organize Congress, and that was after the election of 1952, which brought the immensely popular Republican Dwight D. Eisenhower into the White House. Their poorest showing came in the election of 1964, when their presidential candidate was a person even some Republicans had difficulty voting for, and their next poorest showing, interestingly enough, was in 1974—an election un-doubtedly affected by President Nixon's forced resignation, the Watergate scandals in general, and the problems of recession and inflation.

Table 11-1 Representation of Democrats and Republicans in Congress, 1948–1974

Congress	Election Year	House of Representatives				Senate			
		Dems.		Reps.		Dems.		Reps.	
81st	1948	263	61%	171	39%	54	56%	42	44%
82nd	1950	234	54	199	46	48	50	47	49
83rd	1952	213	49	221	51	47	49	48	50
84th	1954	232	53	203	47	48	50	47	49
85th	1956	234	54	201	46	49	51	47	49
86th	1958	283	65	154	35	66	66	34	34
87th	1960	263	60	174	40	64	64	36	36
88th	1962	259	60	176	40	68	68	32	32
89th	1964	295	68	140	32	67	67	33	33
90th	1966	248	57	187	43	64	64	36	36
91st	1968	243	56	192	44	58	58	42	42
92nd	1970	255	59	180	41	55	55	45	45
93rd	1972	240	55	192	45	57	57	43	43
94th	1974	292	67	143	33	61	61	39	39

Democrats in Control. Being the majority party meant that in 1973 the Democrats in the House were in a postion to pass any measure that met their concept of desirable public policy and to defeat any that was not to their liking. This they could do on the floor provided that (1) serious divisions within the ranks did not occur and (2) Democratic members were present on the floor when their votes were needed. There is nothing in the record to suggest that they were unable to meet the second of these two conditions.[3] With respect to the first, however, the story is somewhat different.

Tables 11-2 and 11-3 provide data which indicate the extent to which the Democrats were able to retain control over proceedings on the floor of the House, to allow passage of motions favored by a majority of Democrats or to defeat motions disliked by a majority of Democrats.

To make it easy to read these two tables, each cell entry has been labeled with a letter of the alphabet. On the left-hand side are counted motions which were accepted or rejected on a *party unity vote*—a party unity vote being defined as any vote

Table 11-2 Motions Passed on the Floor of the House of Representatives, 1973 (N=360)

	Party Unity Votes		Bipartisan Votes	
DEMOCRATIC SUCCESSES (*N* = 320)				
Motions Offered by Republicans	(A)	2	(B)	18
Motions Offered by Democrats	(C)	61	(D)	239
Totals		63		257
DEMOCRATIC REVERSES (*N* = 40)				
Motions Offered by Republicans	(E)	16	(F)	0
Motions Offered by Democrats	(G)	24	(H)	0
Totals		40		0

Table 11-3 Motions Defeated on the Floor of the House of Representatives, 1973 (N=181)

	Party Unity Votes	Bipartisan Votes
DEMOCRATIC SUCCESSES (*N* = 130)		
Motions Offered by Republicans	(I) 60	(J) 23
Motions Offered by Democrats	(K) 15	(L) 32
Totals	75	55
DEMOCRATIC REVERSES (*N* = 51)		
Motions Offered by Republicans	(M) 6	(N)
Motions Offered by Democrats	(O) 42	(P) 3
Totals	48	3

upon which a majority of Democrats voted against a majority of Republicans. On the right-hand side are counted the number of motions which were accepted or rejected by a majority of both parties. Let us, for convenience, refer to votes in the latter category as *bipartisan votes*.

In 1973, there were 226 party unity votes and 315 bipartisan votes. In any session, many motions win broad acceptance from the members, as may be seen in Table 11-4, which provides data on party unity voting in both House and Senate for each year since 1962. Not shown in the table is the fact that in 1973, roughly 40 percent (198 out of 541) of the motions made on the floor found better than 80 percent of the members aligned on the same side of the vote. On only 35 of the 541 motions could the vote be described as close—*close* meaning that the winning side mustered no more than 55 percent of the vote.

Each table indicates also whether a motion was offered by a Republican or by a Democrat. Motions upon measures passed by the Senate and sent on to the House are counted as having Democratic sponsorship, since, it is reasoned, a Senate measure strongly disliked by the Democratic leadership would stand little

Table 11-4   Party Unity Votes in Congress, 1962 to 1974

	SENATE			HOUSE		
Year	Total Roll Calls	Party Unity Roll Calls	Percent of Total	Total Roll Calls	Party Unity Roll Calls	Percent of Total
1962	224	92	41%	124	57	46%
1963	229	108	47	119	58	49
1964	305	109	36	113	62	55
1965	258	108	42	201	105	52
1966	235	118	50	193	80	41
1967	315	109	35	245	89	31
1968	281	90	32	233	82	35
1969	245	89	36	177	55	31
1970	418	147	35	266	72	27
1971	423	176	42	320	121	38
1972	532	194	36	329	89	27
1973	594	237	40	541	226	42
1974	544	241	44	537	158	29

chance of coming to the floor for a vote. As it happens, all Senate measures were passed by the House, and a majority of Democrats voted for them.

The data in these two tables permit two slightly different interpretations of how well the Democratic majority succeeded in maintaining control of voting on the floor. If we look only at the total of votes identified as Democratic successes—votes on which the outcome was that preferred by a majority of Democrats —we see that the Democrats were successful in 450 instances. Noting that the number of successes was far greater than the number of reverses, it is easy to conclude that in 1973 the Democratic majority did succeed fairly well in controlling proceedings on the floor, and thus, in controlling the definition of the substance of public policy.

However, if we probe a little more deeply, we are less sure. For one thing, we are counting as Democratic successes all bipartisan motions—those upon which a majority of *both* parties agreed. If we pass these by, this reduces the number of Democratic successes to 138 of the 541 votes taken on the floor. Further, the entries in cells E, F, M, and N indicate that 22 motions offered by Republicans were disposed of in the way the Republican members wished and over the objection of the Democrats, while cell entries G, H, O, and P say 69 motions offered by Democrats were disposed of contrary to the way the Democrats would have liked. We can still say the Democrats were more often successful than not in controlling voting on the floor, but it does seem more appropriate to call it a limited success.

Consensus and Division.   It is also apparent that there is a high degree of consensus among House members on matters of public policy. Cells B and D indicate that roughly two-thirds of all motions accepted on the floor were agreed to by a majority of both parties. At many points in our earlier inquiry we have remarked upon the absence of sharp cleavages among the American people. Why then should we be surprised to see considerable consensus among members of the House on matters of policy? The answer, of course, is that we should not. Sometimes cleavage appears, and sometimes it follows party lines. It appeared on 103 of the 360 motions accepted on the floor. It appeared more often on motions that were rejected, occurring on 123 of the 181 motions rejected by the House.

Some issues come before the House every year. They include appropriations for government agencies; an always-large request for support of the national defense; routine housekeeping matters, including such things as creating a committee or increasing a committee's funds (in 1973 this included a million-dollar appropriation to the Judiciary Committee to begin its inquiry into the impeachment of the president); questions of foreign policy; efforts to protect the environment; support for farm program's; and in recent years, notably 1973, the energy crunch.

Consensus is highest on housekeeping matters, defense appropriations, and appropriations for the upkeep of government departments. It is a little less in evidence when it is a question of action to protect the environment or, as in 1973, dealing with the energy problem, or a proposed revision of the farm program. It least often appears when the question is regulation of the economy or federal support of welfare programs, broadly defined. Questions touching upon the minimum wage, medical care, health insurance, federal aid to the cities, the food stamp program, and the legal services administration are examples of issues that encourage the greatest cleavage in voting and—no surprise here—upon which cleavage is most likely to follow party lines. Generally speaking, Republicans are less inclined than Democrats to favor a continuing federal role in the management of the economy or in the development of federally supported welfare programs. If votes on the floor fairly represent the attitudes of the congressmen doing the voting, it seems fair to say that congressmen overall are more conservative than liberal, that Republicans are more conservative than Democrats, and finally—recall here the findings from the 1972 election study—that *conservative* and *liberal* take on definitions much closer to those evident in the attitudes of older than of younger voters.

HIGH-CONSENSUS ISSUES IN 1973.   In 1973, voting on the following motions garnered support from at least 80 percent of the House members, including a majority of both parties:

> To extend for one year programs of the Law Enforcement Assistance Agency.
> To authorize 600 million dollars for the National Science Foundation.
> To continue appropriations for the Departments of State, Justice, Housing and Urban Development, the Treasury, Interior, and the Atomic Energy Commission.
> To provide supplemental and continuing appropriations for a number of executive departments.

LOW-CONSENSUS ISSUES IN 1973.   Thirty-five motions produced a vote which was not only close, but which followed party lines. In 16 cases the outcome was that favored by a majority of Democrats; in 19 cases the vote was a reverse for the Democrats. Included in this group of motions, which are especially interesting because they suggest the clear limits of the power of even a majority of the majority party to control policy output from the House, were:

> A motion to restrict poverty lawyers working in the legal services program from efforts to influence administrative decisions by federal, state, or local government agencies.
> A motion to restrict both the partisan and nonpartisan activities of lawyers who receive more than half of their income from legal assistance activities.
> A motion to restrict the use of government limousines by officials of several executive departments.

A motion to delete an authorization of $800 million for grants to state and local agencies to be used as subsidies for urban mass transit operations.

A motion to ban the allocation of petroleum for busing of students to schools farther than the school nearest to their home.

A motion to extend to the 1977 model-year cars the same vehicle emission standards demanded for the 1975 model-year cars.

CONDITIONS FOR DEFEAT OF THE MAJORITY PARTY. Democrats most often suffered a reverse when either or both of two conditions were met: when a motion was offered by a Republican (thus making it easier for other Republicans to stand together behind it), and/or when its substance made it attractive to southern Democrats. The combination of a large majority of Republican votes plus a majority of Southern Democratic votes produced most Democratic reverses. This conservative coalition was able to use its sufficient votes to indicate its dislike for

striking workers
urban transit subsidies
school busing
lawyers engaged in the legal services program

House Voting: Generalizations

Studies of Congress from the last 20 years have found far greater consistency than inconsistency in voting from one Congress to the next. Even a brief look at voting in the House in 1973 provides support for a number of generalizations that are in line with the findings of earlier studies:

Voting in Congress reveals consensus more often that cleavage.

Consensus appears most often on issues upon which the people at large reveal consensus.

Party divisions appear on fewer than half the votes taken on the floor, and more often on measures that are defeated than on measures that are passed.

The majority Democratic party is most successful in having its way when success is a question of securing the defeat of motions offered by a Republican member.

A reverse for the majority Democratic party most often occurs because of unity in the ranks of Republicans and defection by a majority of southern Democrats.

Some issue areas are more likely than others to produce cleavage along party lines. They include measures which may be broadly defined as efforts to increase the federal role in management of the economy.

In short, congressmen most often divide along party lines on precisely those issues which Americans at large see as the source of the sharpest differences between the two parties. They demonstrate consensus on those issues upon which Americans as a whole are least divided.

The Influence of Party

Does this mean that most congressmen pay close attention to what their constituencies want? or indeed that constituencies pay close attention to what their congressmen do? It may mean that congressmen merely vote their own preferences, and that there is a neat correspondence between their own preferences and those of their constituents—which is why they were able to get elected in the first place. It may also mean that the party organization in Congress is stronger than we sometimes think, and that party pressures upon individual congressmen encourage some measure of party voting. There are three possible sources of influence: party, constituency, and self. How do they combine to produce the final decision of the congressman to vote yes, vote no, or be absent?

The Influence of Party Leaders.   One possible source of unity for each party, and thus a source of possible cleavage, is afforded by the existence of a leadership group for each party in each house.

Sometime in advance of the opening of the new session, the members of each party in each house assemble in party caucus, separately of course.[4] One of the purposes of the meetings is the choosing of party leaders. The posts to be filled include speaker of the House, president pro tempore of the Senate, and in both houses, the majority and minority party floor leaders, the party whips, and the assistant whips. In the House both parties choose their floor leaders and whips by majority vote of the caucus. The Democratic caucus also has the responsibility for choosing the assistant whips, but the Republicans leave the choice of their assistant whips to the discretion of the man they choose as whip.[5]

In the House, each caucus chooses a candidate to run for the powerful and prestigious office of speaker of the House. The minority party normally offers as its candidate the person already chosen to be the minority floor leader. Choosing between the two competing nominees becomes the first item on the agenda of the new Congress. With voting following party lines, the outcome is never in doubt. The candidate offered by the majority party wins, and the candidate of the minority party retires in graceful defeat to occupy the post which everyone knew all along he would hold—the post of minority floor leader. The Republicans in the House also have a policy committee, and its chairman is chosen by the Republican caucus.[6] Some members on this Committee serve *ex officio,* including all the party officers, while 18 members, constituting a majority of the membership of the committee, are chosen by Republican representatives coming from districts that lie within each of nine zones into which the party has divided the country in an effort to guarantee every section of the country some voice on the committee.

In the Senate, the choice of the person to be president pro tempore of the Senate is actually the choice of a majority of the majority party. In the Senate, as in the House, both parties also choose floor leaders and whips. Both parties in the Senate also have policy committees.[7] Policy committees for both houses were authorized by one version of the bill which became the Legislative Reorganization Act of 1946. However, Democrats in the House, and particularly Speaker Sam Rayburn, wanted no part of them, but did agree that the Senate might have them the following year. The original hope was that these committees might play a dominant role in developing policy positions for the parties, but in actuality the committees are a long way shy of being able to perform that function. As a result, the real policy-making committees in the Senate, as well as in the House, continue to be the standing committees.[8]

The speaker, the president pro tem, the floor leaders and the whips, the three policy committees, and the caucuses, together constitute the nucleus of party leadership in Congress. How effective they can be in leaving a party imprint on legislation appears to depend upon several conditions.

Conditions of Leadership Influence.   In the most thorough of all studies of party leadership influence, Froman and Ripley outline six conditions as relevant to the ability of party leaders to be influential upon policy making. The six conditions are:

1. Leaders must be committed to passage (or defeat) of a measure, they must have reliable information about it and about how their party members feel about it, and they must be willing to commit a sufficient quantity of scarce leadership resources to carry the day.

2. Leaders are more likely to be successful on a procedural than on a substantive measure. We have already observed that greatest cohesion occurs on the important procedural question of organizing each chamber at the beginning of a new session of Congress. On other questions, the record shows considerable variation. On some roll calls—sometimes called "hurrah" roll calls because many members in both parties support them; bills dealing with communism and national defense have been good examples—leaders of both parties can muster considerable support. The record of the past 20 years contains few examples of opposition to the passage of such measures, changing only slightly in the late 1960s as widespread criticism of the Vietnam War began to develop.

3. The more visible an *issue* is to the public, the harder leaders must work to keep the party united. Party influence is most likely to be substantial when other, contrary influences are absent. A highly visible issue of public policy is frequently emotion-laden and can generate considerable pressures, and a congressman who might be inclined out of party loyalty to support the position advocated by party leaders, may find he is unable to do so.

4. A similar condition is associated with the visibility of an *action*. Some legislative decisions are made quietly, privately, well beyond the range of the public eye. On these, leadership influence can be great. Others, like the civil rights act of the past decade are acted upon under conditions that guarantee that maximum public attention will be focused on the action. On such measures as

these party leaders may well find that their ingenuity and other leadership tools are taxed to the limit.[9]

5. Constituency pressures are never far in the background. The pressures generated by constituency may indeed be the single most important influence prompting a congressman to deviate from positions taken by leaders of his party. Members like to be loyal to the party, but they also prefer being reelected over being defeated at the next election. It requires no genius for a member of Congress to know that supporting the leadership on a controversial issue could mean committing electoral suicide. No one in Congress feels the pull of constituency more often or more strongly than the white southern Democrat. When they feel obliged to answer the call of constituency, these Democrats can prove particularly troublesome for the Democratic leadership, because these same Southerners have traditionally occupied commanding positions on the standing committees of Congress, thanks to the operation of the seniority rule. From this vantage point, they are in an excellent position to obstruct legislation not to their liking.

6. Lastly, membership in a state delegation sometimes demands behavior that is not in accord with the wishes of party leaders. The members of a state delegation are likely to sit near each other on the floor of the chamber, to travel together, to eat together, to have many things in common, including a shared experience with the politics of the same state, and all this makes the state delegation a reference group, and hence a factor in voting.[10]

In sum, we may say, quoting from Froman and Ripley, that party leadership influence is likely to be greatest when

(1) leadership activity is high; (2) the issue is more procedural and less substantive; (3) the visibility of the issue is low; (4) the visibility of the action is low; (5) there is little counter pressure from the constituencies; and (6) state delegations are not engaged in collective bargaining for specific demands.[11]

The Decline of Party Voting.   Party influence on voting varies greatly with issues. The important work done by Turner,[12] Mayhew,[13] Clausen,[14] and Kingdon [15]—to name just four students who have examined the matter closely—all make that point. There is no surprise here. What we have already seen in the studies of party leaders made by McClosky [16] and by Soule and Clarke [17] discourages any expectation that party influence would be equal across all policy issues upon which a congressman must vote.

A congressman votes with his party, that is, he votes on the same side of a motion as do a majority of his party, about 60 percent of the time. On many of these votes, however, a majority of *both* parties agree. As Table 11-4 indicates, since 1962 the number of party unity votes has gone up and down, from a high in 1966, when 50 percent of the votes in the House were party unity votes, to lows in 1970 and 1972, when only 27 percent of the votes in the Senate were party unity votes. Is party voting on the increase or on the decrease? It is not easy to discern a trend in data for the recent period, but what one can say is that, compared to an earlier period, party voting has clearly declined.

When Julius Turner made his path-breaking study of voting in Congress in the interwar period, he found that 90 percent of the members of one party voted in opposition to 90 percent of the members of the other party roughly one time in five. The exact figure was 19 percent of the time. When Edward Schneier updated Turner's study, carrying it forward through the year 1967, he found that the figure had dropped to 9.4 percent, and that in the period from 1960 to 1967 it had fallen to 5 percent. In 1973, 90 percent or more of the Republicans voted in opposition to 90 percent or more of the Democrats in the House *only three times*. Obviously, party leaders are finding it harder than ever to develop cohesion among their members. A major reason underlying this development is the number of occasions when southern Democrats have refused to vote with northern Democrats; the number is increasing, and causes for the defection by southern Democrats encompass a wider range of issues than ever before.

When majorities of each party disagree, we may count on seeing at least 10 percent of each party defect to the other side. In sum, votes which divide the parties most sharply (party unity votes) are also most likely to divide the parties internally. Recall in this connection what was said earlier about the McClosky findings that party leaders are *not* most united on those issues that most clearly distinguish them from the opposing party.

Other differences appear between the period Turner studied, from 1921 until 1944, and the more recent period. Turner found that those issues which most sharply divided the parties were the instrumental issues—patronage, and questions involving the organizing of the legislative chamber. In the postwar period, the differences between the most partisan and the least partisan issues are less extreme. Perhaps the greatest difference, however, is to be seen in the increase in partisanship evident in the postwar period in voting on issues involving the regulation and control of major power groups in American society. In their attitudes toward organized labor and business, northern Democrats and Republicans have grown farther apart. To an increasing extent, the Democratic party—Democrats of the South not included— has become the party of labor, and the Republican party the party of business. On issues involving labor, Southern Democrats are sometimes divided, but they are frequently found voting with the Republicans.

Another change evident is an increase in the cohesion of northern Democrats in the postwar period. The contrast between voting in the two parties is not as sharp as it might be in this same period only because southern Democrats have shown an increasing tendency not to go along with their northern Democrat colleagues, but to defect to the side of the Republicans.

Voting by Same-State Senators. Another intriguing bit of evidence that party does influence the way a member of Congress votes comes from an inspection of the voting records of senators who come from the same state but belong to different parties. When senators from the same state belong to the same party, they usually vote the same way about 80 percent of the time. When they belong to different parties, they seldom vote alike more than 40 percent of the time.

The number of states sending a mixed delegation, one Democrat and one Republican, to the Senate has increased in recent years. Thirteen states did this in 1958. Twenty-one did it in 1974. Pairs of senators from different states differed a lot in the extent to which each of them voted in opposition to the other senator in the delegation. Senators Edward Brooke and Edward Kennedy of Massachusetts, Republican and Democrat respectively, agreed with each other more often than they disagreed. On the other hand, Frank Church and James A. McClure of Idaho, and Gale McGee and Clifford Hansen of Wyoming, were far more likely to disagree than to agree with each other when it came time to cast a vote. This is not a clear-cut evidence of the influence of party over constituency, but it does suggest that these pairs of senators representing the *same geographic area* did have clearly different perceptions of what was demanded of them in the way of prudent political behavior:

Constituency Influence

It is easy to say that constituency, like party, is an influence upon a congressman's voting behavior. Congressmen say it is, and there is no reason not to believe them; and they do spend considerable time responding to the demands made by the home folks upon their time and energy. On our own, we may conclude that we see the influence of constituency at work when a congressman from one party replaces a congressman from the other and yet, on some issues, votes exactly like the man he replaced. Southern white Republicans who replace Southern white Democrats, yet vote like them on civil rights, are always cited as examples of the pressures of constituency. Yet what is the constituency doing the pressuring, and how is the pressuring done? That question is not easy to answer.

It may be the number of voters who supported the congressman in the last election. But if an election is close, may not the congressman have a special concern for the *marginal* supporter, in part because he does not want to lose any supporters who gave him victory and in part because he would like to increase his margin of victory the next time? On the other hand, the constituency to which he pays heed may be what he perceives as the dominant interest in the community, the farmers (if farming is important), or the union workers, or, say, those whose preoccupation is with race. Actually, we need not be too concerned with finding a perfect definition for *constituency,* for our concern is with *constituency influence upon voting.* Whoever or whatever it is that a congressman chooses to pay special court to in the name of constituency, if that courtship has an influence upon his behavior within Congress, then let us say—until proved wrong—that this is constituency influence in operation.

Voters have limited interest and information about what "their" congressmen do. (More on this later.) We might expect that congressmen would have an interest in seeing that they had accurate information about what "their" constituents want. Yet in fact, the information they have about what presses on the daily lives of their constituents is not always accurate or reliable. It is often no more than a gathering of impressions rather than a systematic review of constituency opinion, and is often gleaned from a reading of the congressman's mail.[18]

Measuring the Relative Influence of Party and Constituency. One way to detect constituency influence is to compare the voting behavior of three groups of congressmen: (1) those who are holdovers, incumbents returned, (2) those who are new but of the *same party* as the congressmen they replaced, and (3) those who are new but of a *different party* from the congressmen they replaced.

If *party* is an influence, voting of congressmen in the first two categories should show minimal change from one session to the next. Minimal change rather than no change is prescribed for congressmen in the second category, to allow for the possibility that newly elected congressmen, who are almost always younger than the people they replace, will reflect a more youthful attitude toward all issues. Voting of the newly elected congressman in the third category, however, should show a significant change, at least in some issue areas.

If *constituency* is influential, voting by congressmen in the first two categories should also show minimal change, while voting of congressmen in the third category should fairly much resemble the voting of the congressmen they replaced. Further, if constituency is important, not only must it force congressmen from similar constituencies but of different parties to vote alike on certain issues, it must also encourage congressmen of the same party to vote the same way on issues. Therefore, we may feel confident that we have evidence of constituency *only if* congressmen in the third category vote similarly to the congressmen of the other party they replaced *and if* congressmen in the second category also vote the same way as the congressmen of the same party they replaced.

Five Major Issue Areas. The procedures and standards just outlined were employed by Aage Clausen in a study of two congressional periods, 1953–1964 and 1969–1970. What he found was that both party and constituency were influential.

Clausen identified five major issue clusters: (1) civil liberties, (2) international involvement, (3) agricultural assistance, (4) social welfare, and (5) government management. These five issue areas were evident in voting in both the House and the Senate, and as much in evidence at the end of the 17-year period studied as they were at the beginning. Apparently there was widespread agreement within the broader political culture on how issues were defined and perceived in this period.

The influence of party is most evident in the government management dimension, which includes policies having to do with regulation of the economy, relations between business and government, the care and use of natural resources, and tax and fiscal policy. A combination of party and constituency influence appears in social welfare and agricultural assistance policy. The influence of constituency is unmistakable in the area of civil rights. The fifth dimension, international involvement, reveals a combination of constituency and presidential influence. Constituency, then, makes itself felt unequally across issues. Predictably it is most in evidence on issues with respect to which there have been readily observable differences among regions for upwards of a century.[19]

A 1958 Study of Influences Upon Voting in Congress.   These findings from Clausen's study are generally consistent with one previous study—the only such study that exists—which searched for the ties that bind congressmen and their constituents. This was a study done in 1958 by the Survey Research Center in 100 congressional districts. Interviews were conducted immediately after the 1958 election with the congressmen from those districts, their opponents (when there were any), and with a sample of voters in each district, and an analysis was done of the congressman's voting in the session that followed the election. The point was to discover what relationships might be found between four variables: (1) attitudes of voters in the district, (2) the congressman's attitudes, (3) the congressman's perception of the attitudes of people in his district, and (4) the congressman's voting record. Votes falling in three issue areas—civil rights, social welfare, and foreign policy—were chosen for close examination.

The conclusion of the study was that a congressman's voting is influenced by his own policy preferences and by his perception of the preferences held by his constituents. His attitudes do resemble the attitudes of his constituents. This was more true in the area of civil rights than in the area of social welfare, and the correspondence was weakest in foreign affairs. The study also indicated that the congressman's voting in these issue areas followed his own policy views as well as his perceptions of the views of his constituents. The congressman does not always have reliable information about how his constituents feel about policies. Indeed, the channels of communication between congressman and constituents would seem to be imperfect much of the time. Constituent and representative have the best chance of knowing where the other stands when the issue is one of civil rights, and the best chance of being wrong when the issue is foreign policy. While we have no recent data exactly comparable to that found in the 1958 study, we may suspect that sometime around 1968 constituents began to have a motivation to learn where their congressmen stood on the foreign policy issue of the war in Vietnam.

According to the 1958 study, constituents had only the most general idea of what their congressmen were doing. Among constituents who lived in districts where there was a contest between a Republican and a Democrat, fewer than one in five voters said they had read or heard something about both candidates, and more than half said they had heard or read nothing about either. The situation has probably changed little since then. A study of legislator perceptions in Iowa in 1967 found no evidence to suggest that those legislators were much better informed about constituency feelings than were the congressmen back in 1958.[20] And in 1970, though a majority of persons interviewed in a national survey said they were interested in the national election and paid some attention to the campaign, 60 percent said immediately after the election they could not recall who had run for Congress.

Personal Belief

Finally, we must consider the matter of self, and the possibility that the most immediate determinant of a congressman's voting decision may sometimes be his own personal convictions, convictions that he may realize run counter to the demands both of party and constituency. That such a thing can occur is well documented, in part because it seems to be so rare. Its appearance is best noted when an issue looms large in the public view, the party lines are drawn, and the vote is likely to be close. The nomination of Judge G. Harrold Carswell to be a Supreme Court justice is a case in point. On that occasion, a number of senators felt the contradictory tugs of party, constituency, and self. One who found himself fighting the pull *both* of party and constituency was Marlow Cook, Republican senator from Kentucky. He elected to follow his conscience, though in doing so, as he put it, he made "the most politically dangerous vote of my political career." He voted *not* to confirm, and in 1974 was defeated for reelection.[21]

NOTES

The first quotation at the beginning of the chapter is from a 1954 presidential press conference and is quoted in David Broder, *The Party's Over* (New York: Harper & Row, 1971), 6. The second is also from Broder's *The Party's Over,* xx. The third is from James Q. Wilson, *The Amateur Democrat* (Chicago: University of Chicago Press, 1962), 357. The fourth quote is from John W. Kingdon, *Congressmen's Voting Decisions* (New York: Harper & Row, 1973), 262. The fifth is from Sidney Verba and Norman H. Nie, *Participation in America: Political Democracy and Social Equality* (New York: Harper & Row, 1972), 284.

1. See Daniel M. Berman, *In Congress Assembled* (New York: Macmillan, 1964), especially chapters 6 and 7; and Barbara Hinckley, *Stability and Change in Congress* (New York: Harper & Row, 1971), especially chapter 5.
2. A convenient place to find the record of voting on roll calls in Congress is the *Congressional Quarterly Weekly Report.*
3. In every session of Congress, however, some number of bills fail because members were absent and the vote was close.
4. On party organization in Congress, see especially Berman, *In Congress Assembled,* chapter 9, and Hinckley, *Stability and Change in Congress,* chapter 6.
5. See Berman, *In Congress Assembled,* chapter 9.
6. See Hugh A. Bone, *Party Committees and National Politics* (Seattle, Wash.: University of Washington Press, 1958), chapter 6.
7. Ibid.
8. Ibid.
9. Lewis A. Froman, Jr., and Randall B. Ripley, "Conditions for Party Leadership: The Case of the House Democrats," *American Political Science Review* 59 (March 1965), 59–61.

10. Ibid.
11. Ibid., 60.
12. Julius Turner, *Party and Constituency,* rev. ed. by Edward V. Schneier, Jr. (Baltimore, Md.: Johns Hopkins Press, 1970).
13. David R. Mayhew, *Party Loyalty Among Congressmen* (Cambridge, Mass.: Harvard University Press, 1966).
14. Aage R. Clausen, *How Congressmen Decide* (New York: St. Martin, 1973).
15. John W. Kingdon, *Congressmen's Voting Decisions* (New York: Harper & Row, 1973).
16. Herbert McClosky and others, "Issue Conflict and Consensus Among Party Leaders and Followers," *American Political Science Review* 54 (June 1960), 406–429.
17. John W. Soule and James W. Clarke, "Issue Conflict and Consensus: A Comparative Study of Democratic and Republican Delegates to the 1968 National Conventions," *Journal of Politics* 33 (February 1971), 72–91.
18. Charles L. Clapp, *The Congressman: His Work As He Sees It* (New York: Doubleday, 1963).
19. Clausen, *How Congressmen Decide.*
20. Ronald D. Hedlund and H. Paul Friesema, "Representatives' Perceptions of Constituency Opinion," *Journal of Politics* 34 (August 1972), 730–752.
21. Richard Harris, *Decision* (New York: Dutton, 1971).

The structure of recent American political behavior . . . makes it very clear that of the two major parties, the Democratic Party is in much the more serious trouble. Its capacity to retain its hold over enough of even its nonsouthern coalitional elements to remain ascendant in American politics is very much in doubt.

For the first time in decades, substantial numbers of Americans are challenging the fundamental assumptions on which their political system rests. They openly deny the legitimacy of existing social, economic, and political structures; they seek change of the most basic kind. Men in power have responded with a vigorous defense of orthodox beliefs and practices. . . . Despite patriotic assertions of massive consensus, the fact is that profound social conflicts characterize the United States as the 200th anniversary of its independence approaches. Tensions, if anything, seem to be growing deeper and more pervasive.

The urban poor, the young, blacks, Mexican Americans, the American Indian—groups with the largest stake in social change—have the least connection with the political structure which is the supposed instrument of orderly change.

Most of the work of the political parties is now done by volunteers, who feel free to come and go as the whim, or issue, strikes them.

Our party system will continue to serve us well as long as we keep the old definition firmly in mind: Politics is the art of the possible. Whatever America finds necessary to do in the years to come, the politics of American democracy will surely make possible.

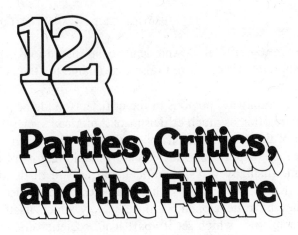

Parties, Critics, and the Future

This is a chapter of summing up and speculation. It considers two broad questions: (1) What is the condition of political parties in America today? (2) Where do they appear to be heading? On the answers given to these questions, people who think of themselves as close students of parties disagree, sometimes vigorously. Those who write about parties, often with obvious affection and some admiration, are seldom satisfied that parties are all that they might be. But rarely do the critics agree in what they prescribe as the remedy for what they see as the soft spots in our parties. This final chapter discusses what parties get criticized for, and comments on the merits and meaning of the criticism.

Criticisms of the Parties

Political parties are among the most criticized of all American institutions. In a way, that is a tribute. Those who criticize often make the point that they are certain that parties are essential instruments of government in modern society, and that their criticism is intended only to suggest changes that will help make parties more effective and democratic institutions. Not all observers, of course, are critics. Even among American scholars—

a group frequently critical of American social institutions—there are those who have much more praise than blame for the American political party.[1]

What is not always obvious in the criticisms made of parties is that they are often as much criticisms of American society itself as they are of the parties. In this book the effort has been made throughout to view parties both as creatures and creators of their environment. In many ways, American parties are distinctively American, that is, they possess characteristics which reflect the fact that they have developed within a society which itself possesses characteristics which set it apart from societies elsewhere. And to the extent that criticism is directed at parties alone, and recommendations are made for change without a careful reckoning of whether such change could be realized without first or simultaneously making changes in other elements of the political system, the criticism may properly be rejected as being either only half thought through or, worse, beside the point.

The Failure to Be Representative.   Of all the criticisms made of parties, perhaps the most justifiable is that they have failed in their obligation to be broadly and directly representative of large segments of the population. The evidence of this failure is easy to document. In the past two decades alone, leaders within both parties have not hesitated to oppose openly efforts to facilitate participation by citizens.

IMPEDIMENTS TO REGISTRATION.   The failure is most glaring in the case of blacks and other ethnic minorities, but it is not limited to discrimination against ethnic minorities alone. For decades, other countries have declared it a duty of the state to see to the registration of voters. In Canada, sometime before each election, lists of eligible voters are stapled to telephone poles in neighborhoods throughout the country. If a citizen finds his name has been omitted, it is an easy matter for him to see that it is added. The initiative and the burden is placed in the first instance upon the state, not upon the citizen. Not so in the United States, where registration procedures have long been among the most complex and cumbersome in the world. Even in the decade of the seventies, a suggestion that persons should not have to take time away from a job to go to register to vote but should be able to do it by mail cannot garner support in Congress. If the history of the demand for registration by postcard turns out to be like the history of other efforts made to facilitate voter participation, probably registration by postcard will be a reality in the country sometime before the decade of the eighties begins, but any effort toward this end will clearly find resistance from some number of party leaders in *both* parties to the very day of its passage into law.

RESISTANCE TO REAPPORTIONMENT.   In a similar vein is the continued resistance of legislators to fair apportionment of seats in legislative chambers. Twelve years after the *Baker* v. *Carr* decision, and despite repeated challenge in federal courts, both chambers of the Mississippi legislature still constitute a classic example of racially gerrymandered legislative bodies. Not only that, the departure from the rule of "one man, one vote" required to create the Mississippi gerrymander is a departure so great that a federal court could have no option but to declare the existing plan unconstitutional, even if racial discrimination were not present. Fair dealing in this instance is surely coming, but it is not on the express track.

THE ELITIST TENDENCY IN PARTY LEADERSHIP.   Nor is the party record much better when it comes to recruitment to the ranks of the party itself. At all levels of government, whether it be Congress, the federal bureaucracy, city councils, or what, those who serve prove the accuracy of an earlier observation made about party leaders: Party leaders enjoy a higher socioeconomic status than the population from which they are drawn. To some extent, as we have seen, this is inevitable. The characteristics which give status—education, income, occupation, and the like—facilitate entry into the ranks of leadership. But there is more to it than that. A problem arises from the observed fact that the status distance which separates leaders from the rank and file can create an impediment to the effective appreciation and representation by leaders of the interests of the rank and file.

THE SLOWNESS OF CHANGE.   Some change there has been. The passage of the Voting Rights Act of 1965 is a classic instance of action by the party in power that promises a substantial change in the environment within which the parties must operate. It created the potential for participation by millions of blacks, Indians, and Mexican Americans, and one dramatic example of the fruits of that Act is the increase in the number of blacks holding public office. In 1974 the state of Mississippi ranked third among all states, behind much more populous Michigan and California, in the number of blacks holding elective public office. Yet change has not come easily. Or quickly. Those who find the pace too slow are quite apt to be among the more severely critical of existing parties. It may not exactly be in the nature of man to resist change, but it does sometimes seem that party leaders would rather continue with things that they know and understand how to use, than to move into less well-known directions.

Criticism of the Parties' Public Policy Role. A second criticism has to do with the role played by parties in the definition of public policy. This one comes in many varieties. The complaint is made that parties don't seem to be able to get things done, that major public problems are being inadequately tended, that parties don't seem to be in charge of the government, even though they are presumably put in charge of it by elections, that the two major parties are too much alike, and that they appear too often to be agents of special interests rather than servants of some broader public interest.[2] The parties are criticized for having an overriding preoccupation with being merely friendly, mediating brokers among competing private power groups, and for failing to assert a leading role in defining a direction for the government and the country to take. In this view, the need is for parties to be *first* in the matter of advancing the public interest; it is not enough for the parties to be merely first among equals, ranking perhaps a bit above the American Medical Association, but no more than equal in power to such notably influential groups as the AFL-CIO, the American Farm Bureau Federation, and the American Manufacturing Association.

In short, the plea is for parties to become more programmatic, to take more clearly opposing stands on large public issues, and to take up more of a leading role in the definition of public policy.

THE LESSONS OF WEST EUROPEAN PARTIES. What shall we make of this criticism? First of all, let us understand that while the criticism is leveled mainly at parties in America, it is not true that all parties everywhere else are distinctively different from each other, either in the stands they take on public policy questions or in the role they carve out for themselves in the shaping of policy.

There was a time, not too many years ago, when college textbooks on government pointed to the British political parties as examples of what parties ought to be, and when textbooks about political parties frequently cited European parties in general (the socialist parties in particular) as examples of coherent, well-organized parties that were programmatic and offered voters a much clearer choice in matters of policy than parties in America.

But that is much less the fashion today. For one thing, European parties themselves are as much subject to change from a changing environment as parties anywhere. And one change that has occurred—a change particularly evident since the end of World War II—is a decided lessening of social and political tensions and a concurrent muting of policy differences among parties. In Austria, for example, this situation has led to elaborate arrangements among parties on how power will be shared.[3] In the politics of the Scandinavian countries, some issues have virtually disappeared as matters for interparty conflict, notably foreign policy and defense questions. The war itself, the experiences which men of all political persuasions shared as members of the underground and resistance movements, the need after the war to pull together in rebuilding, and then much later, a new prosperity that gave ordinary citizens more chance to spend their leisure time on things more exciting than politics—all these, it is said, have contributed to a decline in political conflict and in policy differences among parties in Europe as a whole.[4]

In Norway, leaders of the two largest parties are even agreed that they no longer disagree much. Here are the words of the leader of the Conservative party: "The area of political disagreement has been greatly reduced. The most important feature is that we have been able to work out certain norms that are accepted by everybody."[5] And here is his counterpart, the Labour party Prime Minister:

"When it really come down to brass tacks, it appears as if we don't have very much to fight about, really. Quite obviously none of the parties are very excited about being too different from the others."[6]

The point is that European parties on the left have in the past taken sharply opposing views of policy from those on the right and in the center. But that is no guarantee that they always will, or that the European parties can serve as reliable models of what a good programmatic party should be.

WHY AMERICAN PARTIES ARE UNPROGRAMMATIC.   But let us return to the criticism of parties in the United States. Is it valid? The answer is yes. But why are they that way? To understand why parties are whatever they are, has been a major concern of this book from the first chapter. Without attempting a recapitulation of the entire contents of earlier chapters, we may say that if American parties have developed as unprogrammatic parties, it has to be because of some distinctive features of their environment. Such as? Such as the relative lack of social cleavages in American society; the heterogeneity of party memberships; the decentralization of party organizations which enables Republicans in one place to look like Democrats in another; the existence of competing organizations, each vitally interested in particular aspects of policy—farmers in farm policy, the Ralph Nader and Common Cause organizations in consumer protection, banks in the money supply and the interest rate, and so on and on; the lack of interest of the labor movement in developing a special attachment to one or the other of the two major parties or in developing a party of its own; the obstacles to the growth of third parties, except as local or regional organizations; and, something of an irony here, the ease with which citizens at large have been able to take part in nominating candidates via the primary, with only the weakest of party attachments required; the low level of interest and information which citizens have about parties and politics (recall that constituency influence was strongest when the issue was civil rights—an issue perceived by congressmen to be especially visible to constituents); the increasing professionalization of the bureaucracy, where policy is enforced and where it is most likely to engage citizen attention; and, too, the increasing tendency of public officials to agree, without reference to party, on how to meet public policy needs.

Can the trend be reversed? It can be, of course. Change does occur. The question, however, is rather whether the evidence suggests that change in the direction desired by the critics is *likely* to occur.

A Scenario for Party Realignment. From what we know about party development, we may suggest that several conditions must be met before parties will begin to take more opposing stands on public policy questions. Partisan attachments must first shift away from support of both parties. The number of Independents must increase. Then some significant number of those who are Independents must elect to support the other party. (Given what we know about the connection between social characteristics and partisanship, we suspect that if such a movement does occur, membership of the parties will be less heterogeneous than before. What exact differences may then exist between the supporters of the two parties is, of course, something we cannot foretell. There are too many possibilities.) Attitude surveys will report a gradually increasing emphasis on issues in deciding election outcomes, similar to that report in 1972, and attitudes toward issues will be counted a part of the explanation for the movement of citizens in and out of parties. Turnout will decline along with trust and, possibly, feelings of efficacy: turnout, because people will see little point in voting; trust, for complex reasons, including a generalized feeling that the system is not working; feelings of efficacy, because citizens decide, for whatever reasons, that government is not responsive. An obvious rearrangement will occur in the confidence citizens have for institutions, although it is difficult to imagine that public confidence in parties as institutions could go much lower than it is right now. If the media, for example, continue to be perceived both as reliable and trustworthy, and as left-leaning in ideology as they are now perceived,[7] their impact both as opinion-forming agencies and as shapers of public policy cannot help but increase. And in the process, party may suffer by comparison. Then, finally, one must not ignore the possible impact of leadership itself. The overriding importance of the removal of President Nixon from office, taken as a symbol of the final settlement of the Watergate affair, may be to affirm public confidence in the workability of the American political *system,* though it does little for public acceptance of parties, especially the Republican party, as the returns from the 1974 election indicate.

THE IMPACT OF NEW SOCIAL CLEAVAGES. Does the above read like a scenario for a realignment of parties? Of course it does. But if it comes, it will be a realignment without parallel, for it will have occurred not in immediate response to a great social crisis such as the Civil War or the depression, but as a response to political events. And it will be distinctive in still another respect. The last realignment occurred principally over acutely felt economic wrongs: money, particularly the lack of it, jobs, prices, wages, the supply of goods, inflation, general economic deprivation. The next realignment, if it occurs, may also be prompted partly by some economic issues, such as the price of gasoline and the broader issues of inflation and recession. But there will almost certainly be other issues. The condition of the cities, the conduct of the schools, the fairness of the tax laws, whether government should be more or less decentralized, the use of leisure, the responsibility of the state for the health of its citizens, the use of land, the protection of the environment, foreign policy perhaps, and that staple of American politics, race relations. Questions of economics are not central to all or even most of these issues. And for this reason they do not separate citizens one from another along income or class lines. On some of these questions the cleavage that appears is as likely to be the less educated against the more educated, occupational group against occupational group, young against old, urban against rural dweller, and even new social cleavages which are not now thought to have substantial political meaning.

THE MAKING OF THE ISSUE-CONSCIOUS VOTER.   A huge inventory of findings—some 30 books and more than 100 articles —have significantly increased our understanding of the possibilities for the emergence of greater issue differences between the parties and about the role of issues in the voting decision.[8] They caution us to remember that the citizen is not isolated from his environment. He responds to it and to changes in it. In the development of an issue-conscious voter, several elements of the environment appear to be particularly crucial—the mass media, the economic system, and the prevailing ideology (or lack of it), as well as the party. If the citizen finds it difficult to find words to express to another the reasons which underlie his issue preferences, it does not mean that reasons do not exist. As Plamenatz wisely reminds us:

> A choice is reasonable, not because the chooser, when challenged, can give a satisfactory explanation of why he made it but because, if he could give us an explanation, it would be

satisfactory. The reasoning that lies behind the choice is often made in private language which the chooser never learns to translate into words intelligible to others because there is ordinarily no need for him to do so.[9]

Finally, the party rank and file may well respond to issues if party leaders begin to speak to the rank and file in terms of issues. As Pomper says, "If the parties do not emphasize issues, or do not present distinct and clear positions, the voters are unlikely to invent party programs. When there *are* party positions and differences, the voters can perceive them." [10]

However, parties—in the form of leaders seizing an opportunity—will move toward a greater concern for and awareness of political issues only when they perceive that that is either what citizens want or will buy. It is Neustadt who reminds us that the president's (supply "party leader's") job of teaching is complicated by the fact that he is not the only teacher in the classroom, and that he must deal with citizens who are often inattentive and are willing to listen to his teaching only when he talks about the things that are already on their minds.

NOTES

The first quotation is from Walter Dean Burnham, *Critical Elections* (New York: Norton, 1970), 166. The second is from Kenneth M. Dolbeare and Patricia Dolbeare, *American Ideologies* (Chicago: Markham), 2–3. The third is from Penn Kimball, *The Disconnected* (New York: Columbia University Press, 1972), 289. The fourth is from David Broder, *The Party's Over* (New York: Harper, 1971), 2. The last is from Clinton Rossiter, *Parties and Politics in America* (Ithaca, N.Y.: Cornell University Press, 1960), 188.

1. Leon Epstein, Austin Ranney, and Clinton Rossiter are just three among many who have kind words to say about American parties. See Epstein's *Political Parties in Western Democracies* (New York: Praeger, 1967); Ranney's "Parties in State Politics," in Herbert Jacob and Kenneth N. Vines (editors), *Politics in the American States* (Boston: Little, Brown, 1965), 61–99; and Clinton Rossiter's *Parties and Politics in America* (Ithaca, N.Y.: Cornell University Press, 1960).

   One of the more relentless attacks upon American parties appears in Walter Karp, *Indispensable Enemies: The Politics of Misrule in America* (Baltimore, Md.: Penguin, 1973). Equally critical, but endlessly fascinating, is Hunter S. Thompson, *Fear and Loathing: On The Campaign Trail, '72* (New York: Popular Library, 1973).

2. David Broder, in the preface and concluding chapters of *The Party's Over* (New York: Harper, 1971), offers well-articulated criticism of the parties along this line.

3. Ulf Torgersen, "The Trend Toward Political Consensus: The Case of Norway," in Erik Allardt and Stein Rokkan (editors), *Mass Politics* (New York: Free Press, 1970), 93–104.

4. Ibid.

5. Ibid., 96.

6. Ibid.

7. R. Wayne Parsons and Allen H. Barton, "Social Background and Policy Attitudes of American Leaders," a paper prepared for delivery at the annual meeting of the American Political Science Association, Chicago, September 1974.

8. The major writings on this subject include Richard W. Boyd, "Presidential Elections: An Explanation of Voting Defection," *American Political Science Review* 63 (June 1969), 498–514; Richard W. Boyd, "Popular Control of Public Policy: A Normal Vote Analysis of the 1968 Election," *American Political Science Review* 66 (June 1972), 429–449; Richard A. Brody and others, "Vietnam, the Urban Crisis, and the 1968 Presidential Election: A Preliminary Analysis," a paper prepared for delivery at the 1969 meeting of the American Sociological Association, September 1969; Richard A. Brody and Benjamin I. Page, "Policy Voting and the Electoral Process: The Vietnam War Issue," a paper prepared for delivery at the annual meeting of the American Political Science Association, September 1971; Richard A. Brody and Benjamin I. Page, "Comment: The Reassessment of Policy Voting," *American Political Science Review* 66 (June 1972), 450–458; Philip E. Converse and others, "Electoral Myth and Reality: The 1964 Election," *American Political Science Review* 59 (June 1965), 321–336; Philip E. Converse and others, "Continuity and Change in American Politics: Parties and Issues in the 1968 Election," *American Political Science Review* 63 (December 1969), 1083–1105; John Osgood Field and Ronald E. Anderson, "Ideology in the Public's Conceptualization of the 1964 Election," *Public Opinion Quarterly* 33 (Fall 1969), 380–398; Carl C. Hetrick, "Issues and Politics: An Exploration in Policy-Motivated Political Behavior," a paper prepared for delivery at the annual meeting of the American Political Science Association, September 1968; V. O. Key, Jr. (with the assistance of Milton C. Cummings, Jr.), *The Responsible Electorate: Rationality in Presidential Voting, 1936–1960* (Cambridge, Mass.: Harvard University Press, 1966); Richard M. Merelman, "Electoral Instability and the American Party System," *Journal of Politics* 32 (February 1970), 115–139; Peter B. Natchez and Irvin C. Bupp, "Candidates, Issues and Voters," *Public Policy* 1968, 409–437; John C. Pierce, "Party Identification and the Changing Role of Ideology in American Politics," *Midwest Journal of Political Science* 14 (February 1970), 25–42; Gerald M. Pomper, "After Twenty Years: The Report of the APSA Committee on Political Parties," a paper prepared for delivery at the annual meeting of the American Political Science Association, Los Angeles, September 1970; Gerald M. Pomper, "From Confusion to Clarity: Issues and American Voters, 1956–1968," *American Political Science Review* 66 (June 1972), 415–428; David E. RePass, "Issue Salience and Party Choice," *American Political Science Review* 65 (June 1971), 389–400; John P. Robinson, "Public Reaction to Political Protest: Chicago, 1968," *Public Opinion Quarterly*

34 (Spring 1970), 1–9; Donald E. Stokes, "Some Dynamic Elements of Contests for the Presidency," *American Political Science Review* 60 (March 1966), 19–28; Herbert F. Weisberg and Jerrold G. Rusk, "Dimensions of Candidate Evaluation," *American Political Science Review* 64 (December 1970), 1167–1185; and Arthur H. Miller and others, "A Majority Party in Disarray: Policy Polarization in the 1972 Election," a paper prepared for delivery at the 1973 annual meeting of the American Political Science Association, September 1973.

9. John Plamenatz, "Electoral Studies and Democratic Theory: 1. A British View," *Political Studies* 6 (February 1958), 9.

10. Gerald M. Pomper, "From Confusion to Clarity," 427.

Index